2004

# Belgium

# Studies in Modern European History

Frank J. Coppa
*General Editor*

Vol. 50

PETER LANG
New York • Washington, D.C./Baltimore • Bern
Frankfurt am Main • Berlin • Brussels • Vienna • Oxford

Bernard A. Cook

# Belgium

## A History

PETER LANG
New York • Washington, D.C./Baltimore • Bern
Frankfurt am Main • Berlin • Brussels • Vienna • Oxford

**Library of Congress Cataloging-in-Publication Data**

Cook, Bernard A.
Belgium: a history / Bernard A. Cook.
p. cm. — (Studies in modern European history; v. 50)
Includes bibliographical references and index.
1. Belgium—History I. Title. II. Series.
DH521 .C66    949.3—dc21    2001050655
ISBN 0-8204-5824-4
ISSN 0893-6897


**Die Deutsche Bibliothek-CIP-Einheitsaufnahme**

Cook, Bernard A.:
Belgium: a history / Bernard A. Cook
–New York; Washington, D.C./Baltimore; Bern;
Frankfurt am Main; Berlin; Brussels; Vienna; Oxford: Lang.
(Studies in modern European history; Vol. 50)
ISBN 0-8204-5824-4

*To Rosemary*
*who has been indispensable to the success*
*of the Loyola New Orleans Summer Study Program*
*in Belgium and whose presence has made Belgium even more enjoyable*

# Contents

# Illustrations

# Foreword

This book was written as a result of Loyola University New Orleans' Summer Study Program in Belgium. Before Fr. David Boileau suggested that we start a summer study program in Leuven, I had only been to Belgium once. Now David, my wife, Rosemary, and I have spent nine summers in Belgium. In addition over 200 Loyola New Orleans students have experienced the richness of Belgian culture and the pleasure of a summer in Leuven. I wrote this book in the hope that it would help introduce students and others to Belgium. I hope that it will bring back familiar memories for the alumni of our program and that the students of our host Loyola College of Maryland, which shares its Loyola International House in Leuven with us in the summer, will also find it useful.

Fr. Boileau, who received his doctorate in philosophy from the University of Louvain, is an old Belgium hand, but after nine summers Rosemary and I also regard Leuven and Belgium as our home away from home.

I am hesitant to quote Martin Conway's observation which seems so absolutely condescending, but which is, nevertheless, quite true especially for Americans. According to Conway, "the history of Belgium has been remarkably neglected by historians of modern Europe." He continues explaining that Belgium's ". . . origins in a diplomatic compromise of 1830, unremarkable geography and seemingly placid political culture have conspired to create an impression of a country hardly worthy of serious attention alongside its larger—and more volatile—neighbors." He adds and I completely concur that "this neglect is unjustified."[1] I hope that anyone who reads this book will agree. Here are dramas of religious and cultural conflict, of nation building, of divergent class interests, of a small state overwhelmed by by a potent neighbor, and, finally, of integration into a larger European Community. These are all important and interesting topics, to which I hope that I in some measure do justice.

# Preface

Belgium is a small, densely populated country with cities and towns spread across its countryside. There has been much development since World War II. However, individuality of appearance and a sense of rural tranquillity has been retained. Belgium has an area of 30,562 square kilometers or 18,991 square miles, a bit larger than the state of Maryland. It has short North Sea shoreline of 60 kilometers or about 40 miles and from the coast to its farthest border in the east Belgium stretches only 290 kilometers or about 180 miles. In addition to the main portion of the country, situated between the North Sea, the Netherlands, Germany, Luxembourg, and France, there is a small enclave, Baarle-Hertog, 12 kilometers inside the Netherlands and completely surrounded by Dutch territory.

Belgium is a country, but not "a nation." It consists of two major nationalities, the Dutch speaking Flemish and the French speaking Walloons. In addition to these two major groups which number approximately 6 and 4 million respectively, there are approximately 70,000 German speakers. The Dutch, French, and German speakers of Belgium, apart from the bi-lingual city of Brussels, largely live in defined areas of the country. The north is Flemish and the southeast is Walloon. The Germans live along the frontier with Germany near Aachen and Monschau. Belgium today is a federal state consisting of geographically separate language communities. The Flemish and the Walloons control the cultural, social, and political life of their separate regions.

The Belgian capital, Brussels, is also the seat of the European Union. For those who believe that the heyday of the nation state has passed, what more appropriate venue for the administrative center of a Europe of regions rather than of nation states.

Belgium and Its Neighboring Countries. Courtesy of the CIA World Factbook

# Acknowledgments

To my wife, Rosemary, I must express my gratitude for her patience and advice. Her assistance has rendered the book more readable. To David Boileau, friend and colleague, who shared his enthusiasm for Leuven with me, thanks. My secretary, Vicki Horrobin, is due special thanks for her always cheerful support and extraordinary effort. Heather Mack, my student assistant, carefully read through the manuscript in an earlier form and offered useful suggestions. Patricia Doran, the Interlibrary Loan Coordinator at the Loyola University Library, provided her talent and assistance on this project, as on others, locating needed books and articles.

I would like to thank Christel Snels, the Assistant Director of the Loyola International House in Leuven, and her husband, Luc, for their friendship and for the valuable insights into Belgium, its society, and culture, which they have shared with me.

I am grateful to Professor Emile Lamberts of the Catholic University of Leuven, who placed me in contact with a number of Belgian historians, who wrote entries for *Europe since 1945: An Encyclopedia,* and to those contributors, who added to my knowledge and understanding of contemporary Belgium.

Grateful acknowledgment is hereby made to copyright holders to use the following copyrighted material:

Bernard Cook, "Belgian Revolution of 1830," reprinted from *Chronology of European History,* pages 819-821, John Powell, editor. By permission of the publisher, Salem Press, Inc. Copyright, c. 1997 by Salem Press, Inc.

Bernard Cook, "Belgium: Neutrality of" and "Belgium, Occupation of," in *European Powers in the First World War,* Spencer Tucker, editor, copyright 1996, reproduced by permission of Routledge, Inc., part of The Taylor & Francis Group.

Bernard Cook, "Eyskens, G.," "Tindemans," "Martens," and "Dehaene," in *Europe since 1945: An Encyclopedia,* Bernard Cook, editor, copyright 2001, reproduced by permission of Routledge, Inc., part of The Taylor & Francis Group.

In Flanders Fields Museum, Ieper, Belgium, for permission to quote from "Eyewitness Accounts of the Great War," from the museum's *Guide to Quotations in Flanders Fields Museum*.

Paul Williamson of London for permission to quote a passage from the archives of his father, Harold Sandys Williamson.

The National Archives at College Park, Maryland, and the Photographic Archives of the Imperial War Museum in London for permission to publish photographs from their collections.

# Place Names with Multiple Forms

The **boldface** form will be used in this book.

| Flemish | French | English |
|---|---|---|
| Antwerpen | Anvers | **Antwerp** |
| Aarlen | **Arlon** | |
| Bergen | **Mons** | |
| Bastenaken | **Bastogne** | |
| Brugge | Bruges | **Bruges** |
| Brussel | Bruxelles | **Brussels** |
| Doornik | **Tournai** | |
| **Dijle** | Dyle | |
| Gent | Gant | **Ghent** |
| Ieper | Ypres | **Ypres** |
| **Ijzer** | Iser | |
| Kotrijk | Courtai | |
| **Leuven** | Louvain | |
| **Leie** | Lys | |
| Liuk | **Liège** | |
| Maas | **Meuse** | |
| **Mechelen** | Malines | |
| Namen | **Namur** | |
| Oostende | Ostende | **Ostend** |
| **Tongeren** | Tongres | |
| Waver | **Wavre** | |

The Provinces of Belgium

# CHAPTER 1

# The Beginning

*Gaul is divided in three parts, one of which is inhabited by the Belgians.
(. . .) Of all the Gauls the Belgians are the bravest, because they live farthest
removed from civilization and human refinement, because merchants do not
often visit them and bring those things which tend to weaken the spirit, and
because the Germans, who live across the Rhine, are quite close and the Belgians continually fight with them.*

—Caesar's Gallic War

## Celts and Romans

The territory, which today constitutes Belgium, was divided geographically until the Middle Ages as it is culturally and politically divided today. The etymology of the Dutch *Vlaanderen* or Flanders is "the flooded land."[1] Much of Flanders was an area of marsh and water through which ran the then navigable Senne, Dijle, Demer, and Leie, and the still navigable Scheldt. To the southeast lay the deep forests of the Ardennes teeming with wild animals, bandits, and, reputedly, malign spirits. The area had been inhabited since 150,000 BC. Although the people of the age of the Man of Spy left flint fragments; the Magdalenians produced cave drawings; Neolithic inhabitants made tombs and domesticated animals; and the Michelsberg people gave a foretaste of the future by digging mines, though for flint rather than coal; it was the Celts of the area, the Belgae, who entered written history. They established a number of fortified towns or *oppida*. Kemmelberg in West Flanders was originally one of the Celtic settlements. The language of the Belgae, akin to Irish and Welsh, provides the basis for many current Belgian place names, such as the Ardennes (Celtic *ard* or high). Before the arrival of the Romans, Germans as they migrated to the west had already begun to enter what is today Belgium, and cohabited the area with the still numerically superior Celts.

Julius Caesar conquered the Belgae and present-day Belgium, the section of Gaul between the basins of the Scheldt and the Meuse Rivers, between 57 and 50

BC. It took Caesar seven campaigns to defeat the Belgae, whose bravery and tenacity won his deep respect. In 15 BC the area became the Roman province of Gallia Belgica or more specifically Belgica Secunda. The area organized as Belgica Prima, which today includes only a portion of the Belgian province of Luxembourg, extended through the present Grand Duchy of Luxembourg, Lorraine in France, and the portion of Germany around Trier. Roman law was imposed on the area; the Latin language began to spread; and Christianity was introduced. In the middle of the fourth century Tongeren became a bishopric under Servatius. Christianity did not become pervasive until the sixth century, but, despite the displacement of Roman rule by the Germans, organized Christianity persisted at Tournai and Maastricht.[2] Despite the withdrawal of the Romans, the conversion of Chlodowech in 496 led to a second Christianization of Belgium spearheaded by Irish monks, led by St. Amand and St. Willibrord, who established the abbeys of St. Baaf and St. Peter in Ghent.[3]

The Romans established an important military base at Tongeren. It was an important post on the paved road joining Colonia Agrippinensis or Cologne and Gallia Belgica with the sea at Boulogne by way of Tournai. Tongeren was arranged with the typical checkerboard street pattern of a Roman *civitas* with villas surrounding it to supply it with grain. It had an aqueduct and a 4.5-kilometer long wall two meters thick and six meters high. Roman Tienen produced choice hazelnuts, still a Belgian specialty, and Destelbergen was in Roman times, as now, noted for its peaches.[4] In addition, both Kotrijk and Velzeke were military posts.

After a catastrophic North Sea storm in 270 AD the Romans evacuated the low-lying coastal area of Flanders. They, however, later returned and constructed a defensive system, the Litus Saxonicum, which included the area around a village (*vicus*), which later became the site of Bruges (Brugge). The Romans again evacuated Flanders when they pulled back from all of Gallia Belgica at the beginning of the fifth century, leaving behind their deserted rural settlements.

## The Franks

During the third century the migration of German tribes intensified. During this period Germanic Franks, Frisians, and Saxons moved into Gallia Belgica. The Frisians took control of the North Sea coast, perhaps as far south as the present city of Antwerp; Saxons settled further south along the coast; and the Franks established themselves first in Batavia in present-day Netherlands and Kempen in present-day Belgium. The Romans, who made a virtue of necessity, accepted the Franks as mercenary allies (*foederati*).

Around 431 Tournai became the capital of the Frankish king Chlodio and his successors known as the Merovingians, after Chlodio's successor Meroveus. Under

Meroveus' successor Childerik, Roman authority was finally repudiated. Chlodow-ech (Clovis), who supplanted Childerik, became a Christian in 496 and gained the support of the Church for his conquest of most of Gaul. As the Romans fell back the Frankish population demographically dominated the area of the lower Scheldt and the Leie, which, devastated by raids, was largely empty. The Franks, however, were eventually absorbed when they settled among the more numerous Romanized Celts in the south and the Romance tongue survived.[5] The Silva Carbonara, at that time running from the Rhine River to the North Sea, served as the frontier between the Franks and the Romanized Celts, called the Wala (old German *wealh*, foreigner or Celt, as in Welsh), and their language *waals*, hence the Walloons. This early boun-dary serves as the basis for the linguistic and cultural division of twentieth century Belgium.

Pieter Geyl, the historian of the Dutch Republic, traced the linguistic frontier of the sixteenth century along

> (...) a line, starting from the shore of the North Sea shore in the neighbourhood of Gre-velingen [Gravelines], following the rivers Aa and Leie, then from a point several miles south of Kortryk, continuing in an easterly direction and crossing the Maas [Meuse] sev-eral miles south of Maastricht. [Writing in 1932 he stated that the line] (...) is still in the main the position to-day. For many centuries that boundary has hardly moved (...)[6]

It is still largely so with the exception of Brussels which became predominantly francophone in the nineteenth century.

A remnant of the Silva Carbonara exists as the Forêt de Soignes or the Zonien-would south of Brussels and extending to the east to just south of Leuven. The lan-guage frontier today runs through the middle of the forest. If a driver heads south through the woods on the way to Waterloo she will notice an abrupt change in signs from Dutch to French as she leaves Flanders and enters Wallonia.[7] The predomi-nance of Germanic or Celto-Roman influence remains in place names. Towns end-ing in -court suggest Germanic roots (-iacas, -iaca, and -curtis) as do -gem or -hem (-inga and -haim), while -ville suggest the predominance of Celto-Romans (-villa).[8]

## The Carolingians

In 751 Pepin III, the grandson of Charles Martel, deposed the last of the Merovin-gian kings, Childerik III. Pepin died in 768 and one of his sons was Charles, who would become Carolus Magnus, or depending on one's linguistic and national pref-erence, Charlemagne or Karl der Große. Charlemagne, who was born near Liège, ruled from 768 to 814. He was crowned emperor in Rome on Christmas in 800. From Aachen (Aix-la-Chapelle) he ruled his Frankish Empire which consisted of

France, Germany, Belgium, the Netherlands, and Luxembourg. The unity of the Frankish lands disintegrated with the death of his son Louis, known as the Pious.

In the 843 Treaty of Verdun, present day Belgium was divided between two of Charlemagne's grandsons, Charles the Bald and Lothar.[9] Charles the King of West Frankland (which would become France) gained the territory west of the Scheldt (Flanders). However, Lothar received a swath of land from Frisia to northern Italy, which included the land between the Rhine and the Scheldt and the Meuse, so, in effect, the better part of present day Belgium. When Lothar died in 855, his second son, Lothar II, received the northern section of the Central Kingdom, which was called Lotharii Regnum or Lotharingia. When Henry the Fowler, the king of Germany, annexed Lotharingia in 925, the Scheldt became the boundary between France and Germany. For the time Bruges and Ghent would be in the orbit of France, while Antwerp, Brussels, Leuven, and Mechelen would be in the German world.

Due to economic and administrative weakness, the Frankish successor states lacked the ability to impose centralized rule. There was a severe shortage of gold and silver, and trade with Byzantium and Islam consumed what coinage there was. Barter predominated and without the ability to tax and amass bullion, the Frankish kings had to rely on the feudal service of the nobles to whom they assigned land. Feudalism, in which power and authority were decentralized, became the dominant political form. Belgium at this time consisted of a number of small, more or less autonomous, principalities. In time the principalities would form the basis of the present provinces of East and West Flanders, Brabant, Limburg, Liège, Luxembourg, Namur, and Hainault.

The efforts of the German rulers after Henry the Fowler to consolidate their power in Lotharingia were frustrated by the dissipation of their energy and resources in futile Italian ventures. Otto I appointed his brother, Archbishop Bruno of Cologne, the duke of Lotharingia. After Bruno's death in 953 Lotharingia was divided into Upper Lotharingia, roughly Lorraine, and Lower Lotharingia, the Low Lands east of the Scheldt. The weakness of the German emperors and the lack of internal cohesion led to the rise of largely independent local nobles in the area. However, the legacy of the attempt of the German Ottonians to rule through bishops would endure in the Prince Bishopric of Liège until the soldiers of revolutionary France overran it in 1794. The German Emperors also continued to appoint the dukes of Lower Lotharingia, though the title bore no fixed power. In the eleventh century that honorific was the prerogative of the lords of the Ardennes, the most famous of whom was Godfrey of Bouillon, whose equestrian statue looks down from the Mont des Arts in Brussels on the Grand' Place. The title, which would be changed from the duke of Lower Lotharingia to the duke of Brabant, then passed to the counts of Limburg, and in 1106 to the count of Leuven. Leuven as suggested by that title was the core of the Duchy of Brabant, but in the second half of the thirteenth century the capital was transferred to Brussels. Eventually, the importance of Leuven in Brabant would also be challenged by the rise of the port city of Antwerp and the episcopal seat of Mechelen.[10]

## The Development and Preservation of Flemish Identity

The rulers of the Belgian provinces engaged in long struggles against the dominance of Germany or France over their principalities. John I, the Duke of Brabant (1261–1294) defeated and temporarily checked the Germans at Woeringen on the Rhine. The struggle against France was not as successful. Nevertheless, after the French victory over the English at Bouvines in 1214, which threatened the commercial ties between Flanders and England, the workers of the Flemish cities took up a spirited struggle for independence.[11] According to Geyl, "(. . .) it was only the unexpected popular strength of the great Flemish towns, Brugge and Ghent, that defeated (. . .) [the French] attempts on Flanders, and, [succeeded] in saving the Germanic character of the most exposed region (. . .) [of Dutch culture]."[12]

There had been urban decay after the Romans pulled back. However, Maastricht and Dinant continued as commercial centers, and Arras and Cambrai continued as administrative centers. Ghent, Kotrijk, and Bruges were originally centers of refuge and the urban impulse, which has characterized Belgian history. The number and the proximity of towns and the interaction between town and country especially characterized Flanders. Most of the towns were small. Hasselt, Saint-Omer, and Huy were all between 40 and 80 acres in area. Tongeren, Saint-Truden, Utrecht, and Rotterdam were between 80 and 200 acres. The larger towns, Bruges, Ghent, Leuven, and Brussels were in Flanders or Flemish Brabant. Despite the onslaught of the Normans in the ninth century Bruges developed as a commercial center on the site of an old Roman rural settlement. The favorable location of Flanders on the trade routes from the coast to the Rhine contributed to the early development of the region.[13] New agricultural techniques: the shift from a two field system to a three field system, in which winter wheat and rye, summer barley and oats, were rotated yearly with one fallow field; the heavy iron plow which replaced the wooden scratch plow; the clearing of woodlands and the diking and draining of marshes and coastal tidal flats to create productive polders, all contributed to agricultural productivity, ended hunger except during periods of crop failure, and supported a growing population.[14] The surplus could feed growing towns, which engaged in production for developing markets.

This growth of towns produced what is known as the "twelfth-century renaissance" in Flanders. The Counts of Flanders realizing the opportunity to draw on this new source of wealth granted charters, investing cities with rights at the expense of local nobles. Citizenship was limited to those who lived within the city walls, the burg, and the wealthiest or most influential of these town dwellers, or burgers, became the elite of a new urban oligarchy. However, the merchants' associations of the urban oligarchs were often challenged by the guilds formed by the skilled crafts to protect the interests of their members.

The new wealth of the counts enabled them to hire and to fire a new type of agent, the bailiff, who carried out their will and enforced their law. The earlier Germanic practices of trial by ordeal and oath were replaced by witnesses as the counts and their agents attempted to combat the tradition of vendetta. According to L.J.R. Milis, "these developments turned Flanders from a feudal principality into a kind of mini-state (even though the word 'state' is an anachronism and should be used advisedly here)."[15] Milis states that when Philip of Alsace died in 1191, "Flanders was a well administered country" with an efficiency which resembled Norman England rather than the inefficiently administered France. Nevertheless, French military prowess at the Battle of Bovines in 1214 bested the Count of Flanders and his many allies, England, the Emperor, and the Dukes of Brabant and Holland. The victory of France led to the eclipse of Flanders, caught between its feudal (political) subordination to France and its economic dependence upon English wool. In this complex conflict between political and economic considerations, the relations between the counts of Flanders and the cities were very frequently strained.[16]

However, in Brabant relations between the counts and the cities, Antwerp, Brussels, and Leuven, were more symbiotic. In Brabant the counts and cities both profited from the levying of tolls on trade between Bruges and Cologne.[17]

### Antwerp

Antwerp grew as a border post, port, and communications center along the line of demarcation between the worlds of the French and Germans. The city was reputedly named due to the fate of its early resident the giant Druon Antigonus. This toll-collecting tyrant demanded tribute of passing ships and cut off the hands of those who refused to pay. A relative of Julius Caesar, Silvius Brabo, reputedly disposed of Druon. The 1887 Brabo Fountain in the Grote Markt depicts Brabo throwing Druon's hand into the Scheldt. Hence "*Hand werp*," or hand throw. Regardless of the validity of that etymology, the name, Brabo, the reputed first duke of Brabant, can be recognized in the name of the province. A more prosaic etymology for "Antwerp" is "*Aan de werpen*," at the wharf.[18] The legend is a graphic indication of the resentment of trades people against the levy of tolls upon their labor by local lords.

A settlement did exist at the site by the second century AD. The Irish Benedictine St. Armand built the first church in 660. Irish monks played a dominant role in the establishment or re-establishment of Christianity in the whole area of the Low Countries and western Germany, which had been overrun by the pagan Germans. In the ninth century the Steen fortress was erected on the riverbank at Antwerp to defend the borders established at the Treaty of Verdun in 843 between the territories of Charles the Bald and Lothar. Ravaged by Northmen in the ninth century, the oldest section of visible Steen wall dates from 1250. The left bank of the river belonged to the French-allied counts of Flanders and the right bank (Antwerp) belonged to the German-leaning dukes of Brabant. The town walls were constructed in the eleventh century by Godfrey of Bouillon (1061–1100), count of Antwerp.

### Iron Baldwin: The Counts of Flanders

The advent of the Vikings or Norsemen, who raided and settled the coastal area of Flanders in the ninth and tenth centuries, led to the development of the powerful counts of Flanders, a product of defensive feudalism. The Frankish kings granted to these counts land and authority for their assistance in containing the Norse threat. Though technically vassals, by the eleventh century the counts of Flanders had become for all practical purposes independent.[19]

The first count of Flanders was the Fleming Baldwin, called Iron Arm, who in 827 abducted and married the twenty-year-old daughter of Charles the Bald, Judith. In the words of L.J.R. Milis, "a proven method for social climbing."[20] Ghent was Baldwin's principal stronghold. The son of Baldwin and Judith, Baldwin II, who married the daughter of Alfred the Great of England, built the walls of Bruges and Ypres (Ieper). He completed the transition begun by his father from a royal administrator to a territorial prince. His successors expanded Flemish territory to the south until checked by the duchy of Normandy, established by the Vikings under Rolo in 911.[21] A manifestation of the interaction of these two territories is the fact that Matilda, the daughter of Baldwin V, became the wife of William the Conqueror, the duke of Normandy.

Strengthened city walls together with circular fortifications erected along the Flemish coast reduced the Viking threat, and in 891 Arnulf of Carinthia defeated the Norse at Leuven and ended their threat to Flanders. In addition to walls and fortresses, the counts of Flanders built the first new roads since the Romans and constructed canals as well. They began pushing into what was then called the "Merciless Forest," and today the Flemish Ardennes, east of Ypres. And along the coast they began to reclaim land from marsh and sea as polders were constructed. The counts also granted the first of charters to cities granting their citizens privileges and exemption from the power of local nobles.[22]

## 's Gravensteen

In Ghent at the confluence of the Lieve and the Leie stands 'sGravensteen, the castle of the Counts of Flanders. In 867 Baldwin Iron Arm built his castle on this site.
Baldwin's castle was intended for protection against the Norsemen. Its replacement,
which incorporated part of Baldwin's castle in its keep, was begun in 1180 by Philip
of Alsace, the Count of Flanders, who had just returned to Ghent from the Cru-
sades. The date MCLXXX (1180) is carved into the entrance to the keep and don-
jon. The castle was at that time intended to intimidate the unruly people of Ghent.
It did not succeed. The people stormed the castle in 1302 at the time of the Battle
of the Golden Spurs. It was stormed again in 1338 by the followers of Jacob van
Artevelde. Until its restoration between 1894 and 1913 the former fortress was utilized as a prison and then, between 1797 and 1887, as a textile mill. Today, however,
it appears much as it was in the late twelfth century.

Gravensteen is particularly important as a cultural monument because almost all
of the extant buildings in the Low Lands built before 1200 are churches. From this
earlier period, Saint Servatius and Our Lady's Church (Onze Lieve Vrouwkerk) in
Maastricht and Saint-Barthélemy in Liège are solid examples of the Germanic Romanesque style. The cathedral in Tournai with its four impressive towers is the most
impressive example of the French Romanesque style which prevailed to the south
and west of the Scheldt. Before brick was utilized in the thirteenth and fourteenth
centuries, the low lying areas of Flanders without stone readily available relied on
wood or even turf for building.[23] As a result those buildings no longer exist.

## Bruges (Brugge)

Bruges developed around a castle built in 865 by Baldwin Iron Arm. Charles the
Bald had pursued Baldwin and Judith but reluctantly accepted their marriage out of
fear that Baldwin would ally himself with the Northmen. He asked Baldwin and Judith to check the Viking advance by setting up a fiefdom at the Viking landing site
or *brygghia* in the marshy land near the North Sea. The castle and the settlement it
attracted became Bruges or Brugge. The city prospered because of its proximity to
the estuary, Het Zwin, which at that time extended to Damme, and to which Bruges
had access via the Reie. In the thirteenth century cloth manufacturing enriched the
town. Its annual fair was one of the most important in Flanders. The importance of
the town can be gathered by Chaucer's frequent references to it. The town also
boasted an important pilgrimage site, the Basilica of the Holy Blood (Heilig Bloed-
basiliek). Though the basilica is crowned with a fifteenth century chapel, it dates
from the twelfth century. The relic of Christ's blood is reputed to have been given to
Dirk of Alsace, the Count of Flanders, by the Patriarch of Jerusalem, in 1147 during

the Second Crusade. It, however, might well be part of the loot taken from Constantinople as a result of the sacking of the city during the Fourth Crusade. Baldwin of Flanders, who became the emperor of Byzantium, might well have transferred the relic to his daughters, Margaret and Joanna, who ruled Flanders during his absence.

## Ghent

Ghent developed around the abbeys of St. Baaf and St. Pieter founded by St. Armand in the seventh century on a sandy rise above the Scheldt. Baldwin Iron Arm built his castle for defense against the Norsemen at the confluence of the Lieve and the Leie (Lys), just above their entry into the Scheldt, around 867. The name of the city might stem from the Celtic word for confluence *ganda*. The growing town was fortified during the eleventh and twelfth centuries. During the thirteenth century a canal was constructed to Bruges.

By the thirteenth century Ghent had developed into the largest center for the production of woolen cloth in Europe. By the middle of the century 4,000 weavers and 1,200 fullers were engaged in its cloth making industry.[24] A contemporary, Matthew of Westminster, wrote "All the nations of the world are kept warm by the wool of England made into cloth by the men of Flanders."[25] 30,000 workers belonged to its cloth making guilds. By the end of the century the turbulent city, whose workers and burgers were at continual loggerheads with the nobles, possessed 50,000 inhabitants and was larger than Paris. The counts of Flanders had granted charters to the city in 1180 and 1191. However, in 1212 the Council of Thirty-nine had asserted the rights of the burgers of Ghent against the patricians, the wealthiest merchants and urban nobles, who supported the count. The burgers established the election of magistrates, who had previously been appointed by the patricians. In 1302 workers from Ghent, led by Jan Borluut, contributed to the defeat of the francophile nobles in the Battle of the Golden Spurs.

## Bell Towers: Symbols of Prosperity and Assertions of Power

As feudalism declined in the twelfth and thirteenth centuries, the prosperous cloth producing and trading towns Ghent, Bruges, and Ypres asserted their autonomy from the French kings. Their town halls and bell towers were symbols of their municipal independence and expressions of municipal pride. W.P. Blockmans calls them "quintessential bourgeois monuments."[26] The bell towers had practical value as well. They served as watch towers, alarm signals, meeting places, and prisons. They were utilized for defensive and civic purposes. They contained fortified rooms in which were deposited the city charters, which spelled out the special privileges granted to or extorted by the town. In Ypres, Bruges, and Ghent the bell towers were attached to the cloth hall, another demonstration of town wealth. The Ypres town hall was the greatest of them. It was completed in 1307 after a century of labor, just in time to coincide with a decline of the town's textile trade. Bruges, the prosperity of which would last longer, constructed its impressive hall and tower in the thirteenth century. In 1300 Ghent had 64,000 inhabitants, Bruges 46,000, and Ypres 28,000.[27]

## Belfort

Across the square from St. Baaf Cathedral in Ghent is the belfry, Belfort, built between 1321 and 1380 above the cloth hall, the Lakenhall, of the cloth makers' guild. From 1402 to 1550 its ground floor room housed the iron chest containing the charters and privileges of the city. Of the tower's 52 bells, 37 were cast in 1660. Its greatest bell was baptized "Roland" in 1314.

Roland, named after the hero of the *Chanson de Roland*, who with his dying breath blew a warning to Charlemagne, rang to warn of approaching danger, whether by invaders or by those who would tamper with the rights of the citizens of Ghent. The weavers of Ghent boasted "*Mijn naam is Roland. 'k kleppe brand, en luide storm in Vlaanderland*" ("My name is Roland. I toll out fire, and ring in a storm in Flanders!"). However, Charles V punished a rebellious Ghent in 1540 by having the giant bell removed and destroyed. He replaced it with an equally large bell, but one without the rebellious connotations of its predecessor. When the latter cracked in the twentieth century it was retired to a pedestal on the Burgomaster Braunplein (square). A replacement was installed in 1948 bearing the provocative inscription "*Als mense luyd es storme int' land*"—"When I sing there is a storm in the land"—which in retrospect could be taken as an ominous prophecy for Belgium's francophones.[28]

On the other side of Ghent's bell tower stands the Stadhuis (city hall) built between 1518 and 1560. It is both a symbol of the municipal pride and the wealth of Ghent in the early sixteenth century. Ghent flourished while Bruges sunk into decay. In 1547 a canal was completed between Ghent and Terneuzen on the Scheldt estuary. Ghent thus acquired direct access to the North Sea. As Bruges lay mired in silt and Antwerp was by-passed, Ghent became the most important city in the Low Lands and among the cities above the Alps second in size to Paris.

## Guy of Dampierre and Regional Rivalries

The prosperity of Flanders not only inspired conflict between the Counts of Flanders and Holland over control of the Zeeland islands and the estuary of the Scheldt, but also led to the involvement of France and England in the affairs of Flanders. Guy of Dampierre, the Count of Flanders, imprisoned Floris I of Holland, who was subsequently murdered. Floris, in his quest for dominance in the Low Lands, had sought the support of the Avesnes family of Hainaut, the principal city of which was Mons, and the king of France. Guy was opposed by the burgers of Ghent for granting a monopoly to the patricians. He was summoned to France and forced to repudiate an alliance with England and to end trade between Flanders and England. This was a disaster for Flanders, which was dependent upon English wool. The desperate Guy turned to his former opponents in Flanders for assistance against the French king. With the support of nobles, burgers and artisans, Guy signed an alliance with England in January 1297. The alliance provided for English military assistance and a restoration of trade. Guy then repudiated his fealty to the French king. However, in February 1297 a French force invaded Flanders and the patricians of Kortrijk, Lille, and Bruges promptly surrendered. In the words of Blockmans, "the county of Flanders ceased to exist and the territory was placed under a French governor."[29]

# CHAPTER 2

# The Struggle with France

*When they wanted to ingratiate themselves with the men of Ghent or of Brugge, the Dukes knew perfectly how to speak Dutch. When they wreaked their vengeance, when they chastised and humiliated, the language that made the Flemings tremble was always French.*

—Pieter Geyl[1]

### Philip the Fair

Philip the Fair, the king of France, was able to occupy Ghent in 1300, and, taking advantage of internal divisions in Bruges, was able to stage a triumphal entry into that city in 1301. However, Flanders was not secure. When magistrates in Ghent re-imposed under the penalty of death or, at least, banishment, an excise tax, the workers proclaimed a general strike. When the patricians sent armed hirelings into the working class neighborhoods, the leaders of the workers called them into the streets. The workers, who had been allowed to possess arms to defend the count, were not at a disadvantage. 10,000 armed workers marched on the Friday Market. Several hundred patricians fled the advancing workers. Some were thrown into the Leie; others managed to seek refuge in Gravensteen. A bloody siege ensued. After a number of patricians were killed or wounded they surrendered. The representative of Philip the Fair, faced with this revolt and unrest in Bruges, decided to agree to the demands of the workers of Ghent in order to deal with simultaneous unrest in Bruges.[2]

### The Battle of the Golden Spurs

In Bruges a grandson of Guy, William of Gulik, proclaimed a revolt under the banner of the lion of Flanders, which today can be seen flying over Gravensteen. When the French occupied Bruges on May 17, 1302, William's forces melted into the city and the next day unexpectedly fell upon individual Frenchmen. Led by the butcher, Pieter de Coninck, and the weaver, Jan Breydel, whose statues now adorn the city's Grote Markt, the workers of Bruges rose against the French.[3] The guilds and their workers wished to retain their economic ties to England, which provided the wool, which they wove.[4] The French occupation provoked a growing hatred of foreigners in the cities of Flanders. It added a deepening cultural divide to the political conflict between the patricians and the common people. The common people spoke Dutch dialects while the urban patricians, who already preferred French, found their adopted language the language of political power.[5] On May 18, 1302, the insurgents in Bruges massacred the French in the "Brugge Matins," killing everyone who could not correctly pronounce "*Schild en Vriend.*" 120 French and scores of francophone nobles and patricians were killed. The parallel to the Sicilian Vespers of 1282 is so close that it probably served as an inspiration to the Flemish workers. The Sicilians, exasperated by the Normans and enraged by a French-speaking soldier who insulted a Sicilian lady on Easter Sunday, had killed any Frenchman who betrayed himself by his inability to pronounce *cece* (chickpea) correctly. Six weeks after their "Matins" the craftsmen of Bruges played an important role in the July 11 Battle of the Golden Spurs, fought in a muddy field near Kortrijk, where 2,000 French knights were slaughtered, mauled by the *goedendags* ("good day," wake up calls), spiked balls on four foot chains, wielded by the workers of Bruges.[6] The Flemish had, at best, only 600 mounted soldiers to the 2,500 armored French knights. However, the Flemish had nearly 10,000 foot-soldiers to the 5,000 French archers. The terrain was to the advantage of the Flemish. The soggy ground impeded a cavalry charge and the French horses were unable to get easily across the stream that separated the forces. According to Blockmans, as the French knights sunk into the morass of Flanders, they were slaughtered by Flemish peasants not attuned to the noble custom of holding their "social superiors" for ransom.[7] The battle received its name from the golden spurs, which along with other plunder, were stripped from the bodies of the dead French knights. Despite the fact that Belgium's national holiday is July 21, the commemoration of the ascent of Leopold I to the throne of a newly independent Belgium in 1831, the Flemish celebrate July 11, the date of this Flemish victory over the French, as the Flemish national day.

### The Treaty of Athis

The French king did not accept the reversal at Kortrijk with equanimity. He launched a new assault, which was successful. A new pro-French Count of Flanders signed Treaty of Athis in 1305. Athis granted an amnesty to the pro-French patricians, transferred some Flemish land directly to France, and required the rebellious cities to pay a large indemnity. The patricians with French support reasserted themselves and to a large extent controlled Ypres and Ghent between 1319 and 1337. However, their control did not go uncontested.

Politco-economic conflict was fueled by a great famine from 1315 to 1317 followed by the first bout of the Bubonic Plague. During the famine the city of Bruges had to bury 2,000 corpses found on the streets of the city. Ypres was compelled to deal with 2,800 corpses in 1316 alone, a figure, which amounted to ten percent of the city's population.[8]

When the coastal area of Flanders rose against the count in the 1320s in a bitter war, Ghent, controlled for the moment by patricians, fought on the count's side. The Flemish peasants revolted against the power of both the ecclesiastical and noble landlords, and there was a period of reciprocal violence in which castles and villages were in turn put to the torch. When the papacy proclaimed an interdict against the peasant rebels they only became more determinedly anti-clerical. Under their leader, Klaas Zannekin, they took over Ypres and drove the patricians out of town. However, in 1328 a French army, which had come to the aid of the Count of Flanders, Louis de Nevres, defeated the peasants and the count was able to use this victory to increase his financial and juridical authority over the cities of Flanders.[9]

### The Hundred Years' War and Jacob and Philip van Artevelde

By 1338 it was abundantly clear that if the greater threat, French domination of the country, was to be avoided, internecine strife within Flanders had to end. The greatest achievement of Jacob van Artevelde, a noble who supported the interests of the merchants and weavers, was that he was able, at least temporarily, to suppress internal rivalries. He showed what could happen if the endless squabbling was put aside and a united front presented to the real enemy.[10]

In 1338 Count Louis de Nevers joined France against England at the beginning of the Hundred Years War. This was a threat to the cloth trade and the prosperity of the city. 60 percent of Ghent's population and 50 percent of Ypres' were engaged in the production of cloth, and for this high grade English wool was essential. Van Artevelde took control of Ghent and the English resumed their shipments of wool, which had been cut off by Edward III of England as an economic sanction. Van Artevelde ruthlessly imposed aldermen of his choice on the smaller towns surrounding Ghent. This urban imperialism was duplicated by Bruges and Ypres, which, joined with Ghent in a consultative and cooperative arrangement called the Three Members of Flanders. The three cities "(. . .) attempted to coordinate a common political course which would subject all of Flanders to their will."[11] They imposed their rule on the surrounding countryside and towns, and protected their own textile industry at the expense of others. If the regulations of the dominating city were not followed, the urban militia was dispatched to destroy the looms and tools of the recalcitrants. Burgers from the three cities asserted the right to be tried only by their own magistrates even if the matter dealt with their activities outside their city.[12]

Van Artevelde's ruthlessness was not limited to the supporters of France or resistance in the countryside. He personally killed two opponents who had disagreed with him in public.[13] David Nicholas writes

> James van Artevelde was a violent man. After his elevation to the captaincy, he lived in a considerable state with an armed escort of brawlers maintained at the city's expense. The chronicler Jean Froissart claims that he ordered his thugs, numbering between sixty and eighty, to kill suspected opponents at a signal from their leader. He had spies, and there were wholesale banishments of persons from all social ranks who opposed his regime. His opponents' property was confiscated as was standard practice at the time.[14]

Van Artevelde, however brutal, mirrored a brutal time. Ghent was riven by factions, which pitted the fullers' guild against the weavers' guild, citizen against citizen, and even relative against relative. Personal and family rivalries were pursued with homicidal violence. Notables maintained their armed bands, each identifiable by their distinct uniforms. In addition to those linked by sentiment and interest, there were mercenaries at hire to the highest bidder, and street gangs ever ready to employ opportunistic violence against the vulnerable. In this climate of violence, a contract killing and its agreed upon fee were regarded as a legally binding obligations enforceable by the courts.[15]

After 1340 van Artevelde directly allied Ghent with Edward III, whose third son Edward of Gaunt (Ghent) was born in the city. The francophile Louis de Nevers was repudiated. Louis was nominally replaced by a Lombard banker, Simon de Mirabello, who had loaned the city a considerable amount of money, and Edward III was publicly acknowledged as King of France in an official ceremony in Ghent's Friday Market.

The arrangement between Ghent and England was mutually profitable. However, in 1345 guildsmen who came to distrust the ambition of van Artevelde and his plan to make Edward, the Black Prince, Count of Flanders stormed his home and killed him.[16] Nevertheless, Philip, the son of van Artevelde, assumed control of the city.

Philip van Artevelde was unrestrained in his opposition to Louis de Nevers' successor, Count Louis de Male, and to his own enemies. Philip had 12 of his adversaries beheaded. He personally murdered his opponent Simon Bette and permitted a supporter to assassinate the former burgomaster, Giselbrecht van Grutere. However, Louis de Male, gained the support of towns such as Aalst, which had been exploited by Ghent. And with the assistance of the King of France, Charles VI, he eventually defeated the workers of Ghent at the Battle of Westrozebeke on November 18, 1382. The count's archenemy, Philip, was killed in the fighting, and Louis established a new administration, the Four Members of Flanders. Nicholas asserts, "above all, the defeat of Philip van Artevelde meant defeat of the Flemish cities' pretensions to independence. (. . .) [It] meant the incorporation of the Flemings into a larger state that revolved in a French rather than an English orbit."[17] Louis sought the cooperation of the cities but counter-balanced them by giving representation to the prosperous countryside surrounding Bruges.[18] Nevertheless, the struggle for Flemish independence would continue, even if in another form.

Statue of Jan Breydel and Pieter de Coninck by Paul de Vigne, erected on the Grote Markt in Bruges in 1887. Photograph by Bernard Cook

# CHAPTER 3

# The Burgundian Period

## Blijde Inkomst

The urban elites of Brabant were able to take advantage of struggles between the dukes of Brabant and powerful local barons to gain a degree of administrative and economic autonomy. In 1312, when the death of Duke John II of Brabant had left in his place a young son, the urban leaders of Brabant formed the Council of Kortenberg. The representatives of the cities asserted the right of the duke's subjects to disregard his authority if he violated the laws and traditions of Brabant. The representatives of the duke were forced to assent to a solemn agreement, the *Blijde Inkomst* or *Joyeuse Entrée* (Happy Entry or Accession). The *Blijde Inkomst*, a declaration of municipal rights, subsequently became a solemn agreement between each new duke and his subjects in which the dukes agreed to respect the laws and traditions and the subjects offered their allegiance. In 1355, following the death of John III of Brabant, his daughter Joanna and her husband, Wenceslaus of Luxembourg, were forced to sign a *Blijde Inkomst*. Both the dukes and the cities, however, periodically violated these solemn agreements. And they were violated in this case. When Louis de Male, who had married another daughter of the former duke John III, invaded Brabant in 1357, the Estates of Brabant, representing the clergy, the nobility, and the urban elite, violated the solemn agreement with Joanna and Wenceslas, which had asserted the indivisibility of Brabant. The Estates recognized the claims of Louis and ceded Mechelen and Antwerp to him.[1]

## Philip the Good

In 1369 Louis' daughter and heiress Margaret married Philip the Bold of Burgundy. Charles V of France hoped to achieve through the marriage of his brother Philip what French arms had failed to achieve. The plan miscarried; the House of Burgundy did not subordinate itself meekly to France, but became a rival.[2] With the death of Louis de Male in 1384, Philip the Bold and Margaret inherited Flanders, Mechelen, and Antwerp. In 1390 Joanna ceded Brabant and Limburg to Philip and designated his second son, Anthony, to be her successor in Brabant. In 1419 Philip's grandson, Duke Philip the Good of Burgundy, became count of Flanders. He also inherited Brabant, Limburg, Mechelen, and Antwerp. In addition, he bought Namur and Luxembourg, and was also able to assert his claim to Holland, Zeeland, and Hainault. Philip the Good had his nephew elected bishop of Liège and his bastard son, David of Burgundy, elected bishop of Utrecht. This was the first time since Charlemagne that one ruler governed all of present day Belgium. For this achievement he is known as the "Father of Belgium." According to Pieter Geyl "if at first (. . .) [the dukes of Burgundy] had been able to use the French monarchy to their own purposes, soon, under Philip the Good, they came into open conflict with the country of their origin, and their design to found an independent state on the flank of France stood revealed."[3]

To combat urban and provincial particularism Philip in 1430 established a new knighthood, his Order of the Golden Fleece. Through this "stroke of genius" he encouraged a national consciousness in the magistrates who served as provincial administrators and sat on his council.[4] He also called together representatives of the clergy, nobility, and cities of the various provinces in a States-General to approve the subsidies, which he required. (In contrast to the representative bodies of individual duchies, which are referred to as estates general, assemblies representing a number of duchies or political units are referred to as states-general.)

Philip the Good did his best to avoid war. The currency remained stable. It was not diluted or shaved to pay for war expenses. Wages rose and prices fell. This occurred especially between 1434 and 1467 and was abetted by a population decline due to epidemics. The impact of the plague, which reoccurred in roughly ten-year cycles, is complex. The death rate among women was especially high and by 1400 men outnumbered women in Flanders by 20 to 30 percent. Consequently the age at which women married dropped. Fewer children were born and among those who were mortality soared. The large number of deaths had the beneficial effect of increasing the standard of living of the survivors. As a result of the shortage of labor wages rose. "This flush of money—coupled perhaps with the hedonistic abandon which can accompany times of great uncertainty—stimulated demand for luxury goods."[5] Trade and production were, as a consequence, stimulated. Despite the seven important outbreaks of the bubonic plague in Flanders between 1348 and 1485, the population of the 17 provinces, including Liège, in 1469 was 2,627,500, of whom 1,684,500 lived in the country and 879,000 in towns. There were 64,000 members of the clergy and aristocracy.[6]

Philip the Good asserted his would-be royal authority. In 1438 he forced Bruges to give up many of its rights and in 1453, after crushing a revolt, did the same to Ghent. 16,000 soldiers of Ghent's worker-army were killed at Gavre. Philip then levied an onerous fine on the city and revoked its special rights. He forced the leading burgers of the city to walk through a city gate with nooses around their necks and to kiss the dirt in front of him.[7] If the cities lost rights, there were the compensations of good government and peace. In fact, the Burgundian period was a golden age of prosperity and culture. Art and architecture flowered. Jan van Eyck, although his official title was *valet de chambre*, was the court artist of Philip the Good. Jan van Ruisbroek from Brabant was Philip's master builder. The Flemish Primitives, with their delight in detail and things, flourished. Their paintings were commissioned by business people and administrators who were "hard-headed practical people, interested in cloth, bills, nails, meat, iron, fruit, jewels, spices, and shoes."[8] The pictures for which they paid reflect their mundane interests and provide a window into the everyday life of this period.

## Charles the Bold

The peace and prosperity fostered by Philip the Good did not long outlive him. His son, Charles the Bold, pursued the policy of his father but with "reckless ambition."[9] He tried to expand Philip's kingdom by annexing Alsace and Lorraine. In the process Charles had to fight Louis XI of France, and in the course of the fighting died in battle at Nancy in 1477. Charles' dream of a large Burgundian dynastic state died with him. More than half of its French-speaking components, including the Duchy of Burgundy, was lost. What remained was a Low Land state consisting of the Dutch-speaking provinces and a few Walloon provinces. The center of gravity of this state was Flanders and Brabant with their manufacturing and commercial centers.[10] Geyl not only regrets the temporary link between the Dutch speaking provinces and the distant French-speaking Burgundian lands but also the continued connection of Dutch speaking provinces with the Walloon provinces. During the Burgundian period the court, the upper nobility, and the bureaucracy were predominantly French speaking. According to Geyl, the continued connection with the Walloon provinces "(. . .) by strengthening the class and official position of the French language in the whole country, helped to corrupt their civilization."[11] A remark which would not be welcomed today by the majority of the inhabitants of Brussels proper, not to mention the inhabitants of Wallonia.

The disastrous and frequent campaigns of Charles the Bold brought the good times to an end. During the 1490s, 53 percent of the population of Ghent was classified as paupers. However, even under Philip the Good prosperity had been relative. During the "Golden Age" of Philip the average urban family was compelled to spend 80 percent of its budget on food. In 1431 in one Ypres ward 679 of the 850 families were absolved from paying taxes because of their poverty and 89 families received assistance. Food, financed by the bequests of the faithful, was distributed in front of parish churches after Mass on Sundays and holy days. Poverty might have meant cheap labor and low wages but in the old textile towns changes in international fashion meant no jobs at any wage.[12]

## The Hapsburgs

Charles' daughter, Mary of Burgundy, was surrounded by foes and an uprising the year of her father's death forced her to assent to the Great Privilege, a recognition of the municipal autonomy of the Flemish cities. According to Blockmans, it was remarkable that the States-General following the death of Charles did not turn to another dynasty. He stated that it was "(. . .) striking that the respective States of the Low Countries [with the exception of Liège, Guelders, and Luxembourg] opted to remain a union of principalities. (. . .) The core regions of the Low Countries (. . .) had reached such a level of political integration that they desired to maintain their mutual ties."[13]

Mary, with her rule challenged by Louis XI of France, sought strength through marriage. She chose the son of the Holy Roman Emperor Frederick III, Maximillian of Hapsburg. This marriage alliance would link the southern part of the Low Lands to the Hapsburgs until 1794, when revolutionary France drove them out. It would also link the Low Lands to Spain following the dynastic marriage alliance formed when Maximillian arranged the double marriage of his son, Philip, and his daughter, Margaret, to Joanna and Juan of Castile. Joanna and Juan were the children of Ferdinand of Aragon and Isabella of Castile, the monarchs of the rising power Spain whose crusading Catholic sentiment had been fueled by the liberation in 1492 of Grenada, the last toe-hold of the Muslims in Spain. When Juan died five months following his marriage, his sister, Joanna, who progressively sunk into mental illness and thus gained the sobriquet "Joan the Mad", became the sole heir to the Spanish Empire, which was eventually inherited by Charles, her son by Philip. This marriage alliance would have fatal repercussions in the Low Lands. The northern seven provinces would, after a bitter struggle against the heavy taxes and the centralizing and anti-Reformation policies of the Hapsburgs, win their independence as the Calvinist United Provinces.

Mary of Burgundy only lived until 1482, but Maximillian was able to assert his authority over the whole of the Low Lands, and Mary had given birth to Philip. Upon Maximillian's election as Holy Roman Emperor in 1494, Maximillian handed over the Low Lands to their son, Philip, called the Handsome. According to Geyl, the Burgundians had helped to create a united Dutch identity. The States-General, which they had established to facilitate the collection of taxes, became the mouthpiece of the Dutch nation. During the reign of Philip the Bold, the dominant element of the Dutch-speaking nation "had already realized their community of interests against the grasping dynasticism of the ruler."[14] However Philip had been able through the threat of violence to repress this national consciousness.

After the death of Mary, "there were violent attempts to subject monarchical rule to some sort of national control."[15] The Flemish resented the effort of Maximillian to regain the French speaking areas lost in 1477 and, especially, the cost of the effort. Local authorities representing the cities and guilds resented the effort to centralize authority and usurp their hard-won legal and fiscal powers. The dynasty which could have served as the impetus for the creation of a Flemish-Dutch nation sought something broader and thus contributed to the sundering of the Dutch people and much suffering. According to Geyl, "the tragedy of the Netherlands history was that the dynasty called to this great task never lost its alien character and always pursued objects not only foreign but inimical to the cause of Netherlands nationality."[16]

When Philip the Handsome unexpectedly died at Burgos in 1506 as he claimed the throne in Spain in the name of his wife, the Low Lands passed to his six-year-old son, Charles. Geyl bemoans the fact that during the Hapsburg period, as during the Burgundian period, "(. . .) a principal factor of Netherlands history was the lack of national solidarity between rulers and ruled. Founded by foreigners, the Netherlands state continued to be ruled by foreigners."[17]

Charles was an exception to Geyl's assertion. Charles was born in Ghent in 1500. Apart from a year in Leuven, Charles spent his childhood in Mechelen. Charles was declared of age by the States-General in 1515. The next year he became King of Spain, and in 1519 the Holy Roman Emperor, Charles V. After the 1525 Battle of Pavia in which his forces defeated those of Francis I of France, Charles forced the French king at the Peace of Madrid to renounce all claims to Flanders and Artois and to relinquish his control over Tournai. Charles' Seventeen [Low Country] Provinces were referred to as the Circle of Burgundy. Through his 1548 Transaction of Augsburg, and 1549 Pragmatic Sanction, Charles established for his Netherlands a centralized administration with its capital at Brussels, Charles' residence.[18] Charles' rule was tempered by the fact that culturally he was Flemish and he respected the tradition of local municipal autonomy. He had to agree to conditions imposed by Flanders, Brabant, Holland, and Zeeland to gain the taxes he requested in 1521 and 1522 to finance war against France. Again in 1542 the States-General agreed on a temporary basis to Charles' request for a "tenth penny" tax on stationary goods and trade. The Seventeen Provinces had been declared an indivisible whole by the Pragmatic Sanction. By this time the political and intellectual elites had developed a consciousness of "the over-all importance of the regions they lived in. To be members of the leading classes in the wealthiest, most densely populated and artistically most creative area north of the Alps reinforced their sense of self-esteem."[19] Institutionally and in terms of consciousness a nation was being formed. The Reformation and, especially, Charles' son, Philip, destroyed the unity of this developing state. Protestantism, despite the opposition of Charles, spread through the Low Lands. The Reformation found wide support in the Low Lands because of the connection of ecclesiastical appointments with political patronage and the worldliness of the clergy. Many lay people, feeling completely neglected by the clergy, turned to private devotion, to lay preachers, and ultimately to proponents of Reformed Christianity.

In spite of Charles' personal sentiment, he resisted brutal repression. Some attribute this to his Flemish character. His son, Philip II, was anything but Flemish or moderate. When Charles handed over the Netherlands and his Spanish possessions to his son, Philip, in 1556, Philip's attempt to quell Protestantism and to assert his centralizing concept of authority sparked revolution. Charles' abdication occurred in Brussels in the Coudenberg Palace.[20] Charles entered on the arm of William the Silent of Orange. After Charles' emotional self-abnegation, Philip announced in Spanish that since he spoke neither Dutch nor French his statement would have to be read for him, a bad start for a sorry period.

# CHAPTER 4

# Four Cities and a Begijnhof (Béguinage)

### The Zenith and Decline of Bruges

Despite the victory of Philip the Good and the suppression of many of the privileges of Bruges by the French, the city reached its commercial acme during the fourteenth and fifteenth centuries under Burgundian rule. Its population reached 80,000. (Its population in 1997 was 120,000.) Bruges was the principal commercial city of the Hanseatic League.[1] According to W.P. Brockmans, "between 1380 and 1480, Bruges was unquestionably the most important trading city in northwestern Europe, the center of an international economic system in which the rest of the Low Countries played a significant but secondary role."[2] The role, which Bruges played in the Hanseatic League and the general participation of Flanders in trade with Germany and England, was facilitated by the mutual intelligibility of the languages spoken by the merchants from the three areas.[3]

Bruges was particularly noted for its tapestry. The tapestry of Flanders was not only exquisite, it was extremely expensive. A tapestry often contained threads of silk, silver, and gold in addition to wool and sometimes took a skilled craftsman months to complete. The tapestries often evoked secular themes of power and authority, and were intended to impress the viewers with the wealth and power of the owner more than the art of the maker.[4] The Bruges market traded in cloth from Italy and the east, furs from eastern Europe, metal from Central Europe, wool, cheese, and coal from Britain, fruit from Spain, spices from Arabia, and wine from the Rhine. As many as 150 ships entered the port daily. In 1464, due to its prominence, it was the site of the first States–General of the Netherlands. Its prosperous merchants patronized artists like Jan van Eyck (1390–1441) and Hans Memling (1435–1494). Van Eyck lived on the present Gouden Handstraat across the canal from the Wednesday Market. He died there in 1441. Memling lived on Sint Jorisstraat.

After the death of Philip the Good in Bruges in 1467, the town experienced a gradual decline. In addition to a general recession in the cloth industry, there was a change in trade routes. There were political difficulties as well. Sovereignty was transferred from the Burgundians to the Hapsburgs. Following the death of his wife, Mary of Burgundy, in a hunting accident, Maximillian, a Germanic foreigner and the first of the Hapsburgs in Flanders, had quartered German troops in the city. In reaction to his revocation of town privileges Bruges held Maximillian prisoner for three months in 1488 in the Cranenburg on the Grote Markt at the corner of Sint Armandstraat. There he had to watch the trials and executions of a number of his men. Maximillian, following his release, responded by favoring Antwerp. In addition the access of Bruges to the sea gradually clogged with silt. The silting had begun in the mid–1300s. The city had then shifted the port to neighboring Damme, the population of which rose rapidly to 60,000, but in the mid–1400 the Zwin outside Damme rapidly silted up. It became impassable to deep draft ships and Bruges was cut off from direct contact with the sea.[5]

The moving of waterways and subsequent silting was a natural process in the tidal estuaries. In the early eleventh century a flood through the estuaries of the Zwin and the Ijzer had prompted the first systematic efforts to tame the sea. In response, the Oude Zeedijk between Oostduinkerke and Lo and the dikes between Brende and Oudenburg and between Blankenberge and Bruges had been constructed. Huge Scheldt floods in 1134 had wiped out settlements but in 1167 Count Philip of Alsace demanded 1,000 workers from the Count of Holland, whom he had defeated, to construct a dike at Damme across a new arm of the Zwin, which had been created by the 1134 flood. The dike building, though it protected towns and facilitated the draining of polders, interfered with tides and contributed to silting.[6]

As the silting progressed Antwerp became the chief emporium of the Hanseatic League and Bruges became in common parlance *Bruges-la-Mort* (Bruges, the Dead). That the decline of Bruges was not abruptly catastrophic for all of its residents is demonstrated by the fact that the merchant Jan van Moescroen commissioned Michaelangelo to sculpt the Virgin and Child, which he donated to the late twelfth and early thirteenth century Gothic Onze Lieve Vrouwekerk around 1514.[7] Bruges, however, did not recover commercially until the construction of the Boudewijn Kanaal and the development of the port of Zeebrugge between 1895 and 1907.

Among the noted residents of Bruges was Charles Stuart, the future Charles II, who set up his court in Bruges in 1656. In the nineteenth century the city was visited by Henry Wadsworth Longfellow, who was particularly impressed by the Bruges belfry, the most prominent architectural feature of Bruges. The lower portion was built from 1282 to 1286, and the octagonal upper section between 1482 and 1487. To Longfellow. the nineteenth century American Romantic, the bells "seemed like a heart of iron beating in the ancient tower."[8]

## Brussels

Brussels developed as a transit point between the cloth centers of the west and Cologne. The first written record of Brussels dates from 966. The village (Broucsella, "place in the marsh") located in a marsh created by the Senne (now canalized and covered—the Boulevards Adolphe Max, Anspach, and Lemonnier) grew because it provided a convenient river crossing on the route between Cologne and Ghent and Bruges. The route was the Steenweg. One section of the route eventually entered the city at the Porte de Schaerbeek and the other through the Porte de Namur and met at the eastern end of the rue du Marché aux Herbes. The Steenweg lined with stalls crossed the Senne near the town wharf, which functioned until the sixteenth century, near the present–day Bourse. The Steenweg then continued to the Porte de Flandre.

In 977 the settlement passed to the dukes of Lotharingia, who erected a castle on an island on the Senne. In 1041 the residence of the dukes was transferred to the Coudenberg, which overlooks the lower city. The new castle, which became the principal palace in all of the Low Lands, was partially located in the present Parc de Bruxelles.

In the first part of the twelfth century the first fortified wall was erected, remnants of which are the towers Noire, Villers, and Anneessens. The town market was set up in what is now the Grand' Place. As the town prospered its merchants grew in self–confidence. The increasingly wealthy bourgeoisie drew up an assertion of their rights in 1312, the charter of Cortenberg. This was confirmed in the *Joyeuse Entrée* of Wenceslas of Luxembourg and Joanna of Brabant in 1356.

New more encompassing walls were erected between 1357 and 1383. They were strengthened in the sixteenth century and remained in place until the nineteenth century, when, with the exception of the Porte de Hal, they were pulled down to make way for the ring boulevards.

While Bruges, Ghent, Ypres, Leuven, and Antwep declined, Brussels became the administrative center for the Spanish and then the Austrian Netherlands. During the latter eighteenth century the Palais du Roi was constructed partly on the site of the former Coudenberg palace which had been destroyed by fire. On the other side of the Parc de Bruxelles the Palais de la Nation, which today houses the parliament, was constructed.

## Ghent, St. Baaf Cathedral, and the Iconoclasts

By 1500 English competition had dealt the cloth trade a fatal blow. Ghent, however, because of its location flourished as a center for the grain trade between France and Antwerp. In addition to the Leie and Scheldt, a canal dug to Terneuzen, now in the Netherlands, was opened in 1547. Due to the carrying trade and a revival in tapestry making Ghent flourished while Ypres and Bruges were in deep decay. However, with the closure of the Scheldt by the United Provinces (Netherlands) in 1644, Ghent too suffered economic decline.

Sint Baafskathedral in Ghent is one of the most magnificent churches in Belgium. A chapel in honor of St. John the Baptist stood on the site in 941. A Romanesque church replaced it in the twelfth century. From the end of the thirteenth century this was progressively transformed into the present Gothic structure, which was completed in 1550. Charles V was baptized in the church in 1500. Ironically Charles considered razing the church in 1540 because architects recommended its site as the best location for the construction of a new castle to over-awe the progressively restive population of Ghent.[9] The iconoclasts inspired by a Calvinist desire to reform and purify the church, including a desire to strip churches of statuary, which to them smacked of idolatry, did much damage to the cathedral in 1566 and 1576. In 1566, spurred by "purifying" preachers near Cassel, 55 churches, abbeys, and monasteries in a 200 square mile area had their works of art, as well as many buildings, destroyed. In Ghent in a 24-hour period seven parish churches, one collegiate church, 25 monasteries, 10 hospitals, and seven chapels were "cleansed." A mob of 400 did the same in 46 surrounding villages.[10] During the 1576 attack Catholics were expelled from the church and it became the site for Protestant worship until the Duke of Parma reclaimed it for the Catholic Church in 1585. In 1578 Calvinists burned a number of Franciscans at the stake and turned their priory into a stable. In 1580 the Catholic religion was officially banned though only 1,500 of Ghent's inhabitants were hard-core Calvinists and they were supported by only a third of the population.[11]

The cathedral contains the *Ghent Altarpiece*, sometimes known as *The Adoration of the Mystic Lamb*, completed by Jan van Eyck in 1432. This work, "the greatest monument of early Flemish painting,"[12] was commissioned by a patrician of Ghent, Joos Vydt, and his wife, Isabella Borluut, who are depicted on two of the panels. The subject of the central portion is the Mystic Lamb of God of the Apocalypse (the Book of Revelation), who saved humankind by his immolation on Cavalry. Depicted is saved humankind gathering with the Lamb at the Second Coming of Christ. Although the many innovative possibilities of oil paint were not discovered all at once, van Eyck "(. . .) was long credited with the actual 'invention' of oil painting."[13] Van Eyck and his brother Hubert were, at least, "the first to utilize fully and systematically" the technique known as "atmospheric perspective." The altarpiece was designed and partially completed by Jan's brother Hubert before his death in 1426. It took Jan van Eyck the next seven years to complete it.[14] In 1566 the altarpiece, which was located in one of St. Baaf's chapels, barely escaped destruction by the iconoclasts. It survived that threat, but its subsequent history has been anything but uneventful. The Holy Roman Emperor Joseph

II, the ruler of the Austrian Netherlands from 1780 to 1790, was offended by the naked portrayals of Adam and Eve. He temporarily substituted clothed versions, which are now located at the entrance to the cathedral's nave. The painting was stolen by the French during the revolutionary period, taken with so much other looted art work to Paris, and only returned in 1815 following the Second Peace of Paris. The outer wings were sold to the Berlin Museum, but were restored by the Versailles Treaty in 1919. Two panels, "St. John the Baptist" and "The Just Judge" were stolen on April 10, 1934. A note led to the discovery of the panel depicting John the Baptist at the left-luggage office of the North Train Station in Brussels, but "The Just Judge" was never recovered. It was replaced by a copy. The whole work was stolen by the Nazis in World War II. It was recovered in an Austrian salt mine and returned to Ghent by the Americans.

### Antwerp: Heyday, Conflict, and Strangulation

Antwerp's cathedral, Onze Lieve Vrouw, the largest Gothic cathedral in Belgium, is a testament to the wealth and self-confidence of the citizens of Antwerp in the fourteenth and fifteenth centuries. Originally a twelfth century Romanesque church, the cathedral was rebuilt in Gothic style between 1352 and 1525. Charles V christened the largest bell in its tower, "Carolus," in 1507.

In the fifteenth century Antwerp rose in commercial importance as Bruges declined. It had profited from a number of floods between 1375 and 1424, which deepened the West Scheldt and rendered it navigable by two-hundred-ton ocean going ships.[15] Antwerp became the principal port of the Netherlands. Since Bruges excluded English cloth out of protectionism, Antwerp became a center for English imports, which were finished and dyed in the city's workshops. Antwerp became home port to four hundred ships and by the early 1500s a thousand merchants and bankers set up operations there. Antwerp and its depot on Walcheren Island in the Scheldt estuary were visited by 2,500 ships annually, four times the activity of the port of London in the early sixteenth century. The Hanseatic League opened a house on the Corn Market in 1468 and moved its offices from Bruges to Antwerp in 1553. At the city's stock exchange, which opened in 1532, currency, letters of credit, and debts could be traded daily. Antwerp became a center for international finance and pioneered practices and procedures, which were copied elsewhere, especially after 1580 when Protestants fled the city and brought its advanced practices to Amsterdam. In 1520 agents of the Holy Roman Emperor were permanently stationed in the city to negotiate loans. The city's renaissance style city hall completed in 1565 mirrored the prosperity of the city's merchants and bankers. The growth of Antwerp as a port and business center stimulated a rapid expansion of the city's population as migrants poured in from eastern Brabant and Flanders. Antwerp, which had only 33,000 inhabitants in 1480, had 55,000 by 1526, and 100,000 in 1568, making it the largest city in the Low Lands.[16]

Antwerp was a magnet for people of culture as well as business. Albrecht Drürer resided in Antwerp in 1520-1521, and it was later home to Pieter Paul Rubens. Pieter Bruegel the Elder, although he was probably born near 's Hertogenbosch in north Brabant,[17] spent his working life in Antwerp and Brussels. His work, in addition to magnificently depicting the popular culture of his time, contains pointed critiques of the growing religious intolerance. *The Blind Leading the Blind* (1568) is a visual parable. In *The Triumph of Death* (c. 1562), amid a ravaged countryside, a swarm of skeletons kill people and drag them to hell. In *The Slaughter of the Innocents in Bethelem* (1566) Herod's murderous soldiers are dressed in the garb of the troops of Philip II.

Antwerp was also "the most important center of activity for printers" during the sixteenth century.[18] Christopher Plantijn set up his printing house there in 1555. His most spectacular accomplishment was the printing of an eight-volume edition of the Bible in Latin, Greek, Hebrew, Syriac, and Aramaic. The printing houses served as magnets for the humanistic scholars of the era. When Thomas More went to Bruges in 1515 to represent English merchants, he was in the process of writing *Utopia*. He met the great humanist Erasmus (1469-1536) at that time, and when he had finished *Utopia*, Jeroom Buysleden, a councillor from Mechelen, wrote its introduction. Erasmus dedicated his *Praise of Folly* to More, and when he established the Collegium Trilingue at the University of Leuven, he did so with a bequest from Buysleden.[19]

The prosperity of Antwerp declined during the reign of Philip II as the religious war and its aftermath ravaged the city. In 1566 iconoclasts pillaged the cathedral. The city's merchants were drawn to Calvinism and William of Orange, who led the Dutch Revolt, which began in 1567, for a time set up his headquarters there. In response to the "Protestant fury" of 1566, Philip II dispatched the Duke of Alba and 10,000 troops to Flanders and Brabant to restore order. On November 4, 1576, Alba's unpaid and mutinous troops sacked Antwerp. "The Spanish fury" with the cry "*Santiago! España! A sangre, a carne, a fuego, a sacco,*" killed 8,000 and destroyed 1,000 buildings.[20] In 1577 William of Orange regained control of Flanders and for eight years Catholicism could not be publicly practiced in Antwerp. An offensive led by the Duke of Parma restored the power of Spain in Flanders and with it Catholicism. In 1585 Parma's forces conquered Antwerp and its future would lie with Belgium rather than the Netherlands. Archduke Albrecht and his wife Isabella presided over a new period of cultural flowering. Rubens' house on the Wapper dates from 1610.[21] However, when the Dutch closed the Scheldt in 1644 cutting Antwerp off from the sea, the city, though it remained an important business center for the southern Netherlands, entered a long period of relative decline.

## *Begijnhofen/Béguinages*

Religious houses for women in the Low Lands date from the Merovingian period. However, the original convents were the preserves of the nobility. In the eleventh century, as Christianity became internalized among the common people, whose ancestors had often only become Christian as a result of compulsion or nominal assent but retained many of their pagan beliefs, a broader spectrum of women sought the support of religious community life. Cistercian convents were set up for non-noble women in the late twelfth century and by the thirteenth century women were joining together in small religious communities. By the middle of the thirteenth century these had become begijnhofen or béguinages, "the most important expression of women's religiosity in the Low Countries."[22] Similar groups existed elsewhere in the West but in the Low Lands they persisted despite the order for their abolition by the Council of Vienne in the fourteenth century.

Béguinages were self-contained lay sisterhoods. The name has been ascribed to St. Begga, the daughter of Pepin of Landen, but stems more probably from Lambert le Bègue. Lambert, a Liège priest, who died in 1187, devoted himself to the bereaved families of crusaders. He encouraged the establishment of communities for widows and other women, who could have the support of a religiously oriented community life without taking vows. Almost all Flemish cities possessed a *begijnhof*. Altogether around 70 were formed between 1230 and 1295. However, today only 30 physically survive in one form or another. Only the begijnhof in Bruges is still occupied by a female religious community.

Leuven possesses the oldest and, probably, most impressive begijnhof, the Groot Begijnhof, founded before 1232 along two branches of the Dijle outside the first city wall, which was erected in the 1100s. The begijnhof in Leuven was on the village model in contrast to the Bruges begijnhof constructed around a court or yard. It was located in an area called Ten Hove near the Wolvenpoort, or Wolves' Gate. After the second city wall was constructed in the 1300s the area became part of Leuven proper. The architectural style of the begijnhof today is predominantly seventeenth century, when the community reached its peak of approximately 300 members.[23]

The beguine movement was rooted in the formal lay religious groups, which arose in the fervor of the 1100s. Some, such as the Waldentians, were branded heretical. Their dedication to private spirituality and the quest for perfection in lay associations generated distrust among the clerically dominated church. The beguines in the Low Countries were allowed to continue after the Council of Vienne because they followed a regimen, which resembled that of the accepted monastic and mendicant orders. Due to their orthodoxy and exemplary life-style they won the support of influential church leaders.

The beguines provided community, security, and support for lay women who wished to follow a life of service and prayer without entering a convent. The association was voluntary and could be terminated at will. It also provided women in a paternalistic period the opportunity to run their own lives and to engage in economic activities on their own. The community at Leuven manufactured thread and cloth, did embroidery and sewing, took in washing, and provided child-care. In 1646 there were 270 female children between the ages of 5 and 16 living in the begijnhof. These boarders and day students were taught to read and write and taught to sew and spin.[24]

The great begijnhof of Leuven was at first part of St. Quentin parish. St. Quentin located on Naamsestraat towers over the begijnhof. In 1250 the beguines' chapel became an independent entity with its own priest and cemetery. The community erected St. John the Baptist church in 1305. But it was subsequently modified, especially between 1421 and 1468, and its interior was given a baroque overlay in the seventeenth century. Today the church serves as the university parish.

The French Revolution destroyed the begijnhof as a living community. The Belgian Social Welfare Council, which had taken possession of the complex, sold it to the university in 1962. The university renovated the property, which had fallen into disuse, and now uses it for student and faculty housing.

# CHAPTER 5

# The Spanish Netherlands

Shortly after Philip's accession in 1556, the Low Lands erupted. Philip's vice-roy, his natural sister Margaret of Parma, and her advisor Antoine Cardinal Granvelle, the bishop of Mechelen, provoked increasing opposition. Granvelle was a strong proponent of a church sanctioned royal authority and advocated repression both of political opponents and religious non-conformists. In addition, there were severe economic problems. Philip's moratorium on the payment of state debt enraged the small investors who had purchased state bonds on the Antwerp exchange. The termination of English cloth processing in Antwerp in 1563 spelled disaster for those who processed it or traded it. Following the winter of 1564–65 the harvest was meager and the price of grain and bread soared.[1] In April 1566 a league of disaffected nobles joined together in the Compromise of Breda. The pro-Spanish Count of Barlaimont disparagingly discounted them as a pack of beggars.[2] The 300 protesting nobles then assumed as a badge of distinction the label "beggars," that was meant as an insult.

There were continual incidents. Philip responded to the fervor of the Calvinists with the Inquisition, and on the Protestant side the "Iconoclastic Fury" exploded in August 1566. An emotional sermon by a Calvinist preacher in Steenvoorde, in Western Flanders, led the congregation to purify a local church of its "idolatrous" statuary. The contagion rapidly spread to Ypres, Ghent, Mechelen, and Antwerp. Calvinist purists raged through churches smashing statues, breaking stained glass, and setting fire to religious artwork and church furnishings. The results of their van-dalism can still be seen in mutilated statues and empty niches.

## Philip Reacts

In 1567 Philip dispatched the Duke of Alba at the head of 20,000 Spanish troops. Alba's Council of Troubles, popularly called the Council of Blood, ordered 1,071 executions and 11,136 punishments of banishment and confiscation of property.[3] In one of his more atrocious moves he arrested and executed the Catholic Counts of Egmont and Hoorn. They were beheaded in the Grand' Place of Brussels for urging a policy of conciliation. The estates of those who refused to defend themselves before the Council of Blood were confiscated. Among those whose estates were seized was William, the Silent, of Orange, a member of the high nobility who had advocated toleration but became a Protestant in 1566, and subsequently led the Protestant resistance to Philip. He had been summoned to defend himself before the Council of Blood, but chose rather to oppose Philip from his possessions in Germany out of the reach of the Spanish king. By 1572 William had gained the support of a number of city councils. Representatives of twelve cities assembled as the States of Holland affirmed the freedom of religion and proclaimed William stadholder, or chief magistrate.

Conciliation was neither the style of Philip nor Alba. A war marked by extraordinary cruelty and brutality lasted from 1568 to 1648. The sacking of the pro-Orange cities of Mechelen, Zutphen, and Naarden led to a backlash. The reaction in Flanders against the Spanish was so strong that William of Orange, now stadholder of Holland and Zeeland, was able to convince the southern provinces to join the north and to affirm religious toleration in the Pacification of Ghent on November 8, 1576. Philip's bastard brother, Don John of Austria, temporarily acquiesced to the demand of a united States-General, and ratified the Pacification. His acquiescence, however, was merely temporary. Radical Calvinists had been unwilling to respect the toleration promised to Catholics and even moderate Calvinists were disinclined to trust that Philip would really allow religious dissent. Aided by the growing misgivings of the Walloon nobility over the rapid spread of Calvinism, Don John went on the offensive. Aided by an army commanded by Alexander Farnese, the Duke of Parma, Don John asserted Philip's authority over much of the south. Despite his zeal to create a homogenous Catholic society, Don John promised that the old political freedom of the provinces would be restored. On January 6, 1579, Walloon deputies from Artois, Hainault, Namur, Luxembourg, and Limburg affirmed their allegiance to Philip and Catholicism in the Union of Arras. For their part, representatives of Brabant, Flanders, Tournai, Holland, Zeeland, and Guelders responded on January 23 with the Union of Utrecht and a declaration of independence from Spain.

### The Duke of Parma

The fortunes of war rather than diplomacy, politics, or free choice, determined the general line of demarcation between the Protestant north and the Catholic south. C. Bruneel writes, "Parma's victories led to the complete restoration of Catholicism."[4] This was facilitated by the fact that "Catholicism was already the deeply anchored faith of most of the inhabitants of the region."[5] The Duke of Parma subdued the rebel cities of Flanders and Brabant one by one, cutting them off and starving them into submission. The resistance of the Calvinist Republic of Ghent collapsed in September 1584 and Brussels gave way in March 1585. At the end of 1584 the duke had decided to lay siege to Antwerp still held by the Protestants. The population of the city was roughly divided into thirds: Protestants, who were drawn both from the property owning middle class and wage earners, constituted a third; Catholics constituted a third; and finally another third who, though alienated from Rome, were reluctant to declare their religious sympathies.[6] The duke of Parma had 10,000 infantrymen and 1,700 cavalry. However, the Calvinists in the city, commanded by Philippe de Marnix, Lord of Sainte-Aldegonde, had a garrison of 20,000. Unable to encircle the city, the Duke of Parma had a blockade bridge constructed across the Scheldt to cut the city off from supplies from the sea or the Calvinist provinces to the north. The bridge completed on February 25, 1585, was quite an elaborate affair. Forts protected both ends of the 800 yard-long structure. The middle section rested on 32 barges chained together and anchored. Both wings of the bridge rested on pilings, which were protected by beams sharpened to points. Twenty galleys provided surface defense. The Calvinists employed a number of innovative devices in their effort to destroy the blockading bridge. Four floating barge-bombs with clockwork fuses were sent down river on April 5. One worked. It blew out 260 feet of the bridge and killed 800 Spanish soldiers. The effort, however, did not achieve its purpose. The duke was able to rebuild and improve his bridge-barricade. A Dutch sortie failed and the Spanish began their advance. The citadel fell on August 17 and the city surrendered.[7] Parma insisted that all Protestants leave Antwerp and the other cities of Brabant and Flanders. Within two years 200,000 people had left. The population of Antwerp, itself, dropped from 80,000 in 1585 to 42,000 in 1589. 150,000 refugees settled in the north where their skills and spirit made a significant contribution to the development of the Netherlands.[8]

### The Division Confirmed

In 1588 Philip's effort to crush the Anglo-Dutch combination failed with his Armada, and, though William of Orange died at the hands of a Catholic assassin in 1584, the Dutch Republic was proclaimed. In 1609 the Twelve-Year Truce virtually recognized the independence of the seven northern provinces. Though the south had accepted the Spanish king as their sovereign and there was a Spanish governor in Brussels, and though the Spanish controlled foreign and military policy, the south had a degree of autonomy. The provincial Estates, at least in theory, had control over taxation, and, after Philip handed over the Netherlands to his daughter Isabella in 1598, the provinces even possessed conditional independence.[9] Nevertheless, during the tenure of Isabella and her husband, Albrecht, the Southern Netherlands had a Spanish governor-general, who surrounded himself with Spanish advisors, and relied upon Spanish administrators. After Albrecht of Austria died childless in 1621, the province reverted to Philip IV of Spain, and Isabella was reduced to the role of governor-general. Though Spain formally respected local and provincial privileges, a policy of centralization was pursued. The Council of State was eclipsed by a royal commission, which contained only two Low Landers, and after 1634 the States-General would not be called together again during the Spanish period.[10]

Under Philip III the Twelve-Year Truce of 1609 gave way to the Thirty Years War (1618–1648). James Howell in 1640 called Flanders the "cockpit of Europe."[11] From that time through the middle of the twentieth century Flanders and Belgium have been the site of numerous battles and campaigns as powerful countries attempted to assert themselves over one another on the rolling countryside of a people who were generally unfortunate bystanders and victims of the wars of others. The French joined the fight in the fourth phase of the Thirty Years War. They took Arras in 1640 and defeated the Spanish at Rocroi in 1643. In order to concentrate upon the French threat, Philip IV signed the Peace of Münster on January 30, 1648. At Münster Spain formally recognized the independence of the United Provinces, and, although free trade was established between the south and the north, Spain accepted the closure of the Scheldt effected by the Dutch who had captured Hulst in 1644. The common wisdom is that "the great cloth cities and trading ports of Flanders declined into provincial backwaters,"[12] while in contrast the Dutch Netherlands became a prosperous and dynamic maritime empire. The Dutch, for their part, had decided, by this time, that it would be beneficial to have the Spanish Netherlands as a buffer between themselves and their powerful ally, France, to the south.

### Economic Recovery

It is perhaps over-stating the situation in Antwerp to refer to it in the 1600s as a "provincial backwater." Antwerp, though the Scheldt was blocked, recovered from its trauma. It served as the financial center for the Spanish Netherlands and as an exchange market between the Protestant north of Europe and the Catholic south. Its stock market, bankers, and insurance brokers were all active and it became the financial and market center for a trading network in the Mediterranean. Its printing industry produced Spanish religious books, which circulated not only in Europe but also in the Spanish American Empire. Its artisans produced devotional prints, art works, and luxury goods. Its factories produced soap and glass and refined sugar and salt.

The textile industry of Flanders and Brabant, which was already declining, was dealt another blow by the turmoil of the late sixteenth century. The lighter cloth of

Verviers proved more desirable than the heavier woolens of the Flemish. However, by 1650 the output of linen had again reached its 1570 level. As in Antwerp, many artisans elsewhere in the Spanish Netherlands turned to luxury and highly finished goods. The tapestries of Bruges gained renewed popularity in the seventeenth century. Goldsmiths prospered in Dinant and Liège. In addition, Liège had profited from its neutrality in the conflicts of the late 1500s and the first half of the seventeenth century. Its iron production flourished. It produced nails and fittings for the shipyards of the Dutch and it produced weapons for all buyers.

Despite the recovery the period of turmoil and its aftermath had adversely affected many. According to C. Brunel, "(. . .) broad segments of the population experienced a decline in their standard of living."[13] Many desperate people turned to usurious moneylenders. To offer some relief and to combat the exorbitant interest rates of the money lenders, Isabella and Albrecht established fifteen pawn shops called "Mountains of Charity," which loaned money at reduced rates in exchange for goods left as collateral. Nevertheless, there were many who were reduced to begging or vagabondage. The "deserter" vagabond was a problem during the wars. The threat to property and life posed by them created a general fear and loathing of the vagabond and resulted in punitive measures being adopted by the government, including condemnation to the galleys.[14]

## Bulwark of Catholicism

Localism in the south did not mean toleration. Archdukes Albrecht and Isabella enthusiastically supported the Counter Reformation. Nevertheless, pockets of Protestantism persisted in East Flanders between Oudenaarde and Ronse around St–Maria-Horebeke and in Etikhove and Colzele. However, Protestant churches were not allowed to have towers and had to be a distance from the public roads. Civil authorities enforced Catholic strictures. In the Ronse area in 1649 a farmer was fined for plowing his fields on Sunday. In June 1650 a widow was fined for soaking her wash on St. John's day. Singing anti-Spanish songs could merit a person five years in a galley.[15]

The Jesuits and other orders played a central role in the Counter Reformation in the Spanish Netherlands. By 1626 there were 1,600 Jesuits in the Spanish Netherlands and they ran thirty-four colleges (secondary schools). These colleges because of their quality attracted the children of the intellectual and social elites and enabled the Jesuits to make a strong impression on the future leaders of the society of the Spanish Netherlands. However, not all Catholics were enamored with the Jesuits. They were not able to challenge the dominance of the University of Leuven, which was staffed by secular priests. Cornelius Jansen, a professor of Theology at the University of Leuven and subsequently bishop of Ypres, took issue with their emphasis upon human freedom and rationality. Supported by the secular priests of the Theology faculty at Leuven and a number of bishops, Jansen stressed the complete weakness of humans and their dependence upon Divine grace. Though Jansenism was condemned in 1642, strong ecclesiastical and political support for Jansen's ideas endured in the Spanish Netherlands.[16]

There is some similarity between the role of Catholicism in Belgium and in Poland and Ireland, where it became a central part of Polish and Irish identity. The church in Flanders was not only an expression of religious feeling but also a sign of the country's survival. When Flanders was seen politically as of minimal importance, its own feeling of identity was preserved by the Catholic Church. The increase in monasteries and convents, the building of fine new churches, and the encouragement of religious devotions and festivities kept the country together.[17]

## Art

During the Spanish period lush, elaborate, decorative art flourished in the Spanish Netherlands. This was the era of Peter Paul Rubens. It was also the time when elaborate baroque churches were constructed to mirror the Church triumphant, or perhaps more kindly to awe the faithful with the glory of God's kingdom. In addition to the construction of baroque churches, older churches were "modernized" with dramatically expressive statuary, generous applications of gold leaf, piles of black and white marble, and curiously elaborate wooden pulpits covered with carvings of fauna and flora.[18]

## French Aggression

After the 1659 Peace of the Pyrenees, which gave France Dunkirk, most of Artois, and several fortresses, the history of the Spanish Netherlands continued to be a story of war between France and Spain and France and the Dutch. France under Louis XIV attempted to annex the Spanish Netherlands and destroy the commercial strength of the Netherlands. In dreary succession came the War of Devolution (1667–1668), the Dutch War (1672–1678), the War of the League of Augsburg (1690–1697), and the War of Spanish Succession (1701–1713). These wars saw siege warfare centering on the fortresses such as Namur and Maastricht.

One of France's prodigious accomplishments during the Dutch War was the capture of Maastricht, considered to be the strongest fortress in Europe, in only 13 days. This remarkable accomplishment was the work of Sébastien le Preste, the Marquis de Vauban, the great French military engineer. He meticulously prepared his assault, first by constructing two lines of concentric trenches around the city to cut it off and defend his force from attempted relief from the outside and from sorties from within the fortified city. He then approached the city with zigzag trenches and additional concentric lines of trenches for the artillery, which was to breach the walls, and for his infantry which was to attack once the walls had been breached. Maastricht fell on July 2, 1673, but, before it did, one of the French casualties was the heroic Charles de Batz de Castelmore, Count d'Artagnan, field marshal and commander of the Company of Gray Musketeers. This d'Artagnan would become the hero of Alexander Dumas' *Three Musketeers.* The striking ease with which the French took Maastricht, so frightened the countries of Europe that it gained for the Dutch allies, who eventually forced the French to give up their most ambitious war aims. It was Spain, which had to satisfy France by ceding to it a generous section of the Spanish Netherlands.[19]

During the War of the League of Augsburg, Namur, because of its strategic position at the confluence of the Meuse and the Sambre and its strong citadel perched upon a steep hill dominating the rivers, was twice besieged. On May 26, 1692, the French launched their attack, under the direction of Vauban, against the Dutch defenders. The conquest of the city took only eight days, but the citadel, commanded by the Dutch military engineer Baron Menno of Coehoorn, held out until the end of the month. Louis XIV was present to watch the battle as was his court historian Jean Racine. And Nicolas Boileau, the famous poet, in his *"Ode sur la prise de Namur,"* celebrated the feat, which cost only 2,600 French, compared to twice as many defenders. Despite French victories at Steenkerke in Hainaut in July 1692 and at Neerwinden near Liège in July 1693, the kingdom of France had become, in the words of Fénelon, a great hospital. Voltaire later wrote that France listened to the *Te Deum* celebrating military victories while it was dying of hunger. William III of Orange took advantage of France's weakness to reconquer Namur. Coehoorn's engineers dug their trenches and tunnels to the edge of the city's walls and the Dutch artillery was then able to smash them in a number of places. On August 4 Duke Louis François de Boufiers, marshal of France, sealed himself and his forces in the citadel. After nearly a month of pounding a general assault was launched on August 30. After thousands of dead on both sides, Boufiers capitulated on September 1.[20]

During the 1695 campaign, Louis XIV ordered François de Neufville, the Marquis de Villeroy, who commanded the French field armies in Flanders, to divert attention from Namur by an assault on Brussels. Villeroy placed 18 large cannon and 25 mortars on the heights over Anderlecht, which gave them a command of the city center. The French then bombarded Brussels for 36 hours. 16 churches and approximately 4,000 houses were destroyed. Much damage was done to the area around the Grand' Place.[21] Following the surrender of the French garrison at Namur, Louis' Minister of War, François Michel le Tellier, the Marquis of Louvois, ordered a systematic program of destruction as the French withdrew from Flanders. He decreed that "Flanders be put in a position whereby she would be unable to contribute anything to Spain for a long time to come."[22] Nevertheless, the guild houses, which surrounded Brussels Grand' Place, were rebuilt in three and a half years.

In 1700, following the death of Charles II, the last of the Spanish Hapsburgs, Louis succeeded in placing his grandson, Philip of Anjou, on the throne of Spain. This threat of French hegemony led to the formation of a formidable coalition, which included England, the Netherlands, and the Holy Roman Emperor. These allies were determined to prevent the amalgamation of France and the Spanish Netherlands, along with the rest of the Spanish Empire. During the subsequent War of Spanish Succession France had to face John Churchill, the Duke of Marlborough, and Prince Eugene of Savoy in the Spanish Netherlands. Marlborough's victory in 1706 at Ramillies, north east of Namur, forced France to give up most of the territory it had seized in the Spanish Netherlands. Though the French took Ghent and Bruges in 1708, Marlborough drove them back with his victory at Oudenaarde in 1709. In the 1713 Treaty of Utrecht France renounced all claims to the Spanish Netherlands and accepted their transfer to the Hapsburg Emperor Charles VI. Thus the Spanish Netherlands became the Austrian Netherlands.

# CHAPTER 6

# The Austrian Netherlands

Sovereignty in the southern Netherlands passed from Spain to Austria in 1713. In spite of the unsuccessful efforts of Emperor Charles VI to introduce a centralized administration utilizing French style intendants, the provinces of the Austrian Netherlands retained the high degree of local autonomy, which they had won in the Union of Arras. Despite the fact that the individual provinces of the southern Netherlands asserted their autonomy by demanding that new monarchs be inaugurated in each individual province, there was a consciousness of the unity of the entire southern Netherlands. This consciousness of collective identity and autonomy was "reflected in the actual structure of the state," with the location of a court and government in Brussels. It was also reflected in the "freedoms and rights" of the church in the southern Netherlands, and in the realm of culture.[1]

## Barrier Fortresses

According to the Barrier Treaty of 1715, the Dutch gained the right to garrison border fortifications at Namur, Dendermonde, Tournai, Menen, and Veurne. This was intended to serve as a barrier against future French encroachments. The safeguard, though costly, because it had to be supported by the taxes of the Austrian Netherlands, proved worthless during the War of Austrian Succession (1740-1748). In 1744 the French invaded and overwhelmed the Dutch without difficulty. Though the forces of Louis XV occupied the area, it was returned to Austria through the Peace of Aix-la-Chapelle, which ended the war in 1748. Louis XV also returned the Manikin Pis, the 1619 statue by Duquesnoy, which had been removed from Brussels by the British in 1742 to prevent it from falling into the hands of the French. "Liberated" by French troops at Grammont, Louis generously returned it dressed in a French uniform and crowned with a French three-corner hat. Because of the uselessness of the Dutch garrisons during the War of Austrian Succession the Austrians after the war refused any longer to pay to maintain them. Emperor Joseph II, finally, repudiated the Barrier Treaty in 1782 and the Dutch troops were withdrawn.

## The People

The life of most Belgians in the eighteenth century was confined and short. The economy was adversely affected by the custom laws of 1670, through which France discouraged the import of luxury items from the Spanish, then Austrian, Netherlands by means of a high importation tax, and the laws of 1680, which, through low customs taxes, encouraged imports into the southern Netherlands from Holland and England. Charles VI imposed criminal penalties against begging and vagrancy but measures to aid the indigent were piecemeal and temporary. The pillory, flogging, branding and banishment did not solve the problem of destitution which was aggravated by the famine of 1693–1694, the "great winter" of 1709–1710, and the "long winter" of 1740, not to mention the devastation of frequent military campaigns.[2] Education languished. In Flanders a bare three percent of the population could read or write. Even before the Enlightenment, learning and books became suspect. At the University of Leuven a sterile traditionalism dominated and the memorization of standard answers passed for academic excellence. Peasants and workers were largely tied to their village or employment. A peasant could not leave his village unless the other villagers were willing to assume financial responsibility for him. Anyone familiar with peasant society would realize how improbable that was. Workers could not leave their employment without permission from civic authorities. Steady employment could not be obtained without a certificate from the previous employer stating that the worker, though in good standing, had to be released. Workers seldom lived long. Brussels' Pachéco Hospital admitted to its charity any woman fifty or older. Few workers reached fifty and those who did were generally too infirm to continue to work.[3] Nevertheless, A. De Gomicourt, writing on the conditions in the 1780s, stated "I know no country where the land is better cultivated than in the Austrian Netherlands. (. . .) All the inhabitants of the town of the Netherlands live, if not in opulence, at least in very easy circumstances which are even better in country districts than in towns."[4] And Jan Craeybeckx argues that "(. . .) society in the Belgium of this period was far from being as torpid or backward-looking as the textbooks and most general history books would have us believe."[5]

Though infant mortality remained high, the population grew significantly after 1740 largely because of the decline of the bubonic plague and the increased utilization of the potato, which greatly improved nutrition. By 1784 the population of the Austrian Netherlands and the prince-bishopric of Liège had risen to perhaps

2,650,000. The Austrian Netherlands was largely rural despite a degree of urbanization that was very high by contemporary European standards. 25 percent of the people lived in cities. The largest city was the administrative center Brussels with approximately 75,000 inhabitants. Antwerp, Ghent, and Liège each had somewhat more than 50,000. Bruges numbered 31,000 and Tournai 26,000. Mechelen, Mons, and Leuven each had around 20,000. 65 percent of the people spoke Dutch and 90 percent of the inhabitants of Brussels were Dutch speakers.[6]

The common people, according to a contemporary, were

> (. . .) creatures of habit, and day succeeds day in an atmosphere of undisturbed peacefulness. The good fortune of the people is its calmness, and life is lived in a straight line. Its affections have no emotion and its pleasures no movement. Its spirit, indeed, has little brilliance; and it may justly be said that it makes greater use of its moral sense than of its intellectual faculties.[7]

If the inhabitants of the Austrian Netherlands were creatures of habit, one of the habits, which the bourgeoisie and artisans had developed over time, was a taste for having their own say and their own way. Adrien de Meeüs describes it as "the republican feelings of the population."[8] A French representative in eighteenth century Brussels said that "the freedom of speech so much talked about in England could not be carried any further that it is here."[9] Due process was the rule not only for Belgians but foreign visitors as well.

## Charles VI

The people and the administrators of the Southern Netherlands took changes in sovereignty in stride. They were quite willing to accept new sovereigns or even occupiers as long as the sovereign or occupying power did not interfere with traditional rights and freedoms.[10] However, when these traditions were challenged, they offered resistance. Emperor Charles VI and his administrator, the Marquis de Prié, were confronted with open rebellion in Brussels led by the guilds. The enthusiasm of the craftsmen and merchants, however, was cooled by the execution of Frans Anneessens, the head of the guild of stonecutters, masons, sculptors, and slate-workers. Nevertheless, Charles removed the widely despised de Prié. In 1725 the emperor placed the Austrian Netherlands under the supervision of his sister, Archduchess Maria Elizabeth. Maria Elizabeth, who was strongly influenced by her Jesuit confessor, Amiot, provided "sensible and energetic" leadership.[11] In addition to the good sense of Maria Elizabeth, a crucial factor limiting Charles' absolutist pretensions was his need for cash. He was forced to spend 50 to 70 percent of the government's income in the Austrian Netherlands on defense and he also depended on his revenue from his new territory to pay the debts Austria had incurred with the United Provinces during the War of Spanish Succession with France. He was, therefore, placed in the position of a supplicant before the Estates of Brabant, continually asking for additional grants and gifts. Because of his need and his inability to forcibly extract wealth from this prosperous area he was compelled to pursue a policy of accommodation and concession.[12]

## Maria Theresa

The death of Charles in 1740 precipitated the War of Austrian Succession in which France and Prussia tried to take advantage of the fact that Charles did not have a male heir. During the war the French who occupied the area drove the Austrian administrators out of the Southern Netherlands. However, Charles' daughter and successor, Maria Theresa, was able to survive the war with most of her possessions, including the Austrian Netherlands, intact. Under Maria Theresa and her popular governor, the bon vivant Charles of Lorraine, economic development was fostered. Roads were paved with cobblestones. Canals were constructed (including the Mechelen-Leuven canal). The Peace of Aix-la-Chapelle removed many trade restrictions, which had hampered the export of goods from the Austrian Netherlands, and selective protective tariffs protected vulnerable domestic producers. Major roads grew from 37 miles in 1715 to 620 in 1789. Particularly important was the Aachen to Ostend highway, which allowed German goods to pass through Belgium and gave the Germans access to Belgian wheat and industrial products. The harbor facilities at Ostend were also improved and the Ghent canal deepened. New coalmines and glass works were established. Coal had been commercially mined in Belgium since the twelfth century. The early mines were generally family operations in which the whole family participated, and the skills and techniques were handed on from generation to generation. The first Newcomen pump was introduced in 1725 and provided the drainage, which enabled coalmines to be sunk deeper than 600 feet. The amount of coal which was mined increased from 400 tons in 1762 to 21,000 tons in 1785. The iron industry grew as well. As early as 1770 Jean-Philippe de Limbourg of Liège introduced the production of iron utilizing coke instead of charcoal.

Charles of Lorraine's successor, Count von Cobenzl, thwarted ecclesiastical censorship by giving precedence to the state censor, who with Cobenzl's support allowed the works of the French philosophes to be disseminated. Cobenzl took advantage of Rome's suppression of the Jesuit order in 1773 to replace the Jesuit colleges with royal Theresian Colleges. Cobenzl, by threatening to tax church property, persuaded the clerical First Estate to limit the resistance of the Estates of Flanders to the fiscal demands of Vienna. According to C. Bruneel, the aim of Cobenzl and the empress was not to "cripple the States" but to ensure that her interests prevailed. The "Teresian Compromise" consisted of a willingness to recognize local conditions and accept local customs as long as her will was accomplished.[13]

## Joseph II

Maria Theresa had warned her son, Joseph, that he should not attempt to interfere with the customs of the Austrian Netherlands. She wrote that the Austrian Netherlands were the "happy country (. . .) which furnishes us with so many resources." She added that even if the people of the Austrian Netherlands tenaciously retain "(. . .) their ancient, and even ridiculous prejudices, they are obedient and loyal and contribute more than our extensive and malcontent German lands."[14]

When Joseph II succeeded his mother, his penchant for well meaning and rational, but ill considered and precipitous change led to turmoil. Ellen Evans wrote "Joseph's enlightened proposals (. . .) were seen by Belgians of all classes not as desirable reform but as totally unwarranted intrusion into a well functioning society."[15] Quite oblivious to public opinion, Joseph informed the Estates of Brabant "I need no consent from you to do good."[16] Frederick the Great rightly observed that it was unfortunate that Joseph always took the second step before he took the first. Joseph's November 1781 Edict of Toleration, which gave Protestants and then Jews the rights of citizenship and a circumscribed freedom of worship, and his plans to rationalize the area's old administrative system led to unrestrained opposition. Nevertheless, further reforms followed in rapid succession. In 1783 he abolished contemplative orders and suppressed 163 monasteries. In 1784 he introduced civil marriage. In 1785 he required sermons to conform to the dictates of the state censor. In 1786 religious confraternities were abolished and he established a General Seminary in Leuven, where all future priests were to be trained to be state servants free of Ultramontanism. In 1787 he attempted to abrogate all traditional regional and urban privileges and reorganize the Austrian Netherlands with new provinces governed by civil administrators.[17] Adrien de Meeüs likened him to a royal Robespierre.[18]

## Revolution

In the process of his precipitous and radical efforts at reform, Joseph succeeded in alienating the clergy, the peasants, the bourgeoisie, the administrators, and the nobility. According to Janet Polasky,

> unlike their French neighbors, members of the third estate [in Belgium] shared privileges
> with the first two estates; all three orders reaped the prosperity of both the traditional

trades, and the growth of new commercial enterprises; and almost universally, all shared devotion to the Catholic Church.[19]

Jan Roegiers and N.C.F. van Sas perceptively enumerated the reasons for the failure of Joseph's revolution from above:

> Political self-consciousness, inside and outside the States, was too great in the Southern Netherlands for its citizens simply to roll over and accept Joseph's policy of uniformity. The wealth and power of important social groups were simply too considerable to tolerate the dangers that Joseph's reforms presented them. The highly Ultramontanist clergy were far too entrenched in society for Joseph to dismiss them so lightly. Moreover, a wide segment of the population was not so backward as to be unfamiliar with the new language of freedom that was hardly restricted to France.[20]

In 1787 the call of a Brussels lawyer, Henri van der Noot, for a tax strike in response to Joseph's violation of the rights of the nation, the *Blijde Inkomst*, won popular acceptance.[21] In addition to ideological reasons, the common people's discontent had been fueled by series of bad harvests which had driven up the price of bread.[22] The red, yellow, and black cockade, combining the colors of Brabant and Hainaut, appeared. Joseph II, who, because of the threat of war against Turkey, had depleted his garrison in Belgium to 22,000, most of whom were Belgians, was forced to rescind most of his edicts. He, however, held firm against the church. By early 1788, after Joseph appointed new ministers and a new military commander and cancelled some of his administrative and judicial reforms, his agents were able to restore order. Under the threat of military force the Third Estate gave way on January 26, 1789. That evening a notice was posted, which declared "The legitimate heirs of the liberty, the privileges, and especially the valor of the Belgians announce the death of their Grandmother Joyeuse Entrée and that of their Grandfather the Constitution of Brabant, both cruelly assassinated."[23] Van der Noot fled to the Dutch Republic where he called for foreign intervention to drive the Austrians from the south and a unification of the south with the Dutch Republic.

The agents of Joseph revoked the authority of the Estates of Hainault, and then that of the Estates of Brabant. Finally, on June 18 the emperor repudiated the *Blijde Inkomst*, the "constitution" of the Austrian Netherlands, which he had promised to respect when he became its ruler.[24] Joseph thus alienated those lawyers and elements of the urban leadership, who influenced by the Enlightenment, had initially supported his reforms, especially the ecclesiastical ones. The Flemish lawyer François Vonck[25] and his followers, the Vonckists, organized *Pro Aris et Focis* (For Altar and Hearth) committed to armed resistance. The Vonckists joined supporters of Van der Noot massed at Breda in the Dutch Republic. 2,800 armed rebels, commanded by Jean André van der Mersch, invaded the Austrian Netherlands on October 24. The Manifesto of the Brabantine People, repudiating Joseph, was proclaimed from the steps of the city hall in Hoogstraten. The Austrian forces attacked the rebels but were defeated at Turnhout and then routed at Ghent. These victories were won through urban guerrilla tactics. The Belgian army was supported by men sniping from windows and women throwing paving stone on the Austrians from roofs.[26] Brussels fell to the rebels on December 12, and by December 22 all of the country with the exception of Luxembourg had been liberated. The States-General of the southern Netherlands was convened in Brussels for its first joint meeting since 1632. On January 11, 1790, it enacted the Act of Union, drawn up by the anti-Josephist Antwerp priest Pierre van Eupen, the new state secretary. The Brabançon Revolt patterned its constitution on that of the United States,[27] and called the new state the Confédération des Etates Belgiques Unis, the United States of Belgium, the first time that the state had been designated as "Belgium." However, Belgium was not united. It was deeply divided, on the one hand, into the Statists, conservative supporters of the Estates, the clergy, van der Noot and his followers, and, on the other, the "democrats," the Vonckist supporters of a new style French "democracy." According to Ellen Evans, "ultimately, the failure of the Belgian revolt to evolve into a full-scale democratic revolution probably owed more to the country's relatively advanced economic stage and a lack of economic grievance in the middle classes than to an excess of traditionalism."[28] The clerical traditionalists were able to mobilize the people against the Vonckists whom they described as enemies of religion and the state.[29] Craeybeckx takes the interesting position that "(. . .) the Brabant Revolution was a welcome diversion enabling the privileged orders, guildmasters and a number of well-to-do burghers to keep the lower orders under better control, or at any rate to use them as a weapon against the progressives and [the] pro-Austrian faction."[30] The ensuing anarchy enabled Joseph II's brother and successor, Leopold II, with the moral support of the anti-French Triple Alliance of the Dutch Republic, England, and Prussia, to restore Austrian control. On December 10, 1790, representatives of the emperor met with representatives of the Dutch Republic, Prussia, and England at the Hague and those states agreed to recognize the restoration of Austrian rule in the southern Netherlands on the condition of the revocation of Joseph's ecclesiastical, administrative, and judicial reforms.[31] By the end of December Imperial troops had re-occupied Brussels.

### The Intrusion of Revolutionary France

War broke out between Austria and France in 1792. The issues transcended the Austrian Netherlands but the war had a fundamental impact upon the future of Belgium. General Charles Dumouriez's army defeated the Austrians at Jemappes on November 6, 1792. The southern Netherlands became a French protectorate on December 15, 1792 and was annexed by France in March 1793. However, a defeat of the French by the Austrians at Neerwinden on March 18, 1793, restored Austrian control until the French under General Jean Baptiste Jourdan were victorious at Fleurus on June 26, 1794. With the surrender of the Austrian fortress at Luxembourg city in June 1795, Austrian rule in the southern Netherlands had completely ended.

### Liège and the Climate of Revolution

Liège had its origin when a chapel was built in 558 where the Légie entered the Meuse. St. Monulphus, the bishop of Maastricht, had directed that the church be built and Liège was an appendage of the diocese of Maastricht until St. Hubert established the diocese in Liège in 720. Bishop Notger, appointed in 972, expanded the ecclesiastical administrative area and also transformed it into a base of secular power. He was made a prince-bishop by Emperor Otto I. The authority connected to the title of prince-bishop would endure for 800 years.

Long before the age of revolution there was continual tension between the merchants and craftsmen of the city and their bishops. The political success of the guilds in Flanders at the beginning of the fourteenth century inspired the artisans and lesser merchants of Liège. Rivalries between the bishops, the cannons of the cathedral, and the urban nobility or patricians enabled the artisans to assert themselves. In 1253 the prince-bishop issued a charter recognizing the right of the people to choose two of their own masters to serve as magistrates. In 1312 when the patricians attacked the priests of the cathedral chapter, who had sided with the guilds during the election of a new bishop, the guildsmen rallied to their support. 200 patricians and ten of the fourteen magistrates were killed by guildsmen inside the church of Saint Martin. The guilds then, at least nominally, gained control of the administration of the city. After the common people of the town, the Liègeois, aided Bishop Adolphe de la Marck against Brabant in 1343, they demanded the establishment of a representative council, the Council of XXII to provide popular input for the whole bishopric. The Council, however, was often rendered ineffective due to factionalism.[32]

Despite the fact that "class conflict remained the central hallmark of political life in Liège,"[33] the economic success of the bourgeoisie eventually enabled that class to assert itself. Coal mines were developed in the area as early as the twelfth century. Lead, zinc, and iron were plentiful and accessible, and the bishopric developed into a very important metallurgical center. In the latter half of the eighteenth century these industries were flourishing. With the aid of pumps and colliery lifts mines were sunk to depths, which were incredible for that time. An interesting peculiarity of the Liège area was *boteresse*. Women with straw and wooded baskets full of coal strapped to their backs and forehead carried coal to merchants as far away as

Maastricht. In the nineteenth century the work of these women, whose loads weighed more than they did, was increasingly rendered obsolete by barges but *boteresse* could still be seen in the early twentieth century.[34]

In the valley of the Vesdre, the wool center Verviers, established in 1651, was a new dynamic capitalist city without guild or municipal restrictions to hinder competition and the exploitation of its "free" workforce. Under Velbrueck who had become prince-bishop in 1772 industry and commerce were fostered, and Liège with 83,000 inhabitants overshadowed Brussels.

Along with industry and material progress grew a passion for "the Rights of Citizens." Liège became a center for the dissemination of newspapers and pamphlets. Inspired by the news of the fall of the Bastille in Paris on July 14, 1789, revolt erupted in Liège.[35] A workers' assembly at Polleur near Verviers in August led to the flight and dethronement of the prince bishop. The assembly promulgated a "Declaration of the Rights of Man," the abolition of feudal rights, and the establishment of universal suffrage. Though the prince-bishop was able to regain control with the assistance of Prussia, revolutionaries, exiles from Brabant and their counterparts from Liège, on January 20, 1792, formed the Committee of United Belgians and Liègeois in Paris. De Meeüs called this fusion of Brabant and Liège exiles "modern Belgium's birthday."[36] Three Belgian corps and a Liège legion fought with the French against the Austrians in 1792. The French were at first hailed as liberators. However, Flanders quickly demonstrated its basic conservatism and its interest in asserting traditional local rights. Walloons, however, led by the radicals of Liège pushed for union with revolutionary France. Following the incorporation of Liège and the southern Netherlands into France in 1793, the homegrown "Jacobins" of Liège tore down St. Lambert cathedral stone by stone, thus eradicating what they perceived to be a hated symbol of the "old regime." An Austrian offensive and re-occupation saved Belgium from the excesses of the Reign of Terror. But the southern Netherlands again fell to the French at Fleurus in June 1794.

# CHAPTER 7

# The French Revolution and Napoleon

*[I]t was not so much France that had annexed Belgium in 1795, but Belgium that had annexed France for purposes of economic expansion.*
—Adrien de Meeüs[1]

*By common consent, the area which accepted earliest and with the greatest ease the gospel of industrialization emanating from Britain and which came closest to the British model, was the Sambre-Meuse region, together with the Scheldt Valley of Belgium and northern France (. . .) The Belgian industrial belt contained early and successful examples of all the key industries of the industrial revolution period.*
—Sidney Pollard[2]

## Belgium as Part of Revolutionary France

Following the French victory over the Austrians at the battle of Jemappes on November 6, 1792, Belgium became an appendage of revolutionary France. Many Belgians welcomed the French in the expectation that their independence, which had been stripped from them by the Austrians in 1790, would be restored. Instead, the French held a plebiscite on the incorporation of the Southern Netherlands into revolutionary France. The French were disappointed by the results. Only 21 percent of the males of the former bishopric of Liège, by far more pro-French than much of the Southern Netherlands, voted for incorporation. Nevertheless, the Southern Netherlands was annexed. When the Austrians were victorious at Neerwinden on March 23, 1793, 10,000 supporters of the Jacobins fled to France, and crowds in Brussels pillaged the houses of the pro-French and burned the liberty tree on the Grand' Place.[3] The Austrians were in control again, but only briefly. The French defeated the Austrians at Fleurus on June 26, 1794. The first 15 months of French rule was a time of ruthless pillage. In fact, this time, propertied Belgians petitioned the French government to annex Belgium as a means to stop the looting of Belgian property, and on October 1, 1795, France again directly annexed the Southern Netherlands. The annexation brought the former Austrian Netherlands, the prince-archbishopric of Liège, and the duchy of Bouillon into France, and thus unintentionally laid the basis for the future union of those three previously politically disconnected territories.[4] As Lode Wils writes

> the foundations of the age-old particularisms of the provinces were destroyed and would not be restored after Napoleon's fall in 1814. In 1795 all enclaves which the Southern Netherlands contained—such as Church Principalities and all sorts of fragmented regions—were fused with the new French departments.[5]

Administration was centralized and rationalized and French became the official language of administration. Belgium was divided into nine departments, which form the basis for the nine provinces of Belgium. "Feudal" remnants such as the tithe, guilds, and internal tolls were abolished.

The Catholic Church, which had been so powerful and propertied, was persecuted and its property confiscated. A civil registry was put in place in June 1796 to replace parish records. All religious communities were closed in the fall of 1796 and their property sold. The Flemish called this the *Gesloten Tyd*, the time of closure. Priests were required to take an oath of hatred for royalty. The churches of those who refused, as most did, were closed. 585 of the resisting priests were deported and 30 of the more outspoken resisters were sent to Devil's Island. Masses were celebrated behind the closed shutters of houses on squares while the faithful gathered outside. On October 25, 1797, the University of Leuven was suppressed and its rector died in prison in French Guiana.

The introduction of conscription provoked a Peasants' Revolt in October 1798, but it was brutally repressed.[6] Henri Conscience, the first author to produce a large number of important literary works in Flemish, published a historical novel based on this revolt, *De Boerenkrijg* (The Peasant War) in 1853. Though Conscience was a patriotic supporter of a united Belgium, he was at the same time anti-French and his work contributed to the formation of a national Flemish identity.[7]

### Belgium under Napoleon

After Napoleon's coup on November 9, 1799, the climate improved. There was an accommodation between the state and the church in July 1801, and the *Code Napoléon*, which would form the basis of the future legal system of Belgium, was promulgated. Napoleon's lasting legacies to Belgium would be this code, civil equality, and the modern bureaucratic state. The modern state in Belgium was imposed from the outside.[8]

Linguistically French was promoted. Whereas French had been fostered as part of a spontaneous cultural process in the eighteenth century, it was privileged by government policy after 1794.[9] After 1804 all public acts had to be published in French. In 1813 the *Bulletin des Lois* ceased to provide translations in Dutch and as a result "the most-used language of the region had been driven entirely from public life."[10] Henceforth Dutch was relegated to the pulpit and private life. This occurred at the very time that the Dutch language was being standardized in the Netherlands. The failure of Flemish to develop into a standardized language can be explained by "the frenchification of the top layers of society" in what would become Belgium. Those who might have been expected to foster the standardization of Flemish "(. . .) increasingly switched to French as their language of culture."[11]

Napoleon's policy toward the Church, which had initially won him support, eventually stirred resentment when Pope Pius VII was abducted and held hostage, when a single French catechism stressing loyalty to the French state, was promulgated, and when Napoleon ousted and exiled the critical bishops of Tournai and Ghent. Seminarians who refused to accept their bishops' political replacements were conscripted and many perished in Russia or at the battle of Leipzig.[12]

Materially the French annexation of Belgium promoted the expansion of industry and the "concentration of wealth in the hands of a few tens of thousand families."[13] The process of modernization continued and economic development was encouraged. The prosperity of Belgium was reflected in the rapid growth of its population. Confiscated church lands bought cheaply by nobles and bourgeoisie provided them with revenue or rents, which provided the capital for industrialization. It also provided ready made factory sites. Monasteries and convents of the Archbishopric of Liège were transformed into glass and arms works.[14] Jan Craeybeckx writes "(. . .) in most sectors of industry Belgium was at a considerably higher level than the average of France or the entire Empire."[15] By 1814 Belgium had 89 blast furnaces; France would not have as many until 50 years later. Supplying the armies of France encouraged Belgian development and produced fortunes for individual Belgians. Because of its labor supply and industries Belgium received the lion's share of French military contracts. By 1810 Belgium produced half of the coal produced in the French Empire. It also produced a quarter of the Empire's iron. The entire empire was a market for Belgium, whose manufacturers and merchants had access not only to the Scheldt but also through the Meuse and canals access to the Rhine and distant cities of Germany as well as France. Antwerp had been hobbled by the closing of the Scheldt by the Dutch at the end of the Thirty Years War in 1648. The French resuscitated the city. The French occupied the city of 40,000 in 1795 and Napoleon, after his ascension, reopened the Scheldt and built wharves. The city, he hoped, would become his pistol aimed at the heart of England, "*un pistolet braqué sur le cour d'Angleterre.*"[16] Though the British easily blockaded the port, Napoleon's work laid the basis for Antwerp's future development.

Liévin Bauwens, a tanner from Ghent, introduced the spinning jenny from England in 1798. Patricia Penn Hilden asserts that the Industrial Revolution in Belgium began with the return of Bauwens from England.[17] Bauwens surreptitiously purchased machines in England, had them taken apart, and shipped them to Belgium in consignments of coffee and sugar. His smuggling enterprise was discovered before he had finished, and he had to flee arrest. He was even pursued across the North Sea by the British anxious to maintain their monopoly control of this technology and its productive capacity. He, however, made good his escape and set up the first mechanized spinning mill on the continent in Ghent.

By 1810 the spinning mills of Ghent employed 10,000 workers. Bauwens and others were able to build on the proto-industrialization of East Flanders. The workers of East Flanders had long grown, processed, and spun flax. The flax yarn was then woven into linen or fabricated into lace by the thousands of skilled workers of the area. The early industrialists were also able to draw on the urban poor, especially those displaced by the French Revolution who had gravitated to the cities but were without steady employment.[18] In fact it was the poor, especially the women and children as young as five, who constituted 70 percent of the mill workers, who provided the hands for Belgium's industrial revolution.[19]

Through the work of Bauwens and his colleagues Ghent, filled with redbrick factories, became in the words of Karl Marx the "Belgian Manchester."[20] It was difficult to discipline workers unaccustomed to the regimen of industrial labor when the hours stretched to 13 or 14 a day. The owners and civil authorities, who were often one and the same, undertook the task of acclimation. Bauwens was burgomaster from 1800 to 1802. The behavior of the workers was monitored outside the factory as well as while they were on the job. The unemployed were arrested, confined in workhouses, and forced to labor for Bauwens' factory at sub-par wages, which he justified because they were lodged and fed at public expense.[21]

In 1799 an English mechanic, William Cockerill, went to work for an industrialist in Verviers. He drew on his experience and knowledge to build spinning machines. In 1802 Cockerill founded his own operation. Cockerill's son expanded their production to a whole array of new productive machinery. The endeavors of the Cockerills spread from wool to coal, steel, and eventually railroad engines, and the father's imitation of British technology grew into an industrial empire, which offered stiff competition to the British in the developing European market.

In spite of the industrial development and the prosperity experienced by the few, the standard of living of the working class hovered around the subsistence level. The wages of ordinary workers generally sufficed to purchase between two and seven pounds of black bread a day. One legacy of the French Revolution was the *Loi Chapelier* of 1791 which, in the revolutionary vein of outlawing privileged corporations, outlawed guilds and combinations of workers seeking to advance their own interests. This prohibition against labor unions was perpetuated by Napoleon's code. The industrial pioneers of Ghent and other Belgian cities were, therefore, able to develop their projects without the interference of guild regulations. Workers were totally at the mercy of employers. At first workers profited from the demand for labor. Bauwens to attract workers, at first, paid them between five and eight francs a day at a time when carpenters could normally earn only two. Many fled the poverty of the Flemish countryside for the factories. However, as a growing birth rate provided new young workers, the situation changed. The shortage of cotton produced by the English blockade also undercut the demand for labor. Unemployment and hunger followed.[22]

## Waterloo

In Belgium enthusiasm for the empire waned as a result of Napoleon's falling out with the pope and the imposition of conscription. The Belgian component of Napoleon's army, assembled by compulsion, rose from 110,000 in 1810 to 160,000 in 1813. As a result, when the Allies entered Belgium in 1814 few Belgians supported Napoleon and none resisted.

Napoleon returned to Belgium in June 1815. He had left his place of exile on the island of Elba in March 1815 and had regained control on France. In a desperate effort to strike a blow at his enemies before they were able to concentrate their forces and close in for the kill, he went on the offensive. Napoleon's forces were able to shove Allied troops commanded by the Prussian Marshall Blücher and by the Duke of Wellington back in engagements on June 16 at Ligny and at Quatre-Bras. However, Napoleon failed to order his troops to pursue the Prussians as they withdrew from Ligney to Wavre on the Dijle. General Grouchy was only ordered to pursue them late in the morning of July 17. Grouchy, who did not know the direction of Blücher's nighttime withdrawal, was unable to prevent him from eventually joining Wellington. In addition, the futile pursuit by Grochy's troops lessened the size of the French force in its crucial engagement at Waterloo.

On the night of June 17 Napoleon and his troops bivouacked several miles south of Waterloo, while Wellington slept in the village. The decisive battle began at 11: 30 A.M. on Sunday June 18 with a diversionary attack by the French on the heavily defended fortified farm, Hougoumont, which anchored Wellington's right wing. This and a French infantry assault on Wellington's center failed. French artillery then stopped a counter-charge by the British cavalry. Marshal Ney sent his cavalry time after time against the Allied line without success, but French infantry, with heavy losses, drove the King's German Legion and two companies of Nassau Germans from another fortified farm, La Haie-Sainte. This set the stage for an attack against the Allied center, but the arrival of the Prussians saved the day. After Prussians, under von Bülow, attacked Napoleon's flank at Plancenoit at 4:30 and the farm, Papelotte, at 6 P.M., Napoleon desperately sent his Old Guard forward at 7 P.M. But Wellington's line held. At 7:30 the reinforced Prussians drove the French from Papelotte, and by 8:15 the whole Allied line went on the offensive. Under a hail of musketry, cannon ball, and grapeshot, the French Old Guard broke. In the subsequent rout Napoleon barely escaped. At 9 P.M. Wellington and Blücher were able to confirm their victory with a handshake on the battlefield.

To commemorate this decisive battle, which determined the future of France and Europe and confirmed the independence of the Netherlands (and even of Belgium, though it was not yet independent), the Dutch government between 1823 and 1826 erected on the spot where the Prince of Orange was wounded a 40.5 meter mound surmounted by a 28 ton iron lion, cast at Liège. The mound was constructed with 290,485 cubic meters of earth dug from the surrounding fields. It was carried and dumped on the growing mound by an army of female workers, who carried the dirt in baskets on their backs.

# CHAPTER 8

# Union with the Netherlands

## The Congress of Vienna[1]

Following the first defeat of Napoleon in 1814, the victorious powers met in Vienna to restore order to a Europe thrown into disarray by the French Revolution and the ambitions of the Corsican egotist. Two elements of the agenda of the powers at the Congress of Vienna were to compensate the countries which had most contributed to the defeat of Napoleon and to establish more secure frontiers around France to discourage the resumption of French aggression. To buttress the area facing France's northern frontier, the Congress of Vienna ceded Belgium's eastern cantons, Eupen, Malmedy, and St. Vith to Prussia, and the rest of Belgium was amalgamated with Holland. There, however, was a curious anomaly. Moresnet, a 900 acre tidbit, was jointly administered by Prussia and first Holland, and then by Prussia and Belgium, as a neutral enclave, which in 1906 had 3,434 inhabitants. The reason for this oddity was a zinc mine at Vieille Montagne owned by a Belgian company. Prussia desired the morsel for strategic reasons, but the Dutch wanted it for economic reasons. Had Germany won World War I, it, and undoubtedly much more, would have become German.[2]

At Vienna it was believed that the commercial economy of the Netherlands would complement the increasingly manufacture-oriented economy of Belgium. However, the Belgians were increasingly dissatisfied and the new construct only lasted about fifteen years. King William was Dutch, Calvinist, and authoritarian.[3] He succeeded in alienating Flemish Catholics, Walloons, and liberals. Commercial and agricultural Netherlands favored free trade, while the industrialists of Belgium favored protection against cheap British goods for their nascent industries. Dutch became the official language except within the Walloon districts and Dutch Netherlanders were favored in the civil service. This upset not only the Walloons but the Flemish elite, which had been schooled in French in the imperial lycées.[4] Belgium, with nearly twice the population of the Netherlands, over three million versus barely two, was assigned the same number of representatives in the States-General. There was no ministerial responsibility. The debt was divided equally although that of the Netherlands vastly exceeded that of Belgium.

## The Constitution of the United Netherlands

The constitution guaranteed freedom of religion, and all ministers, including Catholic priests, were to be paid by the state. But Catholic leaders objected to wording in the constitution, which they interpreted to be a threat against processions and other public ceremonies. The bishop of Ghent, Maurice de Broglie, forbade Catholics to swear their allegiance to the new constitution. However, with the Belgians at first divided between Catholics and anti-clericals, conservatives and liberals, William was able to find a majority in the parliament to support his policies. When William attempted to take control of education including the seminaries, the attitude of the public changed. The government established a state institution at Lier, not far from Antwerp, to train teachers for the south. Simon Schama, though very sympathetic to the efforts of the Dutch, wrote that "(. . .) there was something unmistakenly condescending about their missionary dedication to bring education to the benighted." He also writes that "from the very dedicated views of King William it was clear that whatever concessions would be made in using French locally in the Walloon provinces, Dutch/Flemish was to be the proper vehicle of the new schooling and a *sine qua non* for all those who aspired to succeed within it."[5]

The University of Leuven had been suppressed by the French revolutionaries in 1797 because of its Catholic character. The university founded on December 9, 1425, by Pope Martin V is the oldest university in the Low Countries, and is today the oldest extant Catholic university.[6] Its average enrollment between 1528 and 1569 had been 622. William sponsored a restored university in 1817. The re-established university opened with 230 students. The restored university initially had only 18 faculty members: seven from the old university, one Netherlander, two Frenchmen, and six Germans. The church rejected the new institution because it was regarded as a Protestant Dutch intrusion. The archdiocesan philosophical college at Mechelen (Malines) served Catholics until the Church once again gained control of Leuven as a result of the Revolution of 1830. New state universities were also opened by William in Ghent and Liège. In Ghent the faculty consisted of three Germans, two Frenchmen, one Luxemburger, and two Netherlanders. At Ghent all the courses were originally taught in Latin, but French soon replaced that dead language. After the revolution a Free University was established in Brussels in 1832 to cater to the anti-clerical segment of the Belgian population.[7]

## *Opposition*

Opposition within Belgium was multi-faceted, but of particular importance was the catalytic impact of the growing population of young Belgian professionals and intelligentsia who felt that their future and prospects were blocked by the Dutch, anti-liberal character of William's regime. The opposition demanded ministerial responsibility, equal access to employment, and freedom of education and the press. Their demand for a true parliamentary regime would have meant the dominance in the Netherlands of Belgium with its rapidly increasing population.

In November 1828 the Catholic faction and the liberals, even the anti-clerical liberals led by Louis de Potter, were able to agree to a parliamentary Union, a pragmatic coalition, based on their common opposition to the government. According to Lode Wils, due to the eighteen year-long occupation by France, liberal ideas had become firmly entrenched in Belgium.[8] Liberals and Catholics agreed that they would stop attacking each other in their newspapers and that their representatives in parliament would oppose all governmental appropriations until the royal government accepted the principal of ministerial responsibility, moved the high court from the Hague to Brussels, and agreed to employ more Belgians in the civil service, foreign service, and military. They also demanded that William put into action the Concordat which he had negotiated with the Papacy in 1827 but had not enacted because of opposition from Protestants in the northern Dutch part of the kingdom. Liberals liked the restraints the concordat placed upon the church. Although Catholics had initially regarded the concordat with suspicion, they were offended by William's unilateral *de facto* repudiation of the agreement and now took offence at his failure to implement it.[9]

The political accommodation between the Catholic and liberal leadership in Belgium had ramifications beyond the Low Lands. This Catholic-liberal union had a fundamental impact upon the formation of the Liberal Catholic views of the French priest Félicité de Lamennais. De Lamennais wrote that the Union between Catholics and liberals in Belgium was a "(. . .) unique means of re-establishing society on its true foundations (. . .) [T]his reunion operating in Belgium (. . .) [is giving] to the world one of the greatest and most beautiful spectacles that has been seen for a long time."[10] The pope and the Dutch king were less enthusiastic.

# CHAPTER 9

# Revolution and Independence

## The Outbreak[1]

King William made a number of last minute tactical retreats. He closed the Philosophical College at Leuven, ceased his demand for government inspection of Catholic schools, permitted French to be used freely in all of Belgium, and recognized life-time tenure for judges.[2] However, passions were driven to a fever pitch by a series of bad harvests and by a crisis of over production that crippled the textile industry of Verviers, Liège, and Tournai. 378,000 of the 752,000 workers in the Belgian provinces of the kingdom were compelled to seek public assistance. The discomfort of the working class had been compounded by a doubling in the cost of living since 1824 while wages remained at their 1820 level.[3]

The explosion came on August 25, 1830, with the performance of Daniel François Auber's *La Muette de Portici* at Théâtre de la Monnaie in Brussels. Popular emotions had been stirred by the success of the July Revolution in France.[4] The singing of "*Amour sacré de la Patrie*"[5] to the tune of "La Marseillaise" brought the theater to its feet and into the streets. The demonstration at the opera led to an explosion by the desperate and exasperated proletariat of Brussels. The bourgeois liberals had not foreseen this and were terrified by the specter of anarchy. They were willing to accept an autonomous administration with William's eldest son William, the Prince of Orange, as viceroy. However, the workers pressed for more. Violent street fighting in Brussels between workers and Dutch troops forced the Dutch to evacuate the city. But for the timidity of Crown Prince William and Prince Friedrick, the commander of the royal army, Dutch authority could have been easily restored with the 6,000 Dutch troops at their disposal. The people of Brussels were not united. Merchants and manufacturers began to have grave misgivings about the economic consequences of independence. There was also concern among the middle class over the aspirations and violence of the lower classes. The discomfort of the moderates was such that a Dutch effort launched on September 23 would have succeeded had it not been for insufficient Dutch resolve.[6] According to John Rooney, "Prince Friedrick could have encircled the city without effort. He had with him three thousand cavalrymen for this purpose that he never utilized. If he had utilized them effectively the city would have been forced to surrendered within days (. . .)"[7]

## The Assault and Retreat

The prince had announced an amnesty for all but foreigners and leaders of the uprising. As he had thought, this led to a precipitous flight toward the French frontier. What he had not anticipated was the "the spontaneous defense of Brussels by the lower classes and the inward flow of volunteers (. . .)"[8] Though the prince's forces had been able to force their entry through the Schaerbeek gate with artillery, their advance to the Parc de Bruxelles was through "a veritable gauntlet" of snipers. Once the Parc had been reached instead of ordering an immediate occupation of the Royal Palace and advance on the Grand' Place, the soldiers were allowed to rest, and in the interim the rebels strengthened their defenses. Meanwhile the troops advancing through the lower city had met determined resistance: barricades were thrown up and torrents of cobble stones and projectiles were hurled from the roofs against the advancing troops. The opposition consisted of "desperate men," numbering at the most 1,700, leaderless or led by "momentary and spontaneous" leaders.[9] The French ambassador, General Valazé wrote that the defenders were "undisciplined rabble," but the royal army was also disorganized and poorly led.[10] Friedrick's dilemma was that he hoped to pacify the city through negotiation, but the burgers, who might have negotiated a compromise settlement with him, had fled. The leaders who remained were all opposed to the royal government. Friedrick and his commanders failed to take advantage of the nighttime withdrawal of the defenders to taverns, and the inactivity of the royalist forces encouraged the insurgent leaders André Jolly, Charles Rogier, and Emmanuel d'Hoogvorst to return to the city and ensconce themselves in the city hall. Nevertheless, the insurgents were weak in numbers and low on ammunition. There was some effort on the part of a bourgeois Administrative Committee to negotiate with Friedrick. However, Friedrick, profoundly discouraged, ordered the royal troops to evacuate Brussels on the night of September 26–27. He had conceived of his mission as a police operation, but was unable to find responsible bourgeois leaders with whom to negotiate. As Rooney wrote, "Frederick was forced to confront the options of either investing the city, bombarding it, or perpetuating negotiations. Never did the Prince realize the fewness of his opponents, nor of their near despair."[11]

The Dutch force withdrew from Brussels after three days of street fighting. The rebels had lost only 188 dead and 590 wounded, and Frederick's losses were less. Had the prince, Rooney writes, "possessed one or two more days' patience, Brussels would have dropped like an overripe plum into his hands."[12] He did not, and the timid rushed to identify themselves with the unexpected victory. Less that five percent of the street fighters came from the bourgeoisie, who would take charge of the situation won by the workers.[13] Bourgeois leaders who had fled returned and a provisional government was set up under Rogier. Belgian soldiers were called upon to renounce their allegiance to the Dutch king and the cities of the south rose, expelled their royal garrisons, and threw their support behind the provisional government. Independence was proclaimed on October 4; and a national congress was summoned to draw up a constitution. The election of the congress on November 3 demonstrated the lack of enthusiasm for complete separation from the Dutch. Of the 46,000 eligible voters, only 30,000 voted. Many did not vote because there were no opposition, anti-revolutionary and pro-union, candidates and of those who voted a third cast blank protest votes.

## Antwerp

In Antwerp the Dutch were still in control. Prince William, once the States-General in the Hague had approved of administrative separation of Belgium from the Netherlands, went there to assume the role of governor-general of Belgium. On the initiative of the prince, King William at first agreed that his son could accept the crown of an independent Belgium if it was formally offered to him. He issued a proclamation recognizing Belgian independence and authorized voting for the National Congress to proceed in the provinces of Antwerp and Limburg. However, the king fearing a negative backlash in the Dutch north and the possibility of the Catholics in the Dutch Brabant joining their co-religionists in the south, revoked the powers of his son. When Belgian volunteers entered the city on October 27, clashes erupted between the Belgians and the Dutch garrison, which had withdrawn into the citadel and arsenal. The Dutch commander, General Tiel Cassé, then ordered the fortress, the forts surrounding the city, and the eight Dutch frigates in the harbor to bombard the city. According to Rooney, "with the first volley, the House of Orange lost forever the throne of Belgium."[14]

## The Powers

Following the bombardment of Antwerp by the Dutch on October 27, the British called for a conference of the powers. The great powers met in London and ordered an armistice on November 4. On November 10 the Belgian congress declared the House of Orange deposed, but expressed its support for a constitutional hereditary monarchy. Lord Palmerston, who had just taken over the foreign office, wanted to prevent Belgium from falling under the control of France and to prevent the outbreak of war. Louis Philippe, consolidating his power in France, was inclined to follow the lead of Britain. Russia, which was confronted with a Polish insurrection, and Prussia, saddled with war debt, accepted this alteration of the Vienna settlement. On December 20 the London Conference declared the dissolution of the Kingdom of the Netherlands, and on January 20, 1831, recognized Belgium's independence. When the Belgian congress chose the second son of Louis Philippe, the Duke of Nemours, to be king on February 3, 1831, the French king acquiesced to the warnings of Palmerston and repudiated the offer.

## The Constitution

The Belgian National Congress proceeded to draw up a very liberal constitution patterned on that of England. However, it laid the groundwork for the dominance of the urban bourgeoisie and fell short of the democratic aspirations of many of those whose struggle in the streets led to the defeat of the Dutch. Nevertheless, the constitution stated that the legitimacy of the new order in Belgium stemmed from popular sovereignty.[15] The parliament was given sufficient power to ensure its dominance over the crown. Local government was given a degree of autonomy from the directives of the central government, and civil and political rights were increased.[16] The principles of religious toleration and separation of the state and church were affirmed.

Liberals conceded to the Church an extraordinary degree of freedom. Church appointments were to be independent of state interference, and Catholic schools were to be independent of state control. The state would provide financial support to the Church, which insisted upon this in compensation for the property and revenues it had lost during the revolutionary period. The Catholics, for their part, agreed to compensation for all religious ministers and accepted the requirement of civil marriage, even for those who wished the blessing of the Church for their weddings.[17]

## Leopold of Saxe-Coburg

Finally on June 4, the National Congress chose Prince Leopold of Saxe-Coburg as king. This was an excellent and politic choice. Not only was Leopold talented and capable, but as the widower of Princess Charlotte of England and uncle of Victoria he had an English connection. By promptly marrying Louise Marie, the eldest daughter of Louis Philippe, he established a French connection.[18] According to de Gruben, "to the small revolutionary country, he brought a kind of pardon from the courts which had accepted him into the family of kings; he was, for them, the sign and the condition of reconciliation."[19]

## The Finale

William was dissatisfied with the settlement drawn up in London, and was encouraged by pro-Orange riots in Ghent and Antwerp fomented by a segment of the merchants in those cities.[20] When he sent the Dutch army across the new frontier on August 2, 1831, and defeated a makeshift Belgian force, a French army, with British approval, forced the Dutch to retire. With William still resisting and refusing to evacuate Antwerp, a combined British and French naval force in conjunction with a French army expelled the Dutch from Belgium. On May 21, 1833, the Dutch were compelled to agree to an indefinite armistice. Finally on April 19, 1839, William accepted a settlement dividing his kingdom into two sovereign states and dividing the national debt between the two. The settlement established a frontier, which with the exception of Limburg and Luxembourg, was basically the frontier of 1790. Though the Dutch were forced to evacuate Antwerp, and the Scheldt was declared open to the vessels of both nations, the settlement allowed the Dutch to collect tolls on Scheldt shipping. After Belgium purchased the revocation of this right in 1862 for 32 million francs, the city again began to flourish. At the end of the twentieth century Antwerp was the second European port, exceeded in tonnage only by the oil port of Rotterdam.

The Grand Duchy of Luxembourg, which had been assigned to the Dutch king by the Congress of Vienna, also revolted in 1830 and sought to join Belgium. The Prussian garrison placed in Luxembourg city by the Congress of Vienna maintained order in the city and its surroundings. The Treaty of London divided the duchy. Though the Belgians claimed all of Luxembourg, only the larger western French speaking section was added to Belgium as the Province of Luxembourg. The smaller Lettisch speaking area remained under William as the Grand Duchy of Luxembourg. The Belgians also received half of the province of Limburg. The other half was handed over to the Netherlands, despite the opposition of its inhabitants.[21] Finally, the settlement offered the new state a guarantee, one that would be dismissed in a most impolitic fashion by the German Chancellor Theobald von Bethmann-Hollweg in July 1914, as a scrap of paper. The Treaty of London declared Belgium an "independent and perpetually neutral state" with this neutrality guaranteed by the signatory powers.[22]

# CHAPTER 10

# The Kingdom of Belgium

## Independent Belgium

*"Haste and speed are seldom good."*[1]
—Belgian proverb

Independent Belgium was provided with a constitutional regime, which was accepted by the Catholics, who with the Liberals had opposed the Dutch regime. Belgian Catholics, after their experiences under Philip II, Joseph II, Napoleon, and William I of the Netherlands, did not have the strong monarchical proclivities, which moved many French Catholics. They supported the constitutional regime as loyally as the Liberals, with whom they differed principally over continued subsidies and rights for the Church. Catholics and Liberals, in fact, ruled together in coalition until the late 1840s. This system was unique. In fact it was opposed by the pope and conservative Catholics elsewhere who did not appreciate the opportunities presented by religious freedom.[2] In the new constitutional system the king was relegated to the role of head of state rather than head of the government, though at times due to circumstances or personality Belgian kings have played a more direct role in day-to-day politics. The constitution guaranteed freedom of the press and assembly as well as religion. The Liberals, though many were nominally Catholic and some even practicing Catholics, were anti-clerical, that is opposed to the domination of education by the Church and to a political role in Belgian society for the Church or its clerics. Many Liberals had profited from the purchase of Church property by their families during the time of the French Revolution. They feared that they might be forced by a clerically dominated government to return their acquisitions. There were also Free Masons, whose organization had been formally condemned by the Catholic Church in 1838, and who brought to the Liberal Party an added dimension of ideological opposition to the Catholic Church.[3] In order to maintain a cooperative atmosphere, the Liberals, nevertheless, agreed to subsidies to the dominant Catholic Church as well as to Protestant and Jewish groups. Time proved the Belgian Catholics right and the Catholic conservatives, who carped from a distance without understanding Belgium, wrong. As Carl Strikwerda has observed, "(. . .) shrewdly, and, as later events proved, correctly, Catholic leaders gambled that the Church's long history of institutional strength, state subsidies, and the nominal affiliation of almost all Belgians would allow the Church to become as strong as an established state church."[4] The freedoms of religion, education, press, and association guaranteed by the constitution freed the Church from state supervision, permitted the free development of religious orders and Church organizations, and enabled the Church to develop a comprehensive system of Catholic educational institutions.[5] The Catholic Church was as a consequence able to regain much of the influence which had been curtailed under the French and the Dutch.

Belgium's advanced constitution and the cooperation between Liberals and conservatives helped Belgium to avoid the traumas which others experienced in 1848, the year of revolution. Under the Belgian constitution, modeled on the written constitution of the United States and the unwritten constitution of England, Belgian citizens were guaranteed greater rights than any other people in Europe at the time.[6] Belgian citizens were free to worship, to associate, to assemble, and to speak. Though Pope Gregory XVI was scandalized by the provision of religious freedom and Metternich was worried by the liberalism of the new constitution, the Belgian elite had things under control. There were limits to Belgium's liberties.[7] Until 1894 the right to vote was restricted to 10 percent of the adult male population.[8] The constitution initially limited the franchise to those who paid 42.32 francs in direct taxes and limited membership in the Senate to the well-to-do. Though the tax requirement was soon modified to grant the vote to more men in the countryside, only around 55,000 Belgians had the right to vote. Workers could not organize and certainly could not strike.

Though the constitution guaranteed freedom of the press that too was not allowed to get out of hand. Belgium accepted French political refugees after the coup of Louis Napoleon on December 2, 1851. When the verbal invective of some of these opponents exasperated Louis Napoleon the Belgian government felt compelled to pass laws outlawing the most offensive anti-French rhetoric.[9] Among the French refugees was Victor Hugo, who worked on his *Les Misérables* while living in an apartment on the Grand' Place.

Physical and industrial modernization continued as well. After the incorporation of Belgium into revolutionary France the walls of Brussels were destroyed and work was begun on the boulevards which replaced them. The city had been the first city on the continent to employ gas streetlights. These were lit on August 1, 1819. Brussels, as the capital and show place of the new Kingdom of Belgium, witnessed feverish development in the nineteenth century. Slums were demolished. The Senne was covered. New streets, buildings, and monuments proliferated. In 1835 the first rail passenger service on the continent was established between Brussels and Mechelen.

In 1846 the Galeries Saint Hubert, the first galleria or glass-arcaded shopping center, was opened in Brussels.

The city also attracted international attention. Karl Marx lived in the city for a time. He and Friedrich Engels completed the *Communist Manifesto* in a cafe in Le Cygne (The Swan), the headquarters of the butchers' guild, on the Grand' Place. Brussels hosted important conferences of the First and Second International, and was the site of the first part of the founding conference of the Russian Bolshevik Party in 1903. The Russian Social Democratic Labor Party about to give birth to the Bolsheviks met at Coq d'Or, a hotel owned by a Belgian socialist. The Belgian Socialist Emile Vandervelde had arranged the site of the meeting. Things, however, quickly went awry. The first session was routed by a plague of fleas infesting the dark and damp meeting room. The fleas were dealt with but the ideological differences of the delegates proved more difficult to handle. After four or five heated sessions on the party program, the police demanded that four of the delegates leave the city within twenty-four hours. This plus the oppressive intrusion of police spies led to a transfer of the conference to London, which bears the dubious honor of being the founding city of the Bolshevik faction.[10]

# 1848

Leopold's reign lasted until 1865. Utilizing "pocket vetoes" and royal decrees he persistently increased the role and the power of the monarchy, giving to the Belgian monarchy the interventionist character, which it possessed until the Second World War. He was able to do this by recognizing and supporting the country's bourgeoisie in their principal interest, making money, with the minimum of interference and restriction.[11] Until 1847 a Clerical-Liberal coalition cooperated in the consolidation of the new country and its governmental system. However, conservative Catholics had been able in 1842 to gain the passage of a law which "essentially handed elementary education over to the church and made religious instruction by clergy obligatory in public as well as private schools."[12] Liberals were enraged by the law. This law and the condemnation of the Masons by the Belgian bishops in 1837 contributed to the emergence of a party system in 1847. The Liberal Party held a general congress in Brussels on June 14, 1846. 320 delegates from all over Belgium approved a program, the Act of Federation. Their appeal to the electorate succeeded and a large Liberal majority was returned in the June 1847 election. Led first by Charles Rogier and then by Walther Frère-Orban, the Liberals, apart from a unionist coalition of Liberals and moderate Catholics from 1852 until 1857, controlled the government until 1884. The Liberal ministry, which took office on August 12, 1847, immediately took steps to alleviate the economic crisis, which had gripped Belgium after 1843. Rail and canal construction were intensified in order to provide employment and economic stimulation. And to forestall the criticism of lower lev-els of the bourgeoisie, the franchise was extended. In 1848 a new electoral law less-ened the financial qualifications for voting and the number of voters grew to 80,000, an increase of 25,000. The level of the bourgeoisie's satisfaction with the regime was borne out by the absence of turmoil in Belgium during the general revolutionary up-heavals of 1848. Belgium's bourgeoisie was satisfied. Whereas many members of the bourgeoisie in Germany and Italy longed for national unity and constitutional gov-ernment, the bourgeoisie of Belgium had "its nation" and "its liberal regime." It had no need of a revolution. Belgium, like England, remained quiet.

Nevertheless, the revolution in neighboring France thoroughly frightened and depressed Leopold. On February 26, 1848, after receiving news of the abdication of France's Louis Philippe, Leopold offered his own abdication to the government. When it asserted its determination to work with Leopold, he nevertheless sent ship-ments of his personal property to England. There was no need. There was a run on the banks; some radical newspapers appeared calling for the ouster of Leopold and the establishment of a republic; and some students in Leuven took to the streets. But the civil guard, which Rogier had instructed mayors to place on alert, did not have to be called out. The greatest threat came from Belgian guest-workers, who had lost their jobs in France, and were sent back to Belgium. A large number, per-haps as many as 6,000 gathered in Lille, where they were armed and stirred up by radical elements of the French provisional government. Two groups of this Belgian Legion entered Belgium at the end of March and one had to be dispersed by regular Belgian army troops at Risquons-Tout near Mouscron.

With the extension of the franchise, the employment projects, and the prospect for a good crop, the voters returned a Liberal dominated parliament on June 13, 1848. The Catholic conservatives were reduced to 23 members, and those tended to be respected Catholic notables who accepted their role as a responsible minority.[13]

# CHAPTER 11

# Industry and Workers

The industrialization, which had been solidly established by the end of the French period, advanced apace. With industrialization the self-confidence of the Belgian bourgeoisie flowered. That class, in turn, shaped "every aspect of social, political, and economic life" in Belgium.[1] It reinforced its social dominance by inter-marrying with Belgium's traditional aristocracy. Members of the bourgeoisie were ennobled by the Belgian monarchs, so that by the second generation many a prosperous and rising bourgeois family could sport its own aristocratic title.[2] Under the direction of this rising bourgeoisie the coal and metallurgical industry of Liège expanded greatly. Among the most important works was the Cockerill complex at Seraing five miles up the Meuse from Liège and the Usines de la Vielle-Montagne, both of which gained international importance. Between 1835 and the beginning of the twentieth century Cockerill produced 60,000 locomotives and other steam engines. By 1904 the Cockerill works were producing annually 150 locomotives, 2,000 steam engines, and 15,000 tons of structural steel.[3] Despite the decline of Belgian heavy industry in the post-World War II period, Cockerill continued into the twenty-first century as the Cockerill-Sambre Unisor Group. The ornamental ironwork and luxury glass of Belgium, which was so acclaimed in the nineteenth century, also regained their previous reputation in the late twentieth century.

Providing the fuel for Belgium's industrial revolution were the mines of the province of Hainaut around Charleroi and the Borinage, the coal communities to the south and west of Mons. By the beginning of the 1820s the number of companies declined but the number of miners who worked for each greatly expanded. In 1807 there had been 46 mines with an average of 162 workers each. By 1837–1838 there were only 30 active mines in the area, but each employed an average of 480 workers.[4] In 1841 38,000 Belgians worked in the coalmines; by 1851 the number was 48,000; by 1860 78,000; and by 1875 100,000. Glass production also flourished in Charleroi. The semi-official land bank, Société Général, after 1835 provided capital to industrial concerns, and development was further assisted by the founding of a national bank in 1850.

The separation of Belgium from the Netherlands caused a crisis at first because it deprived Belgian manufacturers of the large market of the northern provinces, which were now a separate country, and the Dutch colonies. However, the early development of a thorough system of railways was an important stimulus to industrial development. In fact continental Europe's first rail line was opened between Brussels and Mechelen (Malines) in the 1830s. The rail lines and the construction of new canals fostered the development of a national Belgian market.[5] In addition the construction of railways, by their demand for iron and coal, fostered the further development of the Belgian iron and coal industries. In 1861 and 1862 commercial treaties with France and England established free trade. A further contribution to development occurred in 1863 when tolls were removed from the Scheldt. In the words of W.O. Henderson, "Belgium lay at the crossroads of Europe and the port of Antwerp had made her a centre of world trade."[6]

## Conditions of Belgian Workers

If prosperity, prestige, and power characterized the bourgeoisie, the workers of Belgium did not profit proportionately from the growth of the country's wealth. According to Emile Lamberts, "the living conditions of factory workers before 1850 were abysmal."[7] In the glass works where twelve-hour shifts were spent in front of the constant heat of fires, the shifts were only broken by a half hour break. In the textile mills of Verviers the workers worked a day shift of 12.5 hours or a night shift of 9 hours. Workers in the rope mills worked up to 14 hours a day. The longer days, however, were usually broken by two breaks of a half hour and a break of one hour. A Napoleonic decree of 1813, which excluded children under the age of ten from the mines, remained in effect in Belgium. In the coalmines of the Province of Liège it was unusual to find a young boy under the age of twelve below ground. Young girls in Liège were employed almost exclusively above ground. They generally did not work in the pits before they were fifteen. However, in the mines around Mons young girls went to work in the mines at the same age as young boys. The youngsters primarily hauled baskets of coal or pulled cartloads of coal on their hands and knees in the low-ceilinged tunnels. The workday varied from eight to 12 hours a day, but sometimes stretched to 15. Any eating had to be done while continuing to work. For this children earned between 50 centimes to 1.2 francs a day. In contrast adult women made approximately 2 francs a day in the mines, and men up to 5 francs a day. Most of the children did not learn to read. It was only the children of master workers who received any education. Most workers saw no utility in their children learning what they themselves did not know.[8]

## The Hungry Forties

In addition to the normal low wages, long hours, and distressing living conditions of Belgian workers during this period, Flanders was struck first by a decline of the linen industry, which was apparent by 1841, and then by an agricultural and industrial crisis between 1845 and 1850.[9] Due to the decline of the linen industry, many who were able to obtain employment in the mills of Ghent felt that they were lucky to be able to eat during the "hungry forties," for 15,000 died of starvation in Flanders between 1846 and 1848. Malnutrition and squalid conditions also contributed to the spread and mortality of disease. Eric Hobsbawn writes, "hunger-typhus ravaged the countrysides of Flanders (. . .) where the village linen-weaver fought his doomed battle against modern industry."[10] Between 1846 and 1848 11,900 Belgians died of typhus. And between 1848 and 1849 another 22,441 died of cholera. The decline of Ghent's linen workers parallels that of the hand weavers in England. Successful machine production of linen was not developed until the end of the 1830s, and, even then, the production of linen was more costly than that of cotton cloth. This mechanization, as in England, did not aid the skilled workers in the trade. The owners of linen mills had to cut their costs to compete with cotton. They did this by lengthening the hours of labor beyond the 12 to 16 hour day of the cotton mill workers and by keeping wages as low as possible. Instead of hiring skilled linen workers managers employed unskilled female workers. In Belgium, which was notorious at the time for its miserable working conditions, the women linen mill workers were the most miserably exploited segment of a miserably exploited work force.[11]

By the 1830s Belgium's miners also saw their wages slashed as employers turned to the cheap labor of women and children and of men convicted of vagrancy. By 1904 Demetrius Boulger would write of the "physical and mental decay" of the miners. "Among these," he wrote,

> it seems as if there had sprung up a fresh race of dwarfs, men under four feet eight inches, women shorter still. (. . .) They are stunted and emaciated, and they are easily distinguishable from the rest of the population as the third and fourth generation of the old mining population.[12]

The story in the cotton mills was similar. In 1846 the average cotton worker earned 656.08 francs a year, while the minimum standard of living was estimated to require 742.56 francs.[13]

Discipline and compliance were maintained through a combination of hunger and repression. Articles 415 and 416 of the new state's penal code, copied from France, outlawed unions, and required that each worker carry a *livret* detailing his or her work history. Nevertheless, Belgian workers occasionally responded to the threat of technological unemployment or de-skilling by attacking in explosive episodes of

Luddite rage the machines, which they regarded as threats to their livelihood.[14] The code also stipulated that the employer was master and that his word was law. The code, incidentally, reduced the legal status of all women to that of minors.[15]

## The Economic Crisis in Flanders from 1845 to 1850

Eric Howsbawm writes that although there was no revolution in Belgium in 1848, "in terms of actual suffering Belgium (or rather Flanders) was probably worse off than any other part of Western Europe except Ireland."[16] The great depression of the middle 1840s was accompanied by a failure of the potato crop. As in Ireland a blight destroyed this staple crop, inflicting an additional burden on those workers who were able to supplement their meager wages with potatoes from a home garden, and driving the price of food so high as to increase the struggle for survival for those who still had wages. There was starvation in Flanders as hungry peasants flooded the saturated job market.[17] Numerous contemporary studies provide a vivid picture of the misery of Belgian workers during this era. From these Georges Jacquemyns constructed a typical week's budget for a family of linen workers in Ghent of the 1840s. The typical family of eight members included four wage earners. Families usually depended upon the work of all of their members over seven. The combined weekly income of Jacquemyns' composite was 12.90 francs: 1.10 francs a day for the husband, who was a weaver; .45 franc a day for the wife; and .30 franc a day for each of the two working children. Food, primarily rye bread, potatoes, lard, milk, butter, and coffee, took 8.40 francs a week. The weekly rent for a typical dwelling of two small rooms on an enclosed damp, dirty, and smelly courtyard or *enclos* cost another 1.60 francs. Everything else, fuel, soap, clothes, light more than consumed the remainder. Families like this one had nothing left for "luxuries." Beds and bedding could be counted among the luxuries they lacked, because workers such as these often slept on straw pallets without sheets and with only a rough cover.[18]

Édouard Ducpétiaux, who was the Inspector General of prisons and relief, provided a list of prices for basic food items. White bread cost 20 centimes a kilogram in 1844, but rose to 41 centimes in 1847. Even rye bread rose from 14 to 34 centimes a kilo. Pork rose from 84 centimes to 1.1 francs a kilo. Dry beans rose from 20 to 35 centimes, while rice rose from 23 to 69 centimes.[19] The conditions in the late forties were particularly hard. But ordinary economic pressure was such that children were sent to work very early. In the mining districts boys and girls were employed above ground at the mines as late as 1904.[20]

Ducpétiaux, a social Catholic who was deeply moved by the distress of the workers, described the conditions of two brothers and a sister living in a two-room dwelling. To survive these three traditional skilled linen workers, who worked in the domestic putting-out system, had as a rule to work from 5:30 A.M. to 10 P.M. [21] In addition to their drudgery and poverty, they shared with many Belgians a single life-style imposed by social and economic conditions rather than choice. In 1840 between 15 and 20 percent of 50 year old Belgian females had never married. The brothers and sister basically lived on bread and potatoes, which was fairly common for Flemish textile workers at the time. Ducpétiaux mentioned a worker with six children, the two oldest of whom worked with their mother. Working from 5:30 A.M. to 9 P.M. this worker was only able to earn only 30 centimes. That plus the earnings of his wife and children paid the rent on three rooms and they could purchase potatoes and rye bread, but no meat nor beer.[22]

## Indigence, Vagrancy, and Disorder

During the economic crisis in Flanders some emergency measures were adopted for the relief of the most desperate, the indigents, who were described by Jacquemyns as "(. . .) those who do not have sufficient income to live and who, as a consequence, are either condemned to a slow death, or, rather in the case in civilized countries, are reduced to live through a contribution, benevolent or obligatory, drawn from the income of others."[23] In Bruges, which in 1848 had 21,239 indigents out of a population of 49,211, subsidized grain was provided to the grain market and baker-ies so that grain and bread could be sold at reduced prices or even distributed freely to the destitute to whom special coupons were distributed. Soup kitchens were set up in 1847 to provide cheap or free soup depending upon the condition of the needy. In Ghent the city distributed funds to relief committees which subsidized the sale of bread to the poor. Ypres, with 3,341 indigents out of a population of 16,262 in 1848, was the most generous. To combat speculation and aid the hungry, bread and potatoes were distributed to the needy during the winter of 1845–1846.[24]

Despite the generally pacific character of the Belgians, dire want did prompt some disorder. Beggars and vagabonds proliferated. Some farmers in 1847 reported that they were visited by 300 beggars a day. Brussels paid to ship beggars back to their hometowns. The mayor of Meulebeke gave the beggars of his town sticks with which they were to drive away non-resident beggars and some towns limited begging to one day a week. However, beggars generally avoided Bruges, which had a poor house. According to Jacquemyns "criminality marched in step with the ex-tension of indigence."[25] There were threatening manifestations throughout the distressed area in 1847, though the appearance of gendarmes or police was suffi-cient to restrain the hungry crowds. When the forces of law and order were not present, there were successful episodes of looting. Bakeries were attacked and looted in Scheepsdaele near Bruges. A Dutch barge loaded with grain was looted by 100 paupers at Laethen-Saint-Martin. At Renaix when a farmer demanded an excessive price for his potatoes he was beaten and a sack looted. There were serious disturbances across Ghent on May 17, 1847. Before order was restored the mayor had been wounded and "almost all of the bakeries" had been looted. Though these collective acts were exceptional, "individual crimes occurred daily."[26] There were many instances of acts deliberately calculated to result in imprisonment with its promise of a roof and food. Those condemned to prison for less than a year increased in Flanders from 3,228 in 1841 to 11,434 in 1847.[27] The number of young people less than 18 years old imprisoned in Ghent grew from 350 in 1845, to 1,345 in 1846, and to 1,898 in 1847. During these three years the number of young females who were incarcerated in Ghent was 922.[28]

Ducpetiaux earlier made a correlation between lack of education, which could be tied to poverty, and criminality. Voicing the moral indignation of the Belgian bourgeoisie, he wrote in 1843 that "the class which has the sad privilege of furnishing the greatest number of malefactors remains, after the commotion which has seized the country for the past twelve years, is as it was before, the ignorant, dirty, and improvident."[29] Of the 3,220 inmates in the four central prisons of Belgium in the early 1840s, 1,972 were illiterate and 472 only knew how to read or write imperfectly. Under Dutch rule elementary education had not been compulsory, but it was free. Early Belgian legislation sought to make elementary education universally available and free for poor children. However, many working-class children did not attend school regularly in the 1830s and 1840s.[30] In 1840 out of the 678,854 children between the ages of six and fourteen, 453,381 attended school, but 225,473 did not.[31]

## Escape

There were few breaks from the tedium and deprivations of working class life. Diversion from the long monotony of underpaid labor was provided by *kermesse*, informal street fairs, and regular religious feast days. With the industrial revolution, however, the number of holidays had declined. The sanctioned free feast days were limited to the Monday after Pentecost, the feast of the Assumption (August 15), and a yearly three-day holiday. A more regular escape from drudgery was provided by drink. To the consternation of the bourgeoisie many workers in Flanders ended their workday at *estaminets* where cheap genever (*genièvre*, Belgian gin) offered compensation for the drudgery and squalid conditions. Boulger disparagingly observed of Belgian miners "the only amusement known to this people is to drink and to get drunk." [32]

In 1843 there were approximately 2,800 breweries in Belgium and the per capita consumption of beer was estimated to be 135 liters. The number of distilleries, which produced genever, increased dramatically in the 1830s from 599 in 1831 to 1,092 in 1835. By 1835 the annual production of genever in Belgium reached 260 million liters. The distilleries of Hasselt alone produced 3 million liters of genever a year. Its price declined with the increased production and consumption. In 1831 a liter of genever cost 92 centimes, but by 1834 the price had declined to 40 centimes. In 1838 there were 71,254 taverns in Belgium licensed to sell hard liquor. Between 1828–1829 and 1835–1836, the per capita annual consumption of spirits grew in the city of Antwerp from 9.85 liters to 20.38 liters and in Liège from 10.98 liters to 14.57 liters. The per capita consumption of alcoholic beverages between 1835 and 1836 in West Flanders was 3.22 liters of wine, 10.65 liters of spirits, and 238 liters of beer; in the province of Antwerp 3.75 liters of wine, 10.65 liters of spirits, and 238 liters of beer; and in the province of Luxembourg 8.32 liters of wine, 13.05 liters of spirits, and 110 liters of beer.[33]

## Mortality

In addition to being generally mean, the lives of the workers and their offspring were also quite short. In Verviers in the mid-1840s where still births numbered approximately 17 out of 60, 40.6 percent of the children died before the age of five, and another 4.2 percent died before reaching 15. The rate of mortality was also high among adults of Verviers, 1 in 26.39 in comparison to the 1 in 47 of nearby Huy. Death following childbirth was high for all of Belgium in the nineteenth century, but particularly high in the mining country. In the 1860s one out of every five female deaths in Charleroi occurred during childbirth. Illness along with injury and loss of work to cyclic depressions were ever-present dangers that could transform the existence of a working class family from bare subsistence to dire want.[34]

## The Reaction of the Bourgeoisie

In this era there were conflicting sentiments among the ruling bourgeoisie but the results were almost invariably the same. A number of the ruling class had been schooled in Saint-Simonianism but their penchant for social engineering had become decidedly conservative. Some devoted themselves to reconstructing criminals and mendicants through the "scientifically" inspired octagonal prisons, which would separate diverse categories of inmates and impose through their shape order upon the lives of the disorderly.[35] Other reformers attempted to re-order public space. Supposedly ameliorative intentions to terminate remaining commons and transfer them to the poor resulted in the liquidation of the commons but in the aggrandizement of the bourgeoisie rather than the relief of the poor. Workers and especially women who had supplemented their wages or eked out a living on the margins of survival by grazing animals and gathering kindling saw their crutches removed with the result that they were made even more dependent on their employers or rendered absolutely desperate. Common land by 1840 had been reduced to 163,000 hectares, and by 1860 to 133,000.[36] The importation of cheap grain from North America and Eastern Europe also impacted the countryside. Between 1870 and 1896 the number of peasants, but especially of agricultural workers, decreased by 36.5 percent.[37]

## Peasants

Nevertheless, at the turn of the century, half of Belgium's population still lived in the country. The size of holdings varied greatly between Wallonia and Flanders. Before the occupation of Belgium by the French in 1795 land was largely divided between the Church and the nobility. In Flanders where peasant tenants worked much of the land of monasteries, the French transferred ownership to those who actually worked the land creating a class of small holders who often had no more than five acres. The exceptions in Flanders often occurred when communes took charge of grazing land or wheat fields and rented or sold them to prosperous individuals from the bourgeoisie. In Wallonia, where many nobles possessed undeveloped lands used for hunting, large units were sold to speculators or were held by towns unable to find anyone with the interest and capital to develop them. As a result in Walloon Brabant, Namur, Campine, and the Ardennes, former owners after the defeat of Napoleon were able to reoccupy or repurchase for nominal fees their former lands. These two developments subsequently led to the larger holdings of Wallonia.[38]

At the beginning of the twentieth century, Demetrius Bolger wrote of seeing the Flemish peasants as

(. . .) grey figures moving along the roads or across the fields while gleams of light alone showed the dawn of the coming day. They wish to be at their work, discontinued late the night before, as soon as there is sufficient light to enable them to resume it. They are working for themselves, and very likely they would grumble if they were asked to do it for a master. But it is not only the men, but also the women who work thus.[39]

Describing the living conditions of the Belgian peasants Bolger wrote that

(. . .) their workaday clothes (. . . .) are generally dirty. All the peasants wear the wooden sabot, yellow in colour and clumsy in form, coarse, grey worsted stockings, short trousers tied with a ribbon above the calf, and a linen smock. The usual headgear of the men is a cap with a peak, and the women have linen bonnets with a kind of hood over the forehead. If their dress is plain, their living is still plainer. Their breakfast consists of no more than coffee and rye bread, their mid-day meal of bread and butter, or grease—tartine— with which they sometimes have cheese or a little cold bacon, and their supper of soup and bread. On Sundays and fête days they have hot bacon, and occasionally rabbits or fish. Fresh meat never comes their way, and is practically unknown. On the other hand, they eat great quantities of vegetables, cooked and uncooked, and dandelion salads are the luxury of the Belgian peasant (. . .) In order to correct the depressing effect of the spectacle of these peasant proprietors in their week-day costumes, when they strike the observer as mere drudges bound in misery, it is well to take a glance at these same people on Sundays, going to mass or returning from it. The whole population goes; there are no non-attendants here, except those persons who are ill or bed-ridden (. . .) All the men wear respectable black suits and boots; the women are well dressed and carry themselves well, and there are bright coloured parasols to protect from the sun the girls and young women who have been toiling in the fields all the week with no protection save a linen hood. It is difficult to realize that these are the same people; but it is quite clear from their animated conversation and laughter that they are far from unhappy or dissatisfied with their lot.[40]

The houses of the Flemish peasants differed from those of Wallonia. In Flanders the houses made of brick and covered with stucco and painted yellow were scattered throughout the country. In Wallonia the peasants congregated in towns and their houses were made of stone. In 1904 Boulger observed that in Wallonia "when the outskirts of a townlet or large village are passed, not a house will be found along the road until the next village is reached." [41]

Even when peasants turned to factories for a living, they often kept their roots in the countryside. Belgium, though urbanized and densely populated, was a country of small and medium sized towns. Many industrial workers continued to live in their villages and commuted to work by means of Belgium's excellent rail system. At their homes they continued to tend large gardens to supplement their income, but also as a tie to their traditional way of life. Ellen Evans writes, "Brussels, for example, was surrounded by small commuter towns. (. . .) [The] suburban-village dwellers retained many characteristics of an earlier way of life (. . .)" [42]

## Improvement of Workers' Conditions

There was eventually some improvement in the conditions of Belgium's non-agricultural workers. Industrial productivity soared during the second half of the nineteenth century and some small share was extended to industrial workers whose numbers had grown from 447,000 in 1846 to 934,000 by 1896 and to 1,176,000 by 1910. Real wages rose by 49 percent between 1853 and 1875 and grew again by four percent between 1896 and 1910. Organization and agitation had much to do with this, though some of the improvement was undoubtedly due to lowered costs of living. The Workers' Party called a general strike in 1892 and the mining districts were rocked by "what was practically an armed rebellion."[43] The owners of the mines relented and agreed to a new and increased wage scale.

More important for the standard of living of Belgian workers at this time than small increases in wages were improved conditions of work and the introduction of minimal social services. Hours of labor were lowered from 12 to 14 hours a day to 10 or 11, sanitary conditions at the workplace improved, and there was an improvement in workers' housing.[44] There was an effort to condemn the worst urban housing and force the workers to less crowded housing in the suburbs, a move made possible by the development of an efficient system of tramways. Sick funds were established at the end the century. Workers who subscribed paid a franc a week, which was supplemented by state funds. In return ill workers received medical care and a franc a day. In 1900 a State Pension Bill was introduced. It provided needy workers who had reached the age of sixty-five 65 francs a year. Though it was estimated that 150 francs were needed for secure subsistence, workers were aided by these state pensions.[45] In 1903 a law was passed which finally required employers to provide compensation for workers injured on the job. As a result of these measures life for workers became less mean and tenuous.

# CHAPTER 12

# From Mid-century to the First World War

### Leopold II

I n 1865 Leopold II succeeded his father. Early in his reign Belgium had to deal with threats to its independence. Prussia and France had earlier attempted to take advantage of Belgium's dependence upon foreign markets for its products. Prussia had sought in 1842 to draw Belgium into its Zollverein, the developing customs union among the German states. Louis Philippe and then Napoleon III had tried to force Belgium to join France in a customs union. A more serious threat developed in the late 1860s. Following the 1866 Seven Weeks War between Prussia and Austria, France desperately sought compensation for the augmentation of Prussian power. Among the schemes entertained by Louis Napoleon was the annexation of the French speaking sections of Belgium. British unease about the possibility of a change in the status of Belgium led to a British initiative that gained the agreement of France and Prussia in August 1870 to guarantee the neutrality of Belgium during the Franco-Prussian War. France acceded in order to court the good will of Britain.

### Localism

Initially both the Catholic and Liberal parties of Belgium shared "a tradition of intense localism and anti-statism."[1] This localism was rooted in a medieval tradition of communal liberties, and during the Spanish and Austrian periods the Belgians wheedled every local right, which they could from the distant monarchs. As Germany and Italy moved toward centralization in the nineteenth century, Belgium pursued a different path. The Belgians reacted against the centralization imposed by Napoleon and William I. Localism was as important an issue in the Revolution of 1830 as was national independence.

Belgian towns retained many rights in the new kingdom. They had the power to levy local taxes. They could grant their own subsidies to religious foundations and schools. They also had control over their own municipal police forces. Belgian provinces too had elected provincial councils rather than administrators appointed by the central government as in France. The king appointed governors who served for life but they acted as chairs of the provincial councils rather than as representatives of the central government.[2]

The Belgian Workers' Party, which was founded in 1885, though explicitly socialist and internationalist, found real impediments to its message of broader than local solidarity. Though organizers had some success within individual industries and towns, Belgian workers "(. . .) did not easily identify their interests with those of other regions, let alone with the workers of other countries."[3]

## Between 1870 and 1914

The last three decades of the nineteenth century and the first decade and a half of the twentieth century constituted a period of marked political, intellectual, and social transformation in Belgium. The impetus for this transformation was the social impact of a maturing industrial revolution coupled with the economic and political shock rendered to the political hegemony of liberalism by the long depression of the 1870s, 1880s, and 1890s. The workers, farmers, and shop owners of Belgium became involved in national politics on a continuing basis in contrast to their earlier involvement, which was short-lived and often limited to the members of a single trade and town.[4] The common people of Belgium started thinking in new ways and developed new values inspired by socialism, nationalism, or a new sort of Catholic consciousness. This was the period in which the Belgian masses entered the political arena and their new ideas and values were formulated into energizing political ideologies. These ideologies provided the motivation and direction for the groups as they entered the political arena. The ideologies of socialism and political Catholicism suggested why the masses should bother with politics and what they could expect when they achieved their rightful political due. According to Carl Strikwerda, as

> collective responses to the problems of industrial society (. . .) [these ideologies promised continuity in the midst of an] increasingly conflict-ridden, individualistic society beset with social and economic problems. Bureaucratic techniques, propagated by business and the rationalized state, provided the organizational form as the masses were wielded into new corporate groups, whether parties, unions, or associations.[5]

This "organizational revolution" provided different interest groups with new sets of weapons against "highly organized foes." As a consequence "formal membership, written rules, organized meetings, and designated officers were utilized by everyone from big business corporations to farmers' leagues and coalminers' unions."[6] In contrast to earlier episodic involvement of informal groups usually led by a member of the upper class there was now organizational continuity and open recruitment of leaders.

This was the period of gestation for post-World War II Belgian society: the formation period for "tightly organized communities" which would "engage in complex bargaining" with one another and create a distinctive political system, which has been labeled "consociational democracy" or "segmented pluralism." The tightly organized communities were based on ideological, political, religious, or linguistic-cultural factors. They are referred to as "pillars," or vertical organizations because they cut through the distinctions of economic and social classes.[7]

## Catholics, Liberals, and Socialists

On June 1, 1879, following their victory in the 1878 election, the Liberals succeeded in passing the Education Act, the *Loi Scolaire*, which secularized primary education. The campaign had been led by Walthère Frère-Orban, a virulent anti-Catholic, and by the Education League, which he headed, supported by the Masons. Public "neutral" schools were to be funded by the communes with assistance from the national government. No financial aid was to be given to Catholic schools. This measure enraged the Catholics. They boycotted the new schools. By 1884 a third of the teachers in communal schools had resigned and had joined the Catholic "free" schools. By 1883 3,885 "free schools" had been established and the percentage of students in Catholic schools rose from 13 percent to more than 60 percent.[8] The reaction against the anti-Catholic legislation of the Liberals led to a victory of the Catholics or, as they were called, the Clericals in the June 1880 election. The new Catholic government was headed by Jules Malou, but its real leader was Count Charles Woeste, who had been a leader of the school strike. The Liberal Party was so marginalized that it never again governed alone and would not participate in a coalition government again until 1917. The Catholic Party, on the other hand, "monopolized every cabinet" from 1884 to 1917.[9]

The attempt of the Liberals to secularize the educational system was the catalyst, which led to the formation of a mass Catholic Party as the small Catholic elite of rural notables and wealthy farmers appealed to lower and middle class Catholics.[10] Though it took time for the disparate Catholic elements to address the problems created by industrialization, a Catholic working class movement would develop in the twentieth century and the Catholic movement was democratized. The educational issue mobilized the Catholics and once the Catholic Party attained power it revoked the 1879 law. On September 10, 1884, a new Education Law provided public support for religious schools. On August 30, 1895, instruction in Catholic religion for Catholic students again became compulsory in all public schools. The 1884 education law required every commune to set up at least one school. The school could be secular or religious, but the secular schools were required to have religious instruction during regular class hours if the parents of twelve students requested it. Teachers could be lay or religious. They were required to have some preparation for teaching but did not have to attend state normal schools. By 1912 18,000 primary school teachers in Belgium were members of religious orders. The sole role of the state was to inspect the standards of the schools and to provide financial support for all of them, religious or secular.

Count Woeste and conservative Catholics were strongly opposed to compulsory education. They insisted on the right of parents and employers to keep young people out of school. In fact, Belgium did not require compulsory attendance at elementary school until 1914. Evans writes that, although the Catholic Party became "not altogether willingly" the advocate of the oppressed Catholic Flemish people, the party "by resisting state teacher-training" and by insisting on the right of parents to keep their children out of school "actually condemned the Flemish-speaking rural population to another thirty years of inferior education and even complete illiteracy (still 40 percent in Flanders in 1910)."[11]

The Liberals, who drew their support from towns and the French-speaking area in particular, failed to evolve into a mass party. Catholic "independents," urban Catholics, particularly in Brussels, who had supported the Liberals, shifted their support to the Catholic Party. However, the Socialists, who formed their own party in 1885, following the defeat of the Liberals in 1884, can be viewed as the mass party successor to the Liberals. The progressive or radical faction of the Liberals, who were in the main journalists, teachers, and lawyers, though small in number, played a significant part in the early socialist movement.[12]

### Belgian National Identity: French versus Flemish

With Belgian independence cultural nationalists encouraged the elaboration of a uniquely Belgian culture. This effort certainly drew on distinctive traditions but in retrospect it can be viewed as a not uncommon effort by nationalists to construct a new nationality and a national culture. The Belgian nationalists wanted the Belgians to have their own national history, art, and literature. Their effort was ultimately divisive, undermining the very national unity, which they desired to construct. These national artificers chose French to serve as the voice of Belgium and to give linguistic unity to the new nation.[13] Despite the call from Flemish intellectuals for a cultural synthesis through an interaction of Germanic and Romance traditions, French was declared the official language of the new country. "In the 10 years following Belgian independence, the public and cultural life of the whole country, including those areas where Dutch was the main language, was largely dominated by French."[14] Secondary and higher education were accessible only to those who knew

French; Flemish/Dutch speakers, if brought to court, could not hope to be tried in their own language.[15] All of this despite the fact that according to the census of 1846 2,471,000 Belgians spoke Flemish dialects compared to only 1,827,000 who spoke French.[16] Though 95 percent of the people of Flanders spoke Flemish, French was the language of the provincial governments and even of some of the municipal councils in Flanders.[17] Flemish if it endured was to be reduced to the tongue of a second-class culture. It was regarded by the Francophone elite "not as a language but as a collection of dialects," and relegated to the role of a "dialect to be used only with servants and animals."[18] The lack of education in Flemish, the language of the majority of the people of Belgium, had disastrous results. In 1848 the illiteracy rate for conscripts to the army from East Flanders was 49 percent compared to a rate of only 11 percent for conscripts from the francophone province of Luxembourg.[19] A parliamentary commission in 1856 recommended education in Flemish be provided in lower level trade schools and that it be taught as a foreign language in university preparatory schools and at the University of Ghent in order that doctors, lawyers, and educators might be able to serve the people of Flanders.[20] Actually the acceptance of standard Dutch as the language of education and literature rather than the Flemish variant was due to the refusal of the Belgian state to support the development of a distinct standard Flemish variant. The Francophone elite "exploited the linguistic chaos in Flanders to put Flemish at a disadvantage and favour French."[21] The only interest of the government was for the development of a standard spelling of the language. However, in the contest for a standard spelling Jan Frans Willems was able to successfully promote the standard Dutch spelling, the Siegenbeek standard, which had become the officially recognized variant in the Netherlands in 1804. According to Kas Deprez, "at a time when spelling was considered to make up the whole of a language, this constituted a crucial victory for the advocates of pan-*Nederduits* [as Dutch was often called before the 1850s when the designation *Nederlands* came into use to distinguish the Dutch language from Low German]."[22] The Siegenbeek standard was adopted in 1864 and Dutch as it was used in the Netherlands eventually became the literary language of the Flemish.[23]

The denigration of Flemish Dutch, or Dutch in general, was almost immediately repudiated by Philip Blommaert who decried the neglect of Dutch in the new state in a pamphlet written in eloquent Dutch. Actually Flemish Dutch was an ancient literary language. A hagiography of St. Servatius was written in it prior to 1200. This pre-dates the literary debut of English with Chaucer's 1387 *Canterbury Tales*. Early printing had flourished in Antwerp, and those printers, who sought to sell their books to the growing class of wealthy traders and merchants, did so predominantly in Dutch. Antwerp had also supported an array of poets and theatrical groups, who wrote and performed in Dutch.[24] In the nineteenth century Hendrik Conscience and Guido Gezelle indubitably affirmed the power of Flemish Dutch in their writings.

Hendrik Conscience, the Flemish romantic and outstanding proponent of Flemish cultural nationalism in the first half of the nineteenth century, published his *Lion of Flanders* in 1839. This book inspired the Flemish flag and anthem and popularized Jan Breidel and Pieter De Coninck, the leaders of the workers of Bruges at the Battle of the Golden Spurs in 1302, as Flemish national heroes. In 1867 a committee was set up in Bruges to erect a statue in their honor. When the municipal authorities intervened and set the date for the 1887 dedication on August 15, thousands of people assembled for a gigantic outpouring of Flemish national sentiment on the anniversary of the Battle of the Golden Spurs, July 11. They marched past the new statue and sang *The Flemish Lion* over and over.[25]

A Flemish "party" had emerged in the 1840s. Its first object was to promote the study of Flemish literature and art with the eventual object of establishing Flemish on an equal footing with French in education and government. In rural West Flanders diocesan priests, who taught the Flemish language and Flemish literature, propagated the identification of the Flemish nation with Catholicism. The Flemish poet-priest, Guido Gezelle, who taught in secondary schools in Roulers and Bruges from 1854 to 1865, stands out among them. He was the guiding light of a Flemish Christian poetic movement, the West-Flemish School. Gezelle called for a rejuvenation of Catholicism by returning to its cultural roots among the people. "This required the study of the past, (. . .) of the vernacular, of the customs and rituals of the common people, in which the religion of the forefathers is reflected, of Gothic architecture, of the liturgy etc."[26] Gezelle, however, advocated a resurgence of *viz Diets* [Old Flemish] rather than standard Dutch. Because of his ardent propagation of the Flemish language, Gezelle ran afoul of the "Fransquillon" (Gallicized Flemish opponents of the Flemish movement) ecclesiastical authorities. He was forced to resign his teaching post. He was assigned to a parish in Kortrijk in 1872, gave up writing for twenty years, and publicly expressed hostility to the Flemish movement. Shepard Clough speculates "the Gallicized higher clergy of Flanders brought pressure upon him to forsake his Flamingant sympathies."[27] According to Clough, "the blanket of disappointment and discouragement which smothered the poetic fire of Gezelle for so many years was finally thrown off."[28] He again began publishing his masterful Flemish poetry in 1893, but his work was cut short by his death in 1899.[29]

Cardinal Desiré Mercier,[30] a leader of the Gallicized episcopacy, asserted in 1906 that Dutch was not a suitable medium for higher education.[31] The privileged position of French did not go unchallenged. Flemish students at the University of Leuven, where the General Catholic Flemish Student Union had much support, demonstrated what they thought of the Cardinal's assessment of their language on May 9, 1909, at the 75th anniversary of the reopening of the university. In front of the stand where the Cardinal was seated with officials of the university, the student band struck up *De Vlaamse Leeuw* (The Flemish Lion), the anthem of Flanders, and students shouted "We demand Flemish at the university."[32]

As Kas Deprez and Louis Vos summarized:

(. . .) the kind of Flemish written by the leading authors, such as Conscience, was not felt
to be good enough; it was full of dialecticisms and Gallicisms (. . .) Dutch was a matter of
self-preservation; a separate Flemish would never be able to stand up to French. In 1864,
the Flemish spelling commission settled for 'one language, one spelling.'[33]

## The Emergence of a Flemish Sub-nation

In 1856 the Belgian government established a Flemish Grievance Commission. In
its 1859 report the commission called for the Flemish provinces to be bi-lingual
with two official languages and the right of the inhabitants to use either in public
life.[34] Though the Walloons resisted bilingualism, students, priests, and intellectuals from the Flemish lower middle class worked to win for Dutch speakers the right
to use their language when dealing with state authorities at least in the parts of Belgium where the majority of the people spoke Flemish. They achieved some recognition of the rights of Flemish speakers in the courts and administration, and the right
to bilingual secondary education for Dutch speakers in Flanders.

According to Vos, "in the last quarter of the nineteenth century, as Flemish ethnic and national identity began to assert itself, a Flemish subnation emerged within
the greater Belgian nation."[35] The champions of this subnationalism promoted a
Flemish Belgian culture and wanted "Flanders to be a home for the Flemish where
they could speak their own language, notwithstanding the continued existence
there of a French-speaking upper class."[36] Flemish activists made a significant advance in 1898 when the government recognized Dutch as one of Belgium's official
languages. This Flemish victory provoked a reaction among French speakers who
protested against the legal requirement that state officials use Dutch when addressing Dutch speakers in Flanders. Nevertheless, by 1913 Dutch was made legally ac-
ceptable for Flemish schools, courts, and local government.[37]

The linguistic conflict had repercussions within the political parties. Each of
the three major parties, the Catholics, the Socialist, and the Liberals had supporters among the Flemish and the French speakers. However, the Catholic and Socialist parties became increasingly identified with specific ethnic constituencies.
According to De Gruben, "in general (. . .) the Catholic party shifted more and
more in the direction of the peasant population of the Flemish part of the country,
whereas the Socialist party was pointed toward the proletariat among the Walloons (. . .)."[38] According to Evans the Catholic Party became identified with the
Flemish cause "reluctantly and almost by default." Catholicism was more deeply in-
grained and seriously practiced by the Flemish than by the Walloons and with the
extension of the franchise, the party's constituency included an increasing number

of Flemish speakers. She adds "neither the Liberal nor the Labor party showed any interest in the Flemish question, associating it with provincial backwardness and obscurantism." Despite the fact that there were Flemish Liberals and Flemish Socialists, the Catholic Party was the only national party willing to represent the Flemish as "an interest group."[39]

Nevertheless, in Antwerp Flemish Liberals and democratic Catholics cooperated and formed a coalition effort, the "Meeting Partij," in 1862 to challenge the French speaking elite, which had run the city. The party dominated the municipal elections in the next decade and established Dutch as the administrative language of the city and province. It was the success of this party, which persuaded the national parliament in 1873 to allow the limited use of Dutch in the courts, in 1878 in administration, and in 1883 in state secondary schools.[40]

## Administrative Separation

The demands of the leaders of the Flemish movement were rather moderate. They called for the equality of Flemish or Dutch with French. The Flamingant leaders, such as Frans Van Cauwelaert, A. Van De Perre, and Kamiel Huysmans, did not question the unity of Belgium. Before World War I "no considerable group of Flemings had demanded the administrative division of Belgium and certainly no group had ever talked seriously about political independence or union with Holland."[41] However, such notions were expressed from time to time. Though those who expressed them were on the periphery at the time, they did point to the future. In 1845 J.C. Theelem, a Flemish intellectual, wrote "nothing can save Belgium from ruin but the administrative separation of the Teutonic (Flemish) and the Gallic (Walloon) parts of Belgium."[42] At the beginning to the twentieth century the Flemish People's Council of the National Flemish Association, founded by Flemish nationalists, discussed the idea of dividing Belgium along linguistic lines for administrative purposes. The idea was echoed by some Walloons. Dupont, a Minister of State, on March 9, 1910, proclaimed in the Senate that "rather than learn Dutch we shall advocate administrative division."[43] Another Walloon, Albert Mockel, wrote in October 1911, "the only means by which Wallonia and Flanders can live in fraternal peace is by the complete administrative separation of the two peoples."[44]

## The Congo

Leopold II's reign, in addition to serving as the gestation period for many aspects of twentieth century Belgian society, was also the period during which Belgium became involved in Africa. Leopold II was an enthusiastic imperialist. He and other Belgian supporters of imperialism had earlier advocated an imperial role for Belgium as a compensation for its constrained frontiers, as a source of markets for its industries, and as sustenance and living room for its people, but Leopold quickly abandoned the idea of a settler-colony in favor of an area to be exploited for his personal enrichment.[45] On September 12, 1876, he convened a congress of scientists and explorers, the Geographical Conference, and founded the International Association for the Exploration and Civilization of Central Africa. This organization, which was purportedly established to suppress the slave trade, was personally financed and headed by Leopold. In 1877 and 1879 Belgians set up posts on Lake Tanganyika. The Belgian component of the International Association was organized on November 25, 1878, as the Committee for the Study of the Upper Congo. Henry M. Stanley, who had just crossed Africa, was hired to establish posts in the Congo region between 1879 and 1884.[46] Stanley persuaded Congolese chiefs to cede land in exchange for uniforms and alcohol. Without the chiefs realizing the ramifications of their actions Leopold was able to amass a gigantic area for which he sought international recognition.[47] In 1882 the Committee was reorganized as the International Association of the Congo. The United States recognized the International Association as the sovereign authority in the Congo on April 22, 1884.[48] At the 1884 Berlin Conference on the Congo the International Association was recognized as the Independent State of the Congo or the so-called "Congo Free State." On May 2, 1885, Leopold was declared sovereign of the Congo Free State, which in effect became his personal possession, not a Belgian colony. In fact, "the fiction that Belgium had nothing to do with Leopold's private affairs was very carefully upheld."[49] Concessionaires were granted large portions of the state, but much of it was set aside as state or crown lands, the private domain of the king. E.H. Kossmann refers to the Congo venture as Leopold's "very private enterprise."[50] The Belgian parliament, though it gave its permission for Leopold to assume the crown of the Free State, explicitly "refused to accept colonial responsibilities."[51]

The purpose of the Congo venture had clearly shifted from international cooperation, exploration and the ending of the slave trade to blatant exploitation. Military force was used to control workers and extract forced labor from them. Agents of the Anglo-Belgian Indian Rubber Company raided villages and held women, children, and elders as hostages, to force the adult males to collect rubber. Congelese were subjected to a rubber tax and specific labor requirements. Resistance was answered with death or the severing of hands.[52] Immense profits flowed into the personal account of the king, who spent large amounts on architectural and urban development and beautification projects throughout Belgium. However, in 1904 Edmund Morel[53] formed the Congo Reform Association in Britain to publicize the horrors of Leopold's rule in the Congo. The growing international indignation over the conditions in the Congo led to intervention by the Belgian parliament. In 1906 the Belgian government forced Leopold to agree to annexation of the Congo by

Belgium. After the details of transferal had been agreed upon, the Belgian state on November 15, 1908, assumed control in the Congo removing it from the personal control of Leopold. Leopold, nevertheless, was able to retain the profits from the enormous crown domain for his dynasty until his death.[54]

Although there is agreement that Leopold's regime in the Congo was bloody and exploitative, there is disagreement over numbers. Many speak of a million deaths. Jules Marchal, the author of *L'histoire du Congo* (History of the Congo), and Adam Hochschild, the author of *King Leopold's Ghost*, both assert that Leopold's exploitative regime was responsible for the deaths of 10 million people in the Congo. Nevertheless according to Marchal,

> The Belgians weren't imperialists; they did not want an empire. The Congo was about one man who wanted money. That's what made it so bad. The state's only purpose was to collect rubber. The king didn't want to exterminate people; he wanted them to work for him.[55]

The transfer of the Congo to Belgian control did not improve conditions. Although parliament was officially responsible for the supervision of the Congo, colonial policy continued to be dominated by the king and the minister of colonies, and the administration within the Congo remained unchanged.[56]

## Socialism and Universal Suffrage

In addition to horrific social problems in the Congo, there were significant social problems in Belgium proper. Due to its coal mines and early development of metallurgy small Belgium in the second half of the nineteenth century was the fourth ranking industrial power in Europe. Along with industrialization came acute social problems and labor unrest. Politically and juridically Belgian workers at first had no redress. They did not have the right to vote and stringent legal penalties blocked the organization of labor unions until the 1860s. Nevertheless, a socialist movement developed. The first mass strikes erupted in the late 1850s. From these strikes there emerged in Ghent a proto-union, the *Broederlijke Wevers* (Fraternal Weavers), soon joined by its female counterpart, the *Zusters Genootschap der Weefsters* (Sisterly Association of Weavers). In 1865 Ghent workers established *Vooruit* (Forward), which with its many social and educational components quickly developed into the largest socialist "parallel" society in the country.[57] It was the forerunner for the *Maisons du Peuple* (Houses of the People) which served as social and educational centers for workers in the industrial towns of the country.

The late 1860s also witnessed the spread of the First International Workingmen's Association, whose Belgian component the *Association Internationale des Travailleurs*

(AIT) was headquartered at Verviers. The government adjusted. In 1866 it revoked the anti-labor articles 415 and 416 of the constitution. Strikes and workers' groups were legalized. The new article 310, however, limited the potential effectiveness of strikes by providing stiff punishments for impeding workers who wished to stay on the job or for interfering with economic activity. Nevertheless, organization was permitted and strikes followed. An 1868 strike of miners led to bloody clashes with mounted troops sent in to control the strikers. The economic crisis of 1873 provoked a number of strikes particularly among the textile workers.

The First International, which was disbanded by followers of Marx in Philadelphia in 1876, continued to operate in Belgium. The AIT, the unions, and the workers' associations provided the amalgam for the Belgian Workers' Party (Partie Ouvrière Belge), which was founded in 1885. The new party quickly replaced the Liberal Party as the major alternative to the Catholic Party. This Belgian socialist party, which became the largest party in the Belgian parliament in 1894, was in many respects the quintessential socialist party. According to Barbara Tuchman it was "the most solidified, disciplined and serious of the European Socialist parties."[58] Nevertheless, despite the strength of the party and the degree of industrialization in Belgium, a smaller percentage of Belgian workers were, at the time, unionized than in Britain or Germany or even in less industrialized France and the Netherlands.[59]

The organization of Belgian workers was difficult because they were largely illiterate and remarkably repressed and exploited. As late as the First World War 10 percent of the Belgian population was still illiterate.[60] The problems of the early industrial revolution existed to a marked degree in Belgium and they persisted. The industrialization of Belgium closely resembled that of Great Britain but poverty remained even more persistent in Belgium. Though Belgium was until 1880 second only to Great Britain among the industrialized countries in terms of the percentage of the population employed in industry (20 percent), and though Belgium in the two decades prior to World War I grew almost as fast as the German dynamo and faster than either Great Britain or France, Belgian performance was accomplished at the expense of its workers. Belgium was known as "the country of low wages and long hours."[61] Belgium also continued to use and exploit a high percentage of female and child workers. In the textile industry, which employed more workers than any other branch of the economy other than agriculture, 54 percent of the workers were female. In 1870 women constituted 36 percent of the whole labor force and they earned a third to a half less than male workers.

The socialists, despite the low level of labor organization, successfully used a major series of strikes between 1886 and 1894 to press their demand for reform and universal manhood suffrage. The general strikes of "*l'année terrible*" (the terrible year) 1886 led the Catholic government to launch an investigation of working conditions. The dismal revelations of the study then prompted Belgium's first labor legislation.

The legislation was passed in 1889 and went into effect in 1892, but it was rather limited in scope. It banned all females and males under the age of ten from underground work, but permission was granted to females already working underground to continue to do so. In contrast to other European industrial societies Belgian women continued to work at "men's" jobs until World War I. Belgian women had for centuries formed an essential part of the work force and efforts to prohibit traditional forms of female employment would have roused very strong opposition. In Belgium it was traditional for women to engage in productive labor. In 1904 Demetrius Bolger wrote "the female half of the community works as hard as the male."[62] The Royal Academy of Medicine fruitlessly lamented Belgian backwardness and failure to follow the ideological shift in France which progressively assigned to women a "biologically dictated," restricted domestic sphere. However, the pro-industry governments of Belgium assiduously dedicated to the "free labor market" were no more willing to restrict the labor of women than to legislate less exploitative conditions for workers male or female. Though hours of labor were reduced, according to Patricia Penn Hilden until 1914 "Belgium had the dubious honor of remaining the only European industrial nation almost entirely bereft of legal limitations on the exploitation of the nation's workers."[63]

If strikes provided the impetus for the first labor legislation, such as it was, they also prodded Belgium toward electoral reform. After a general strike was proclaimed in April 1893, the government on April 22 introduced universal male suffrage. The votes, however, were weighted according to age, income, education, and marital status. All males over twenty-four received one vote; men over thirty-four who had families and paid property taxes received a second vote; men, who were professionals, or owned more property received a third vote. The weighted vote gave approximately two or three votes to approximately two fifths of the adult males and left the other three fifths with a single vote. Nevertheless, Socialists were able to gain a considerable number of seats in the parliament. Universal suffrage was also of great benefit to the Catholics, but almost completely eliminated the Liberals who represented the urban bourgeoisie.[64] The Liberal delegation in the Belgian parliament declined from 61 to 20 members. On December 24, 1899, proportional representation was introduced to protect minorities. This saved the Liberals. The Liberals and Socialists took advantage of this to form an alliance and to push for the principle of equal votes. Between 1901 and 1905 there was another period of intense strike activity. The labor and social unrest was accompanied by acts of terror, especially dynamiting, ascribed to the anarchists. A political general strike from April 14 to 24, 1913, ended with the assurance that the electoral system would be revised. The reform was delayed by the war, but on May 6, 1919, unweighted universal manhood suffrage was established and some women received the right to vote. The vote, at that time, was given to "war widows, who had not remarried, widowed mothers of sons who had been killed in the war, and women who had been imprisoned by the Germans."[65]

## Social Catholicism

In response to the social problems experienced by Belgian workers, and in view of the socialist challenge, some Belgian priests, even before the publication of the social encyclical *Rerum Novarum* by Pope Leo XIII in 1891, attempted to set up Catholic labor organizations. Father Antoine Pottier labored among the industrial workers of Liège and Verviers with little success. This was due as much to opposition from the conservative Catholic elite and a timorous and conservative hierarchy as it was to socialist sentiments among the workers. After the establishment of universal, if unequal, manhood suffrage in 1894, Adolf Daens, a priest in Aalst, and Florimond Fonteyne, a priest in Bruges, organized a splinter movement, Daensism, to promote the interests of the lower middle class, workers, and farmers of Flanders. The hierarchy was not pleased by what they regarded as radicalism and the two priests were made to pay for their social concerns.[66] More successful was Joris Helleputte,[67] one of the organizers of the *Boerenbond*, the Flemish Farmers' League, which developed into a very successful union of farmers. In 1913 the Confederation of Christian Syndicates was founded under the leadership of Father Rutten to serve as a national federation for the Catholic unions, though it was largely Flemish.[68] The Confederation of Christian Syndicates and the *Boerenbond* set up savings banks, insurance societies, cooperatives, youth organizations, printing houses, and unions, all of which became elements of the Catholic "pillar" in Belgium. Though the social Catholics were regarded with hostility by conservative leaders of the Catholic Party, such as Woeste, they sowed the seeds within the party that would eventually produce Belgian Christian Democracy.[69]

Leopold II , King of the Belgians, 1865–1909. Courtesy of the National Archives (131-No23–6)

# CHAPTER 13

# World War I

### The German Violation of Belgian Neutrality[1]

Following the Belgian Revolution of 1830 the British and French worked out a compromise establishing an independent and perpetually neutral Belgium. In 1867 Napoleon III had sought to bolster his popularity in France by annexations at the expense of Belgium. However, Britain, at the outbreak of the Franco-Prussian War, successfully pressed Prussia and France to reaffirm treaties guaranteeing Belgian neutrality. Belgium faired less well in 1914. Belgium played a key role in Germany's Schlieffen Plan, which called for a massive maneuver of encirclement driving through Belgium into the French rear.[2] Alfred von Schlieffen, the German Chief of Staff under whom the German war plan was developed, was not troubled about the prospective violation of Belgian neutrality. He believed that the war would be won so quickly that adverse international reaction would make no difference. He also questioned the "true" neutrality of Belgium, which fortified its frontier with Germany but not its border with France. Friedrich von Holstein of the German Foreign Office, responding to a query from Schlieffen in 1900, replied that the Foreign Office would have to acquiesce to strategy and offer justifications for the proposed violation rather than oppose it. Theobald von Bethmann-Hollweg, who became German Chancellor in 1908, knew about the planned violation, but lamely asserted that he had never had an opportunity to discuss it with the military.

On July 29, 1914, Bethmann-Hollweg, seeking British neutrality, assured the British ambassador that in the event of war the integrity of Belgium would be preserved, but he hinted that Belgian neutrality would have to be violated. Edward Grey, the British foreign secretary, labeled the offer a "disgrace," and on July 31 asked France and Germany to agree to respect the neutrality of Belgium unless it were first violated by the other. The British position was quite hypocritical. As Niall Ferguson has argued, "if Germany had not violated Belgian neutrality in 1914 Britain would have."[3] Early on August 1 France gave a definitive assent, but Germany refused to bind itself. On August 2, after its declaration of war on Russia, the German ambassador in Brussels, von Below-Saleske, presented an ultimatum to the Belgian Foreign Minister M. Davignon demanding the right of passage for German troops. If Belgium did not resist, its integrity would be assured and it would be compensated at the expense of France after the war. However, if the Belgians resisted, they would be treated as an enemy. The Germans gave the Belgians only twelve hours to respond. On August 3 King Albert appealed to George V of Great Britain for diplomatic support. Expecting an invasion of Belgium, the British Cabinet sent Grey to the House of Commons where in a rousing speech he won its support for war if Belgium were violated. Early on August 4 Grey demanded an immediate affirmation from Germany of Belgian neutrality, but Bethmann-Hollweg responded to the British ambassador that Britain would certainly not go to war over "a scrap of paper."[4] At 2 P.M. Grey was informed that Belgium had been invaded. In fact, the German army had crossed the frontier at dawn on August 4 at Gemmenich, only 50 kilometers from Liège. The British issued an ultimatum to Germany to stop its invasion by midnight. When that deadline passed, Britain entered the war.

In a speech before the Reichstag on the day of the invasion, Bethmann-Hollweg, insisting that Russia had forced Germany into a defensive war, claimed that the threat of a French attack had compelled it to violate Belgian neutrality. He, however, accepted the protests of the Belgian government as "legitimate," and added "we shall try to make up for this injustice—I speak openly—this injustice we are committing, once our military aims have been accomplished."[5] Nevertheless, Germany quickly asserted claims to Belgian territory, and its tenacious adherence to demands for Belgian territory impeded efforts to secure a mediated end to the conflict.[6]

## The German Attack

*"Necessity knows no law."* —Bethmann-Hollweg[7]

*"No might is right. ( . . .) Right is a moral force."*
—Cardinal Mercier,
Catholic Primate of Belgium[8]

The Germans advanced on the railhead of Liège, which "with its twelve bridges over the Meuse ( . . .) was the gateway to Belgium, and ( . . .) the key to Paris."[9] But the central fortress and six surrounding forts of Liège blocked the German advance toward France through the plain to the north of the Ardennes.

The first Belgian village to be entered by the Germans was Gemmenich located on the border near Aachen. There they distributed a proclamation from General Otto von Emmich. The commander of the invading force promised that there would be no atrocities. However, following the death of a German soldier outside the town, the Germans responded by executing hostages, by pillage, and by arson. The German intent was to terrify the Belgian populace and to forestall resistance. Ironically, as German troops moved through Malmédy, which had been given to Prussia by the Congress of Vienna in 1815, they began to pillage the German town. As a result of its Walloon appearance, they thought that they were already in Belgium.[10]

Albert had informed the parliament one-hour after the beginning of the invasion of his determination to resist and he assumed command of the Belgian army.[11] Belgian civilians, despite German reprisals, did resist. They blew up railroad tracks and tunnels and the bridges over the Meuse. Guerrillas, some in private automobiles, conducted hit and run attacks against the advancing Germans.

## The Assault on Liège

Germans attempted to seize the bridge over the Meuse at Visé. They failed, but were able to gain the other side of the river further upstream at Lexhe. The bulk of von Emmich's men, however, were forced to cross the river on pontoon bridges under Belgian fire. By nightfall elements of General Karl von Bülow's Second Army had breached the outer defenses to the north of Liège. However, the ring forts inflicted heavy casualties on the Germans on August 5. After the Germans had captured the smaller forts, General Erich Ludendorff of the Second Army led a brigade into the city on August 6 and forced its surrender on August 7. This battle saw the first strategic bombing of a city by air in the First World War. On August 6 the Zeppelin L6 flying from Cologne dropped bombs on Liège. The attack killed nine civilians but had little material effect. In fact the airship was hit by Belgian ground fire and eventually crashed near Bonn.[12]

Though Liège had fallen, the Belgians in the large forts continued to fight. The Germans then put their gigantic 305mm and 420mm siege howitzers into action and after ferocious pounding the resistance of the Belgians in the surrounded forts ceased. General Gérard Mathieu Leman, the commander of the Belgian forces in and around the city, ordered Fort Loncin, which he had made his headquarters, destroyed on August 15 rather than hand it over to the Germans. However, before his order could be carried out the German bombardment crushed the fort, which was then taken by German attackers. General Leman survived to be carried unconscious from the rubble and was sent to imprisonment in a German POW camp. On August 16 the final forts, Hollogne and Flemalle, hoisted the white flag.[13]

## Belgian Resistance

The preoccupations of Belgium in the years before the war were economic and political. "It did not believe and did not wish to believe in the possibility of war."[14]

Every year when the military budget came before parliament it was met with "pacifist declarations and customary attacks against 'militaristic folly.'"[15] The government, however, was not oblivious to threats. With difficulty it had gained approval in 1906 for the funds necessary to construct a new ring of forts around Antwerp. The same year it had directed the military to draw up contingency plans to deal with a possible German invasion of Belgium. In 1912–1913 the parliament authorized compulsory military service and a program of reform and modernization for the army. However, these changes were to be accomplished over a period of five years.[16] The compulsory military service was intended to create a potential force, including reserves, of 350,000 men. However, by 1914 the Belgian army had only reached a total of 200,000.[17]

The Belgian war plan called for Belgium's field army of 117,000 to concentrate west of the Meuse. It would defend Antwerp but attempt to avoid a head-on clash with a numerically superior force. In addition 67,000 men were to man the forts around Liège, Namur and Antwerp. Those forts begun between 1880 and 1887 were built to form a ring around each city. The forts, constructed with masonry and earthen ramparts and covering, possessed semi-spherical armored gun-emplacements. Liège and Namur, which commanded the principal crossings on the Meuse River, were vital to the defense of Belgium.[18] Behind the "moat of the Meuse" Antwerp formed what could be considered the modern equivalent of the keep of the kingdom.

The Belgian army reserves were called up on July 29 after the French army moved into position along the Belgian frontier. On July 30 the Belgians began to provision their fortifications and forbade the export of horses and vehicles. On July 31, after announcement of mobilization by the Netherlands, Belgian mobilization was officially declared and the Belgian State Railway suspended the movement of trains into Germany. On August 1, as Germany declared war on Russia, the Belgian government bought the whole supply of wheat on the Antwerp market. On August 2 when German troops invaded Luxembourg, the French cut all rail lines entering both Germany and Belgium. On the night of August 2, after the reception of the German ultimatum, guards were posted on the bridges across the Meuse at Liège and Namur and the civic guard was called out.

As the German Army attacked at 8:02 A.M. on August 4, the Belgian field army was positioned near Leuven (Louvain) behind the Gette. Before the forts of Liège fell the First and Second German Armies were already pushing against this line. Given the slow response of the French and the failure of the British, as yet, to act independently of their Gallic ally, the main Belgian force of 65,000 led by Albert withdrew into Antwerp. There as it waited for British support, it could at least threaten German communications. From the port city it did conduct sorties against the flank of the German invading force. The Germans took Aerschot and Leuven on August 19; entered Brussels on August 20; and the same day invested Namur.

Namur, with its citadel overlooking the confluence of the Meuse and the Sambre, was a fortified position from the beginning of its history. It was a strong point of the Aduatuci mentioned by Caesar. In 1692 the French directed by their great military engineer and master of siege warfare Vauban took the town. In 1695 William of Orange retook it. In 1887 the construction of nine forts ringing the city and the citadel fortress made it supposedly impregnable. The fortresses, however, were undermanned and five of them fell on the first day of the German assault. The concentration of German artillery broke the resistance of the rest by August 25.

The Germans, driving toward Antwerp, had shoved their way into Mechelen (Malines) but were driven out by a Belgian counter-attack from Antwerp on August 25. This thrust, though it was ultimately repulsed, provided significant assistance to the British and French. It helped to ease German pressure at Mons and along the Sambre because it led the Germans to commit four reserve divisions and Landwehr brigades to the Antwerp front. The confusion, which the Belgian breakthrough at Mechelen caused the Germans in nearby Leuven, forms an important part of the tragic three-day pillage of Leuven.

## Leuven

According to Arnold J. Toynbee "the destruction of Louvain (Leuven) was the greatest organized outrage which the Germans committed in the course of their invasion of Belgium and France."[19] Germans billeted in Leuven and newly arrived reinforcements were apparently in an anxious state as dusk approached on the night of August 25. Artillery fire could be heard from the fighting around Mechelen and rumors made a Belgian entry into Leuven seem imminent. Apparently mistaking new arrivals moving down the main street running from the railroad station for Belgians, Germans billeted along the street opened fire on fellow Germans. The confusion and anxiety of the German soldiers were probably heightened by looted wine. All hell broke loose. The Germans believed that they were the targets of franc-tireurs and responded with enraged violence and abandon. In and around Leuven 2,441 houses were burned; 2,722 were looted; 251 civilians were killed, the majority summarily executed or just murdered without any pretext of judgment; and 831 civilians were deported to an internment camp in Germany. Almost 40 percent of the destruction occurred in the city itself. Sint Pieterkerk, which was constructed between 1425 and 1497 on the site of two earlier Romanesque churches both of which had been destroyed by fire, was put to the torch. The Germans also burned the renowned university library housed in the old Guild Hall, constructed between 1317 and 1345 by town's then powerful cloth guilds. The extent of the arson can still be measured by the presence of concrete plaques with the date 1914, a burning torch, and a bayonet displayed on the facades of so many re-built buildings in the town.[20]

## The German Drive Continues

The Germans began their siege of Antwerp on August 28 with an assault on the outer forts. Nevertheless, on September 9, at a crucial point during the First Battle of the Marne,[21] the Belgians provided assistance to their Allies by launching another sortie. The Belgians advanced to Vilvoorde, ten miles from the outer ring of Antwerp's forts. Though the sortie was quickly blunted and driven back, it led the Germans to cancel the transfer of one division to the south and to delay the movement of two others. In conjunction with the German defeat along the Marne this Belgian effort contributed a blow to the morale of the Germans.

The Belgians in Antwerp were still a bothersome factor when General Erich von Falkenhayn replaced General Helmut von Moltke as the German Chief of Staff on September 14. A crucial mistake of the Germans was not to secure control of the Belgian coast and the French Channel ports when the Allies were in retreat and the coastal area was completely open to the Germans. The opening of the German assault on Antwerp had awakened the British command to the brilliance of First Lord of the Admiralty Winston Churchill's plan to send British troops to Belgium where a minimal force could have a maximum effect. Churchill was belatedly allowed to send a brigade of British marines and two brigades of new naval volunteers to Antwerp and on September 19 the regular 7th Division and 3rd Cavalry Divisions commanded by General Sir Henry Rawlinson were landed at Ostend and Zeebrugge. They were to move overland toward Antwerp. The Dutch, who controlled the mouth of the Scheldt, refused to allow the British to send the troops directly by water to Antwerp. The Dutch asserted that this would have violated their status as a neutral country. The Dutch later showed their consistency when they closed the lower Scheldt to German warships especially submarines, thus denying them the facilities of Antwerp. The British advance guard arrived in Antwerp on October 4. Though the insufficient British forces could not prevent the fall of Antwerp on October 10, they delayed its collapse and covered the retreat of the Belgian army down the coast of Flanders. All of this impeded the German occupation of the coast until the main British force had reached the Ijzer (Yser).

General Hans von Beseler's German troops penetrated the outer ring of Antwerp's forts at an unguarded point on the night of October 5 and moved up to the inner ring of obsolete forts constructed in 1859. As the German artillery began to pulverize their outdated masonry, the Royal Naval Division and the remnant of the Belgian field army retreated down the coast of Flanders.[22] During the evacuation of British and Belgian military units from the city, the Dutch again denied them the use of the Scheldt, and as a result 33,000 Belgian soldiers and British marines, separated from the main force as it retreated, were forced by the advancing Germans to cross into the Netherlands, where Dutch authorities, who wanted to offer no provocations to the Germans, interned them.[23]

The Antwerp campaign witnessed an important military development, which had been forecast by the ineffectual bombing of Liège from the air on August 6. In September and October the British Royal Naval Air Service conducted what probably was the first effective strategic bombing raids from a field near Antwerp. Planes flying from Antwerp bombed Zepplin hangers near Düsseldorf and destroyed one Zepplin.[24]

The Germans took Ghent on October 12, Bruges on October 14, and Ostend on October 15. Though the Germans crossed the Ijzer (Yser) on October 24 they were stopped. The British along with the French and the Belgians blocked the German advance and preserved the southwestern corner of Belgium. In this 10 by 25 mile miniscule Free Belgium Albert set up his wartime headquarters at La Panne. On October 29 the Belgians, dug in behind the Dixmunde-Nieuport rail embankment, opened the sluices at Nieuport and placed the flooded polders between themselves and the Germans. On October 30 the Germans attacked with five divisions but "after a few hours of fighting, the Germans realized that it was impossible to continue the attack, as their soldiers were up to their knees and unable to throw themselves down for protection from Belgian fire."[25]

Because of the low and sodden character of the land on the Belgian front, where 150,000 men were crowded together along a lake of stagnant and putrid water, disease became rampant among the Belgian soldiers. The absence of clean water and the abundance of rats and filth promoted disease. A third of the Belgian soldiers who died on the Ijzer front died of disease, compared to a death rate from disease of only a sixth elsewhere on the Western Front.[26]

The British Regular Army for its part stopped the Germans at Ypres (Ieper). Ypres, however, became its "tombstone."[27] "From failing hand they threw the torch,"[28] and many more would follow them to the grave. With the failure of the Germans to break through, the trench line was consolidated from the North Sea to the Swiss frontier 350 miles away.[29] Four dismal years of war of attrition followed. The Ypres salient was the center of years of bitter fighting which left it in ruins. The Cloth Hall, constructed between 1260 and 1304, was destroyed by artillery fire on November 22. It was reconstructed between 1933 and 1934. But during the four years of fighting Ypres and the area around it was transformed into an uninhabitable lunarscape. The Germans, who held the Messines (Mesen) Ridge from 1915 to 1917, were able to keep the city and the Allied lines under observation and fire.

On April 22, 1915, the Germans used lethal poison gas for the first time in the West at Bixschote and Boesinghe near Langemarck. The gas took Algerian and French Territorial troops by surprise and they fled in panic. However, the 1st Canadian Division with its flank gone stood its ground. These soldiers "provided a rock past which the German tide could not flow."[30] Few of the Canadians survived, and many who did survive had suffered such damage to their lungs that they had to spend the rest of their lives in veterans' hospitals. It was during this offensive between April

22 and May 25 that the British were pushed back to Sanctuary Woods. In a dressing station John McCrae of the Royal Canadian Medical Corps was moved to write "In Flanders Fields" as a memorial to his dead comrades. Hooge Chateau on the Ypres front was also the site of the first tactical use of flamethrowers in modern warfare.[31]

The Third Battle of Ypres, an Allied offensive in the summer of 1917 to prepare a rolling action against the German coastal positions, foundered in the mud of Flanders in a monstrous display of the butchering incompetence of much of the military leadership. The farmers of the pre-war Ypres area had depended upon an elaborate drainage system to enable them to farm the land. When the drainage system was destroyed and interrupted by the fighting and trench work "the rain lay on the ground, and the clay dissolved into a clinging mud, thick, glutinous, and all-conquering."[32] The 4,283,550 shells fired by the British in their two week long preliminary bombardment, the heaviest British bombardment of the war, destroyed what was left of dikes and drainage ditches and turned the soggy land into a quagmire.[33] The "elastic defense-in-depth system" of the Germans "with a zigzag series of strong points and thick-walled mutually-supporting concrete boxes"[34] largely survived and awaited the hapless troops of the British Empire. In fact, many of the thick-walled German pillboxes, now used as sheds or animal shelters, still remain, imperviously dotting the Belgian countryside around Ypres. In their struggle against the muck British engineers laid plank roads and duckboard tracks to get men and supplies to the front, but the men on them were easily targeted by the Germans. The offensive, which General Douglas Haig expected to break through to Ghent, by its end in October, at a cost of a quarter of a million casualties, gained only four and a half miles, the Menen road, Polygon Wood, and the remains of the village of Passendale (Passchendaele). Siegfied Sassoon wrote "I died in hell—-they called it Passchendaele." On the stone archway at Menen Gate visitors can look at the 54,896 names of soldiers from Britain, Canada, Australia, New Zealand, South Africa, and India who perished on the Ypres front and whose remains were never found.

### Christmas 1914 on the Belgian Front

The absurdity of war, and the First World War in particular, was dramatically manifested at the first Christmas on the Western Front. Frank Richards, a private in the 2nd Royal Welch Fusiliers, stationed on the Lys, wrote:

> The German Company-Commander asked ours if he would accept a couple of barrels of beer. They had plenty of it in the brewery. He accepted the offer with thanks and a couple of their men rolled the barrels over and we took them into our trench. The German officer sent one of his men back to the trench, who appeared shortly after carrying a tray with bottles and glasses and drank one another's health. Our Company-Commander

had presented them with a plum pudding just before. The officers came to an understanding that the unofficial truce would end at midnight. At dusk we went back to our respective trenches.[35]

At Pervijze the Germans asked the Belgians to forget the war for an hour to commemorate the birth of Christ. The Belgians accepted the offer and Christmas Eve was a celebration of brotherhood. The Germans offered the Belgians presents including wine, but the Belgians were embarrassed that they could not reciprocate. After the routine of death had resumed, the Belgian post commander, Sub-Lieutenant Naviau, was stripped of his rank for tolerating fraternization with the enemy.[36]

At Diksmuide German and Belgian soldiers exchanged presents and sang Christmas carols. The day after Christmas the spontaneous truce was repeated. German soldiers shouted "Comrades, don't shoot" and three German officers mounted the trench with a monstrance from the hospital of St. John in Diksmuide. A Belgian chaplain threw a rope across to them and pulled the monstrance in a linen bag across the ice of the Ijzer.[37]

## Hitler at Ypres

A German who would have a disastrous impact on Belgium, received his "baptism of fire"[38] at Ypres. Adolf Hitler of the 16th Bavarian Reserve Infantry Regiment, the List Regiment,[39] who described his war experience as "the greatest and most unforgettable time of my earthly existence",[40] saw his first action at Ypres on October 29, 1914. Within four days his regiment was reduced from 3,500 to 1,700 men. It was at Ypres that he won the Iron Cross and it was at Ypres that he was gassed. He wrote of his experience there in 1917:

> With three weeks of drumfire the Englishman prepared the great Flanders offensive. (...) [T]he regiment clawed its way into the various holes and craters, and neither gave ground nor wavered. As once before in this place, it grew steadily smaller and thinner, until the British attack finally broke loose on July 13, 1917. In the first days of August we were relieved. The regiment had turned into a few companies: crusted with mud they tottered back, more like ghosts than men. But aside from a few hundred meters of shell holes, the Englishman had found nothing but death.[41]

On the night of October 13, 1918, on a hill near Wervick, south of Ypres, Hitler's unit withstood several hours of bombardment with British gas shells. By morning Hitler had been severely affected. He wrote, "I stumbled and tottered back with burning eyes." When he reached the regimental command post around 7 A.M. he could hardly see. A few hours later he had succumbed to blindness. "My eyes had turned into glowing coals; it had grown dark around me." Hitler's blindness, however, would only be temporary. He was recovering at a military hospital in Pasewalk near Berlin when the war ended.[42]

## Churchill on the Ypres Front

Hitler was not the only future leader to be steeled by battle in the fields of Flanders. Winston Churchill stepped down as the British First Lord of the Admiralty in November 1915 amidst the disaster of the Gallipoli campaign, which he had promoted. From January to May he commanded the 6th Royal Scots Fusiliers battalion posted next to the Ploegsteert Wood about six miles south of Ypres. Churchill spent much time in the front trenches. At one point his lookout post, "Convent," was destroyed by German shells. While at the front he wrote from his reserve headquarters, "Maison 1875,"

> [T]his is now the third time in a fortnight that our bedroom has been pierced by shells (. . .) and riding across the ploughed field shrapnel kept pace with us in the air. One lives calmly on the brink of the abyss. But I can understand how tired people get of it as it goes on month after month. All the excitement dies away and there is only dull resentment.[43]

## Artists and Authors

Britain's "official" War Artist, Paul Nash,[44] found his inspiration at Sint-Elooi near Ypres in April 1917 and a few months later during the Third Battle of Ypres. As a result of his experience, he wrote of

> the grave which is this land; one huge grave. (. . .) I am no longer an artist interested and curious. I am a messenger who will bring back the word from the men who are fighting to those who want the war to go on forever. Feeble, inarticulate will be my message, but it will have a bitter truth, and may it burn their lousy souls.[45]

Harold Sandys Williamson, whose paintings are also exhibited at the Imperial War Museum in London, saw action on the Ypres Front in the summer and fall of 1917. He wrote:

> I was gazing down on Sanctuary Wood, where we had lain two days ago, and on Zillebeke, now as ever under bombardment. I could see the white road stretching away until it vanished towards Ypres (. . .) the plain below still shimmered in the sun. Men moved mere specks in the landscape, and, far away, lorries on the roads were being shelled. I noticed that nothing could move unseen by me, and I realised that I sat where for years the enemy had sat and had observed our every move within the fatal Salient.[46]

Erich Maria Remarque, too, briefly served in Flanders as a lance-corporal in the

2nd Guard Reserve Division. His experiences would be immortalized in his *All Quiet on the Western Front*, the quintessential novel of the First World War. Ernst Jünger, another German author, though not as well known to Americans as Remarque, served in Flanders with the 73rd Hanoverian. Jünger, like the thousands of young Germans who died at Langemarck in October 1914 at the *Kindermord bei Ypern* (the slaughter of the children at Ypres), was motivated by romantic enthusiasm. Jünger, overwhelmed by emotion, enlisted just after receiving his *Abitur* (secondary school leaving certificate) though he had to wait for three days at the overwhelmed recruiting office.[47]

## Belgians and the War in Africa

Although Spencer Tucker is certainly right that "fighting in Europe alone decided the war,"[48] the First World War saw significant fighting in the Middle East and in Africa. Though the Germans in Africa posed no threat to the Belgian control of the Congo, a number of German imperialists planned to absorb the Belgian colony into a German dominated *Mittelafrika* following a German victory. At the beginning of the war German gunboats on Lake Tanganyika sank a number of Belgian boats. Belgian troops for their part assisted the French and British in the conquest of German Togoland and Cameroons. Following the war the Belgians were awarded sections of German East Africa bordering the Congo, which their forces had occupied in 1916. The territory became the Belgian colonies of Ruanda and Urundi (Rwanda and Burundi). These colonies became independent as two separate countries in 1962. However, the Belgians contributed to the subsequent tragic history of Rwanda by continuing the German practice of privileging the Tutsi minority at the expense of the majority Hutus.

## German Atrocities[49]

The German response to the resistance of the Belgian government and people was brutal. There were atrocities. Hostages were taken and, at times, used as human shields. Individuals suspected of being guerrillas, of performing acts of sabotage, or of giving active support to Belgian soldiers were summarily executed. Houses, towns, and parts of cities were put to the torch. Among those executed were priests and women. Belgian officials were ordered to stay at their posts and take their orders from the Germans. Individuals, such as Burgomaster Adolphe Max of Brussels, were imprisoned and deported for acts of independence. However, the extent of German atrocities was exaggerated both in number and type by British propaganda.

Historians have debated the whole question of German atrocities in Belgium. John Horne and Alan Kramer wrote of "the undoubted conviction of the ordinary

German soldier that franc-tireurs really existed."[50] "According to international law," Nicoletta Gullace has written,

> a conquered people did not have the right to resist its invaders. In anticipation of an imminent invasion, a civil population could rise up against the enemy in a levée en masse; yet, once an invasion was successfully completed, civilian resistance would lose its legality and be regarded as guerrilla warfare—a form of opposition that could be punished with sever reprisals.[51]

Nevertheless, German soldiers' diaries have revealed fearful brutalities. In Schaffen, north of Leuven, 50 civilians, who had taken refuge in a church tower from which German soldiers had been fired upon by a machine gun, were executed. Over 600 civilians were executed in and around Dinant, and in the single largest mass killing between 150 and 200 civilians were executed on August 23 in Leffe outside Dinant.[52] Altogether as many as 5,500 Belgian civilians were executed by the Germans.[53]

## The German Administration

On August 26 the Germans, claiming to be following the provisions of the 1907 Hague Convention, appointed Field Marshal Colmar Freiherr von der Goltz Governor General of Belgium and Dr. von Sandt chief of civil administration. On November 27 Goltz was transferred to Constantinople and General Moritz Ferdinand, Freiherr von Bissing, held the post until his death on April 18, 1917. The final Governor General was General Alexander von Falkenhausen.

The whole country was administered under martial law. Belgian civil servants on the advice of the Belgian government-in-exile remained at their posts and administered much of the day to day affairs of the occupied country. The Germans attempted to keep the Belgians isolated and uninformed. Belgian civilians had to have a permit in order to move about. Ironically, a consequence of the war was the subsequent requirement for all Belgians to carry identity cards. The use of telephone and telegraph were forbidden. Communication with the outside world was only permitted through letters handled and censored by the Germans. Censorship and information control was pervasive, but clandestine newspapers, such as Libre Belgique and Flambeau, were printed and circulated.

## A Flemish University at Ghent

The four universities refused to open for class in the fall of 1914. The professors not only objected that there could be no question of academic freedom in such a context, they also asserted that it would not be proper to teach men who could only be in class by shirking their duty to join the Belgian army.[54] Three of the universities remained closed for the duration, but the Germans in an effort to court the Flemish transformed the University of Ghent into a Flemish language university and reopened it. The Germans propagated the idea that the Flemish were an oppressed nationality, and that they intended to liberate them and welcome them into the German family.[55]

Flemish nationalists had agitated before the war for university instruction in Flemish. However, only at Ghent and Leuven were there courses teaching the Flemish language, and at those universities only through the intermediate level. There were no courses taught in Flemish. At the turn of the century Flemish nationalists, led by Frans van Cauwelaert, had called for the University of Ghent to become a Flemish university, but the proposal had met with determined resistance from the francophones.[56] On December 31, 1915, the German Governor General ordered the reopening of the University of Ghent as a Flemish University. A German professor from Munich, Von Dyck, was made rector, and the professors of the university were told to resume teaching, but in Flemish. A large majority refused, and two of the most distinguished, Paul Fredericq, who was a leader of the Flemish cultural movement, and Henri Pirenne, the most noted Belgian historian, were deported to German captivity for their resistance. When efforts to recruit a faculty in Belgium and the Netherlands produced no success, Germany resorted to a German faculty reinforced by a few young Dutch instructors. The recruitment of students was equally difficult in spite of generous scholarships, not to mention beer permits. In 1916–1917 the university had only 138 students. Following the defeat of Germany, teaching in Dutch was initially terminated at the university; all degrees given by the Flemish university were nullified, and the recipients of those degrees were banned from re-entering the university. Teaching in Dutch as well as French was begun in 1923, and in 1930 the university again became a Dutch language university. [57]

## The Council of Flanders

The Inquiry Commission established by the Wilson administration to provide information to assist the United States in the formulation of specific peace proposals concentrated a number of its studies on Belgium. Its programmatic statement asserted that

> Belgium has become the pivot of German policy. Obviously the control of Belgium, besides its commercial advantages, would make it possible for Germany to prevent England from ever again landing an army in France and would thus leave France absolutely

at her mercy. This is probably even a stronger motive than the control of submarine bases. It is interesting to note that Bethmann [-Hollweg] frequently toyed with the idea of an 'administrative division of Belgium.' Such a division would mean Flemish adminis-tration of the Flanders coast with the possibility at least that the Flemish could be drawn into the orbit of German influence.[58]

In fact on March 21, 1917, the German administrator, von Bissing, established two administrative regions for occupied Belgium: Flanders with its capital at Brus-sels, and Wallonia with its capital at Namur. Flemish was decreed the official lan-guage in the Flemish district.[59] The Germans stated that they were responding to a request made by the "Council of Flanders."[60] On June 4, 1918, the German admin-istration proclaimed Flemish the language of instruction in all state-supported schools in the Flemish part of Belgium.

"Fueled by the *Flamenpolitik* of the German occupier, radical activists developed a Flemish nationalism that was overtly anti-Belgian."[61] On February 4, 1917, the ultra-Flemings of the Council of Flanders, representing the Flemish Assembly, re-quested the separation of Flanders from the Walloon part of Belgium. On Decem-ber 22, 1917, the Council declared the independence of Flanders,[62] and on January 20, 1918, at a meeting of at the Alhambra Theater in Brussels it designated mem-bers of local and provincial councils. The more extreme Flemish nationalists known as the Activists supported these acts. On November 11, 1917, they repudi-ated the Belgian government located at Le Havre and demanded the establish-ment of an independent Flemish state. However, most Flemings supported the Pas-sivist group, which refused to cooperate with the Germans in any action that might divide the country. The city council of Flemish Antwerp on January 29, 1918, declared that Belgium had always been bi-lingual, and that it wished to de-velop its Flemish character only on the basis of the full equality of the French and Flemish speakers and without damage to the integrity of the country. Many local officials refused to support separatism and were deported to Germany. In February 1918, 46 of the 48 members of the Court of Appeals in Brussels ordered the prose-cution of two of the leading members of the Council of Flanders for disloyalty. The Germans responded by dissolving the court and ordering the arrest and deporta-tion of its three presidents. In reaction the Court of Cassation and other Belgian tribunals refused to operate any longer. Communal councils were so unanimous in their support of the judges that the Germans forbade further consideration of gen-eral policy by communal councils.[63]

The majority of the advocates of the Flemish subnation remained loyal to the kingdom. A number of collaborators were tried for treason after the war; others, however, sought refuge in the Netherlands and Germany.[64] The expatriate nation-alists called for the destruction of the Belgian state and its replacement by a greater Netherlands, which would be associated with Germany. Their nationalism became ethno-centric and exclusive and they collaborated with the Germans again during the Nazi occupation of Belgium.

## The Flemish Soldiers' Movement (Frontbeweging)

There was also a Flemish movement within the Belgian Army. Belgian soldiers were principally poorly educated Flemish speaking laborers and farm workers,[65] who suffered from home sickness since they were away from home for the first time in their lives. Flemish priests, teachers, and students, who were serving with the army as stretcher-bearers or orderlies, organized a vibrant social and cultural life among them. The Flemish speakers, who experienced isolation in an army whose language of command (French) was incomprehensible, felt at home in the "Circle of Friends" clubs formed for soldiers from particular towns or regions. In these social and educational centers the discrimination which the Flemish speakers experienced in the army became a burning issue. The French-speaking officer corps had ignored a 1913 law which had mandated the use of Flemish as well as French in the army. Instead of addressing that problem, senior Belgian officers, fearful that the German effort to win over the Flemish might take root among the Flemish soldiers, took disciplinary action against Belgian soldiers who were active in the Flemish speaking movement. They banned political organizations within the army and Flemish pamphlets, and French speakers were favored for promotion. Despite this obstruction the Flemish soldiers' movement (*Frontbeweging*) became the most important Flemish wartime political movement. The Flemish movement produced a number of open letters to the king demanding the legal rights of the Flemish.[66] One dated July 11, 1917 appealed to the king:

> Trusting in You, who, at the outbreak of the world war, reminded the people of Flanders of the Battle of the Golden Spurs, we, Flemish soldiers, the army of Flanders, that is to say the army of the Ijzer, address You to say that we are suffering, and why we are suffering; to tell You that we are ready to sacrifice our lives for our country, but that our sacrifice may not serve to subjugate our people further; and that instead it must allow them to breathe freely, and to live freely.[67]

Joseph De Cuyper, an army doctor, in his war diary expressed the frustration of the Flemish fighting for Belgium. He wrote

> despite everything the newspapers have written, the government takes no account of the people of Flanders, who are the majority of the Army; and anti-Flemish sentiment grows stronger and stronger. These movements are very incorrectly called "Flemish." In reality they are protests against the preferential treatment which French speakers enjoy in general, and the injustice which many of the officers show towards their Flemish soldiers.

"Flemish nationalism," therefore, is only a vague description of a very deep-seated movement which has shown itself in the army for some time.[68]

Despite the reasoned protests of the *Frontbeweging*, the king and the Belgian government did not correct the affronts to its Flemish soldiers, and the conflict continued to divide the country long after the war.[69] Had the German military behavior been more restrained and their occupation policy less harsh, they might have made greater inroads among the Flemish.

## Belgium under German Occupation

Although the Germans attempted to close off the Dutch border with an electrified barbed wire barrier, 40,000 Belgians made their way across the barrier to join the Belgian army on the Ijzer front. As a result of an historic quirk one tiny part of Belgium remained unscathed and unoccupied: the small enclave, Baarle-Hertog, 12 kilometers inside the Netherlands and completely surrounded by Dutch territory. Other than this diminutive anomaly, the blockage of transportation, communication, and credit brought commerce and industry to a complete standstill. This placed the Belgian people in a precarious position. In 1914 Belgium was the most densely populated European country with approximately 700 people per square mile. Due to the density of its population, its agriculture, though intensive and highly productive, was insufficient to feed the country's population. 60 percent of its grain had to be imported, and this was paid for by export of manufactured products.[70] At the end of July and the beginning of August cash reserves and a large part of negotiable securities had been removed from banks. Subsequently, banks, placed under German control, stopped payment or limited withdrawals to small amounts. As a result businesses and the wealthy were unable to negotiate their accounts at will. Since the Belgian National Bank had shipped its assets and plates to London, the German administration denied the National Bank the right to issue bank notes, and on December 22, 1914, empowered the Société Général de Belgique to resume the issuance of currency. In the meantime a number of towns issued vouchers payable within the limits of their own municipalities.

In October 1915 the Germans began conscripting Belgian workers to do military work within Belgium. On May 2, 1916, they forbade the continuation of relief work that had been implemented by the Belgian National Committee for Relief and Alimentation to combat unemployment. To the Germans this relief work was unproductive and inhibited their effort to draw Belgian workers to Germany to supplement the depleted German labor force. Between June 1915 and March 1916 the Germans had been able to recruit only 12,000 Belgian workers for work in Germany. Though voluntary recruits increased after May, they still fell short of German needs. In October 1916 the Germans resorted to forced deportation and by the end of their occupation had deported 120,000 workers.[71] Cardinal Mercier protested against the deportations. He was supported by neutral states and even by Socialists in the German Reichstag. As a consequence, in February 1917, the Germans ceased the "systematic massive deportations," and most deportees were sent back to Belgium by the summer of 1917.[72]

The Germans imposed war contributions on the Belgians, which far exceeded the cost of military administration. They also systematically stripped Belgium of machinery and raw materials. Much of the requisitioning was done without compensation or with totally inadequate compensation. In addition there was rampant pillaging by German officers and men. By the end of the war the number of cattle in the country had been cut in half. 1,500 of the pre-war 2,500 coke ovens had been destroyed or dismantled, and only 11 of the country's 57 pre-war blast furnaces remained.[73]

## The Kaiser's Flight

At the end of the war a drama was played out on Belgian soil. The German military headquarters in the west was at Spa. At the end Kaiser Wilhelm was there attempting to bolster the morale of the army command and trying to avoid the pressure from the government in Berlin to abdicate. Prince Max von Baden, the last chancellor of the German Empire, in order to save the monarchy attempted to persuade Wilhelm by telephone to hand over the crown to his grandson. The Kaiser was enraged and sought the support of the army command. They at first supported his decision to hang on. However, the military mutinies in Germany spread; the Bavarian monarchy was overthrown on November 7; and with the Spartacists poised to seize power in Berlin, Friedrich Ebert and his Majority Social Democrats pressed Max. Max contacted the Kaiser on November 9 and insisted. When that appeal failed Max took matters into his own hands and announced the abdication of the Kaiser. Wilhelm desperately asked the military to join him in a march on Berlin. General Ludendorff, because of his opposition to the Allies' armistice terms, had been forced to step down as assistant to the Chief of Staff, General Paul von Hindenburg. Ludendorff was replaced as First Quartermaster General by the pragmatic Württemberger General Wilhelm Groener. Groener realistically informed the Kaiser that he was deluding himself if he thought that the German army in defeat would follow him in a quixotic gesture. Hindenburg, who was a master at passing the buck, reluctantly concurred with his Quartermaster General. Wilhelm then boarded his personal train and headed into exile in the Netherlands.[74]

## Albert Triumphant

While Albert remained in the unoccupied corner of south western Belgium, the Belgian government-in-exile, which had set itself up in Le Havre, France, grew upset with his disagreement with Allied war goals. The king insisted that the Belgian Army stay in Belgium and remain independent. He was unwilling to allow the British Field Marshal Sir Douglas Haig to utilize the Belgian Army to strengthen his offensive at Ypres in 1917. Albert hoped for a compromise peace rather that a complete defeat of Germany. In reaction to the king's support for a negotiated peace and the resumption of Belgian neutrality, Baron Charles de Broqueville, the wartime premier, broadened the cabinet. He added Socialist and Liberal ministers to his government and terminated the thirty-year monopoly of the Catholic party. Albert gave way and placed the Belgian Army under Allied command. General Marshal Ferdinand Foch, who became the generalissimo of the Allied forces in 1918, appointed Albert commander of the Flanders Army Group in autumn 1918. The king led the final Allied offensive in Belgium and triumphantly entered Brussels on November 22, 1918. That day he gave a speech, which he hoped would promote reconciliation and unity in Belgium. He called for the replacement of the weighted vote with universal and equal manhood suffrage, legislation to improve the condition of Belgian working people, a reform of the legal code, and for the Flemish the continuation of a Dutch university at Ghent and the promotion of real equality for all Belgians. Though his call for universal manhood suffrage would be answered, there was too much anger toward the Flemish nationalists for his call for reconciliation to be welcomed.[75]

Albert I, King of the Belgians, 1909–1934    Courtesy of the National Archives

Ruins of Leuven (Louvain) Courtesy of the Photographic Archives of the Imperial War Museum (Q53271)

Ruins of the Cloth Hall in Ypres Courtesy of the Photographic Archives of the Imperial War Museum (E [Aus] 1171)

Sanctuary Woods Courtesy of the Photographic Archives of the Imperial War Museum (E [Aus] 1234)

# CHAPTER 14

# Between the Wars

## Versailles and Reconstruction

On November 22, 1918, when King Albert and the Belgian army marched back into Brussels, "all Belgium was in a sad state."[1] Of all the participants in World War I, Belgium, which had not wished to be part of the struggle, suffered proportionately the greatest physical destruction. More than 100,000 houses had been seriously damaged or destroyed. More than 300,000 acres of farmland had been transformed into a barren and dangerous wasteland. As late at the 1990s Belgian ordinance crews were still disarming lethal shells turned up by farmers and construction crews. Thousands of heads of livestock had been killed or shipped off to Germany. 2,400 miles of rail line had been destroyed and out of the 3,470 locomotives in Belgium in 1914 only 81 operable ones remained. Toward the end of the war the Germans had shipped 50,000 tons of machinery a month to the east. Of the 51 steel mills operating in 1914, 26 were destroyed and 20 damaged.[2] The total estimate for destroyed property was placed at $7 billion in 1919 United States currency. The country, however, made a remarkably swift recovery. By the mid-1920s devastated sections of a number of cities had been rebuilt.

The antagonism of Belgians was not only directed toward Germany. Many Belgians resented the neutrality of the Netherlands during the war and what they perceived as Luxembourgeois sympathy for Germany. Belgium therefore attempted to gain territory which had been denied to it at the time of its independence. Its government asked the peacemakers at Paris to transfer to it Dutch-Limburg and Flemish Zeeland from the Netherlands and the entire Grand Duchy of Luxembourg. The only result was to sour relations with the Netherlands. Despite Belgian covetousness Luxembourg agreed in 1921 to form an economic union with Belgium, the Belgian-Luxembourgeois Economic Union. However, in 1927 Dutch nationalists defeated a treaty, which would have resolved disputes over the shared waterways of Belgium and the Netherlands.[3] Though Belgium's territorial ambitions with regard to the Netherlands and Luxembourg were denied, the Versailles Treaty, in addition to reparations, awarded Belgium the districts of Eupen, Malmédy, and St. Vith, which had been granted to Prussia by the Congress of Vienna. Belgium was also awarded Rwanda and Burundi, sections of the former German East Africa. On September 7, 1920, Belgium discarded its tradition of neutrality in favor of a military alliance with France. During this period it cooperated closely with France in questions of foreign policy, including participation with France in the 1923 occupation of Germany's Ruhr basin. On May 22, 1926, a treaty with France and England formally terminated the Treaty of 1839. The Belgian government, however, changed its mind after Hitler re-militarized the Rhineland in March 1936. It gave France a one-year notice of its intention to again seek its security through neutrality. The victory of the Nazis in Germany, nevertheless, had led the government to take precautionary steps. 150 million francs were dedicated to the construction of a fortified arc from Antwerp and along the Meuse to Namur. After Hitler violated with impunity the Versailles prohibition against troops or military installations in the Rhineland, Belgium not only resumed neutrality, it also extended the military service of Belgian draftees from seven to eighteen months.

## The Flemish Question between the Wars

During the war the Germans had courted the Flemish, who were deeply dissatisfied with the second-class status which had been accorded to their culture and language. There was a surge of Belgian nationalism in the immediate aftermath of the war, but the spread of education and economic improvement among the Flemish, and the shift within Belgium in 1918 to an equal vote for all Belgian men contributed in the long run, since Flemish population growth was outstripping that of the Walloons, to growing strength for the Flemish movement. In the process, according to Louis Vos, "for many Flemings patriotism and loyalty towards the nation shifted from Belgium to Flanders, Belgium came to be looked upon as a mere state whereas Flanders was considered to be the real nation."[4] The moderate Flemings in the Catholic Party, led by Frans van Cauwelaert, pushed for Dutch to become the only official language in Flanders, while the nationalist but democratic *Frontpartij* (the Front Party or Flemish Front), founded in 1919, but in 1933 transformed into the authoritarian Flemish National League (VNV), called for self-rule for Flanders and closer ties with the Netherlands. In 1919 the party received six percent of the vote in Flanders. At its highest point in 1939 it received 12 percent of the vote in Flanders.[5]

Step by step the demands of the moderate Flemish nationalists were enacted into law. On January 1, 1922, a law went into effect which finally granted recognition to Flemish as an official language on a par with French. The Germans had transformed the University of Ghent into a Flemish language university. Though this had ended with the departure of the Germans, on July 27, 1923, the Belgian government re-established Flemish as an official language of that university. The university again became entirely Dutch speaking in 1930. A transformation which was decried by a francophone parliamentarian from Brussels as "an act of scientific vandalism."[6] On July 18, 1932, new language laws made French the administrative language only in the Walloon provinces, while Flemish became the administrative language in Flanders. In Brussels and Brabant there were to be two sets of higher officials, one French and one Flemish. Also in the secondary schools instruction was to be given in the predominant language of the district. In 1935 the Flemish were given the right to court proceedings in Dutch, and in 1938 the army was directed to set up monolingual units. As Vos has written, "Belgium had opted for dual monolingualism instead of overall bilingualism."[7] However, the language laws, lacking any mechanism for enforcement, were frequently ignored, increasing calls among the Flemish for a decentralized federal state.[8]

## Belgian Politics between the Wars

During the inter-war period the political scene was dominated by the Catholic and Socialist parties. The contest between these two antagonistic communities produced a large degree of political instability. The reforms introduced after World War I had destroyed the dominance of the Catholic bourgeoisie within the Catholic party. During the inter-war period the Catholic party lacked any clear direction. It was not only divided between its francophone and Flemish adherents, there was a deep divide between its Christian Democratically oriented worker component and the more conservative bourgeois elements. These divergent segments "could agree on little more beyond the defense of the interests of the Church and antipathy to the twin historic adversaries of atheistic liberalism and Marxist socialism."[9]

There were eighteen different governments between 1918 and 1940, sixteen of which were coalitions. There were six cabinets composed of Catholics and Liberals, who joined together at these times in a common front in defense of property and middle class or, perhaps, Christian values, against the Socialists; nine composed of Catholics, Socialists, and Liberals; and one composed of Catholics and Socialists. In the November 16, 1920 election the Catholic Party lost its majority though it still held 73 seats to the 70 of the Socialists. On November 28, 1921, however, the Catholics, who possessed the largest party between the wars, the Catholic Union, regained their majority. The Catholic vote was undoubtedly strengthened by the partial enfranchisement of women. The vote was given to "war widows, who had not remarried, widowed mothers of sons who had been killed in the war, and women who had been imprisoned by the Germans."[10] However, support for the Catholic Union and its nemesis, the Socialists, fluctuated. The seesaw favored the Socialists on April 5, 1925, when they reached their high point of 39.43 percent; then the

Catholics on May 26, 1929. The Catholic Union was a conglomeration of segments rather that a unitary party.[11] In 1921 it had guaranteed representation to each economic group among its constituency: the upper middle class, the middle to lower middle class, farmers, and workers. In Flanders it was more democratic. In Wallonia it was more conservative. It defended the role of the church in Belgian society, state support for church schools, support for families, private property, inter-class cooperation rather than class warfare, and national unity.

The first post-war coalitions introduced a number of reforms based upon an agreement made between King Albert and the representatives of labor at Loppem Castle in 1918. The eight-hour day was introduced; the right to strike was guaranteed; arbitration councils were set up; prices were regulated; and a progressive income tax was instituted.[12] The success of the Socialists in 1925 produced a "Roman-Red"coalition, but after its fall the conservatives dominated Belgian politics until 1935. However, concessions had to be made to the Christian Workers'Alliance, including an elaboration of social security laws and subsidies for families.

Even before the Great Depression, Belgium suffered a financial crisis. World War I had cost Belgium 12 percent of its pre-war wealth. German reparations fell far short of expectations and inflation was endemic. In July 1926 the king was given dictatorial powers for six months to deal with economic problems. The franc was devalued and stabilized at one-seventh of its pre-war value. The devaluation transformed the franc into an undervalued currency and greatly stimulated exports. As a result Belgium's traditional industries regained their pre-war level of production. Technical improvements and profits from mining enterprises in the Congo also stimulated the recovery of metallurgy. The Flemish area experienced growth and a new level of prosperity symbolized by the formation of the General Bank by the Agrarian League (Boerenbond) in 1928. The coalfields of Limburg grew in importance, but principally served the industry of Wallonia. The opening of the Albert Canal between Antwerp and Liège in 1935 facilitated this connection. Trade with the Congo stimulated Antwerp and American automotive plants were set up in its proximity.[13] In July 1932 in an important early step toward trans-national integration, Belgium, the Netherlands, and Luxembourg agreed to more toward free trade through a gradual reduction of tariffs. However, Belgium was shaken by the shock waves, which buffeted Europe after the crash of Wall Street in October 1929. By 1936 Belgian exports had shrunk to 43 percent of their 1929 level. The fledgling auto industry collapsed and textiles were hard hit. By 1930 76,000 people were unemployed. By 1932 the figure had risen to 340,000. As the economic crisis deepened, it was accompanied by political unrest and the growth of radicalism of the right. To combat the growth of fascist formations, the government on July 12, 1934, outlawed the formation of paramilitary units and the wearing of uniforms by political organizations.

Elsewhere in Europe the political effectiveness of the Left in the 1920s and 30s was undermined by the split between the Communists and Socialists, which had occurred following the Bolshevik Revolution in Russia. Belgium was one of the few places in Europe where the Socialist Left had a constructive impact. On November 11, 1918, King Albert had agreed at Loppem Castle to a program of social reform and, despite opposition from conservative Catholics, to a franchise reform that granted all adult men an equal vote.[14] The new system of franchise plus proportional representation undercut the possibility of single party government and encouraged compromise. The Belgian Socialists decided, in the face of the Depression and the threat from the radical right, to form a political alliance with the conservatives.[15] According to Emile Lamberts both the Christian Democrats and the Socialists, though they had been initially sharply critical of the status quo, had been integrated into bourgeois society by this time. A democratic and social consensus had been reached which Lamberts characterized as a "neo-corporatist" approach to government.[16] The Socialists proposed a Plan of Labor, authored by Hendrik de Man, which rejected revolutionary Marxism in favor of a mixed economy and governmental economic planning. In the Catholic camp, Paul van Zeeland, the vice-governor of Belgium's National Bank, advocated a plan, inspired by the British economist John Maynard Keynes and Franklin Roosevelt's New Deal, which called for government intervention in the economy and the formation of a mixed economy. On March 25, 1935, van Zeeland formed a government of national unity. It was given power to rule by decree for a year in order to deal with the desperate financial crisis. Van Zeeland devalued the franc again and managed to balance the state budget. Unemployment was lessened through an elaborate public works program and Belgium's banks were regulated.

Though van Zeeland's coalition fostered recovery, unrest continued on both the Communist left and the radical right.[17] In the May 1936 election Léon Degrelle and his radical right-wing Rexists won 11.49 percent of the vote and 21 seats, and Staf De Clerq's radical right-wing Flemish National Alliance (*Vlaams Nationaal Verbond*—VNV) 7.1 percent of the vote. Martin Conway has observed that "in the largely static world of Belgian electoral politics, this result was nothing less than a revolution."[18] Many voters from the francophone and particularly the rural constituency of the Catholic party expressed their frustration and anger at the failure of their party to protect their interests in the midst of the Depression.[19] There were also many among the elite in Belgium who, as in many other countries, had lost faith in nineteenth century style parliamentary government to deal with the problems of twentieth century society. They sought "to change the political system from within in order to create more effective and 'depoliticized' structures of government."[20]

The Rexists, who seceded from the Catholic party and sought support among young Walloon Catholics, were named for the Catholic weekly *Rex*, which in turn was named after *Christus Rex*, Christ the King. Degrelle, the son of a prosperous brewer from Bouillon, had briefly attended the University of Leuven before quitting to become editor of *Rex* and director of the Rex publishing house. He had joined

the Catholic Association of Belgian Youth, an apolitical Catholic Action organization supported by Cardinal Mercier. By 1930 when the group influenced by Charles
Maurras' *Action française* turned to politics the Church withdrew its support. In
1936 Degrelle left the Catholic Association and founded the corporatist Rexists,
the slogan of which was "Unity, Authority, and Discipline." The expulsion of the
Rexists from the Catholic socio-political sub-culture or "pillar" marginalized the
movement and its adherents. They were excluded from "the sources of influence,
patronage, and power" provided by the Catholic "pillar." This exclusion reinforced
a process of radicalization in which the Rexists sported their exclusion as a badge of
honor. The movement "gloried in the hostility which its actions inspired and saw its
exclusion from power as proof of ideological rectitude."[21]

Originally suspicious of Nazi Germany, Degrelle and the Rexists eventually
viewed the defeat of Belgium in 1940 as vindication of their opposition to the existing order in Belgium. During World War II Degrelle, who portrayed his movement
as a champion of "European Civilization" in a great "European Civil War," formed
the Walloon Legion, which became the 28Th SS Division of the Waffen-SS. Degrelle commanded this unit, which was never larger than a regiment, on the Eastern
Front. After the war he reached Spain where he died in exile in 1993.[22]

Martin Conway very perceptively identified the orientation and source of the
Rexists. According to Conway,

> Rex is one of these movements which needs to be considered on its own terms rather
> than as a Belgian "variant" on some standard fascist model. Its origins in the Catholic
> student world of the University of Louvain place it at the heart of the revival of a more
> militant form of political Catholicism which took place in many areas of Europe during
> the inter-war years. This revival was led by young Catholic intellectuals who proclaimed
> that the solution to the problems of the modern era lay not in the atheistic doctrines of
> liberalism or Soviet Communism but in a political and social structure modeled on dis-
> tinctively Catholic ideals. Drawing their inspiration from the series of encyclicals issued
> by the papacy from the late nineteenth century, Catholic radicals from countries as di-
> verse as Austria, Italy, Spain, Portugal, and Lithuania sought to found political move-
> ments which, by defining themselves as against both liberal democracy and modern to-
> talitarianisms, advocated a "third way" of strong central government combined with a
> devolved structure of guilds and corporations.[23]

Depending upon one's perspective, it could be argued that it was their tragedy or
their destiny to become linked to the crimes and horrors of Nazism.

Despite the success of the radical right in the May 1936 election, Van Zeeland
was able to reorganize his government, this time even with the support of the Communists, and on June 24 he introduced a comprehensive social improvement program. Similar to the French Popular Front's Matignon Agreement, the Belgian program established a minimum wage, the 40 hour work week in larger industries, paid

holidays, and increased unemployment benefits. Zeeland's espousal of full employment and progressive social policy laid the basis for Belgium's post-World War II mixed economy. Nevertheless unrest continued. On October 22, 1936, martial law was proclaimed to counter the violence of the Rexists and Degrelle was arrested. A year later on October 24, 1937, the effort to construct national unity collapsed. Van Zeeland resigned after being charged with corruption in connection with the National Bank. There was a lengthy cabinet crisis before Paul Janson, a Liberal, was able to form a new government.[24] Then on May 13, 1938, a new coalition was formed under the leadership of the moderate socialist Paul Spaak. Though municipal elections indicated a decline of both right and left-wing radicalism, the Liberals, Catholics, and Socialists had increasing difficulty working together. There was a prolonged cabinet crisis. New elections on April 2, 1939, although confirming the decline of the Rexists, about whom Cardinal J.-E. van Roey had expressed deep misgiving in 1937, did not otherwise improve the political situation.[25] On April 18 Hubert Pierlot formed a Liberal-Catholic government. It would be the last government formed before Germany again invaded Belgium.

Conway has rightly observed that the parliamentary system in inter-war Belgium was regarded by many as deficient and even impotent to serve the needs of the Belgian people. This was not only the sentiment of the Rexists and their supporters, it was shared by King Leopold and historically more respected figures such as Spaak.[26] There was a crisis of authority in Belgium similar to those experienced elsewhere in Europe in the inter-war period. According to Conway, "the resurgence in liberal democracy after 1945 has disguised the extent to which during the previous twenty years the tide had run in the opposite direction."[27]

Léon Degrelle    Courtesy of the National Archives (306-NT-42A-1)

# CHAPTER 15

# World War II

### Hitler's Decision

*Dutch and Belgian air bases must be occupied. (. . .) Declarations of neutrality must be ignored.*

—Hitler, May 1939[1]

*We have an Achilles heel: The Ruhr. The progress of the war depends on the possession of the Ruhr. If England and France push through Belgium and Holland into the Ruhr, we shall be in the greatest danger. (. . .) Certainly England and France will assume the offensive against Germany when they are armed. England and France have means of pressure to bring Belgium and Holland to request English and French help. In Belgium and Holland the sympathies are all for France and England. (. . .) If the French Army marches into Belgium in order to attack us, it will be too late for us. We must anticipate them. (. . .) We shall sow the English coast with mines which cannot be cleared. This mine warfare with the Luftwaffe demands a different starting point. England cannot live without its imports. We can feed ourselves. The permanent sowing of mines on the English coasts will bring England to her knees. However, this can only occur if we have occupied Belgium and Holland. (. . .) My decision is unchangeable; I shall attack France and England at the most favorable and quickest moment. Breach of the neutrality of Belgium and Holland is meaningless. No one will question that when we have won. We shall not bring about the breach of neutrality as idiotically as it was in 1914. If we do not break the neutrality, then England and France will. Without attack, the war is not to be ended victoriously.*

—Hitler to his Military Commanders, November 23, 1939[2]

*I am instructed by the Government of the Reich, to make the following declaration: In order to forestall the invasion of Belgium, Holland, and Luxembourg,*

Leopold III, King of the Belgians, 1834–1944 and 1950    Courtesy of the National Archives
(306-NT-99008)

*for which Great Britain and France have been making preparations clearly
aimed at Germany, the Government of the Reich is compelled to ensure the
neutrality of the three countries mentioned, by means of arms. For this purpose, the Government of the Reich will bring up an Armed Force of the greatest size, so that resistance of any kind will be useless. The Government of the
Reich guarantees Belgium's European and Colonial territory, as well as her
dynasty, on condition that no resistance is offered. Should there be any resistance, Belgium will risk the destruction of her country and loss of her independence. It is, therefore, in the interests of Belgium that the population be called
upon to cease all resistance and that the authorities be given the necessary in-
structions to make contact with the German Military Command.*

—Ultimatum delivered to the Belgian Government by the German
Ambassador after the German invasion had commenced,
May 10, 1940.[3]

## Belgian Preparations

Between the wars the Belgians had modernized a number of the pre-war forts
around Liège and Namur. They also constructed new fortresses during the
1930s at Eben Emael, Tancremont (Pepinster), Neufchateau, and Battice.
Though Eben Emael was the best known, it was not Belgium's only modern fort.[4] It
was located at the juncture of the Albert Canal and the Meuse and dominated the
bridges at Vroenhove and Veldwezelt and the roads leading west from Maastricht. It
was reputedly the strongest fortress in Europe, but it had a fatal flaw. The Belgians
had failed to complete their plans to cover the roof with mines and barbed wire.

## The Germans Attack Again

Belgium remained neutral when the war broke out in September 1939. Though Belgium mobilized its army, it refused to allow British or French troops to cross its frontiers and even refused to agree to joint staff talks. In January 1940, when a German
military plane was forced by weather to land in Belgium, plans from the German
General Staff for an invasion directed toward France through the Netherlands and
Belgium fell into the hands of the Belgians. Though the Belgian army was deployed
along Belgium's frontier with Germany and the Maastricht appendage of the Netherlands, King Leopold and the government still sought to forestall a German attack
through diplomatic means. The Germans, nevertheless, invaded on May 10, 1940,
and Belgium was rapidly overrun. 500 parachute and glider troops, led by Captain
Koch, dropped during the early morning darkness, to seize the "impregnable" fortress
of Eben Emael and to take the two nearby bridges intact. The bridges would have

been destroyed by their Belgian defenders if the Germans had merely attempted to drive across the fifteen miles of the Maastricht appendage, which separated Belgium from Germany at that point. Seizing the fortress and the two bridges enabled the Germans to sweep past Liège. A force of only 78 parachutists led by Lieutenant Witzig landed on the roof of the fortress. They overpowered the anti-aircraft troops stationed there and quickly blew up the armored cupolas and the artillery casemates. In the process of disabling Belgium's premier fortress the Germans lost only six men. The small German force was then able to hold the fort's garrison of 1,200 at bay until the German ground forces arrived 24 hours later. Though the Belgians had blown all of the other Albert Canal and Meuse bridges, General Höppner's 3rd and 4th panzer divisions crossed the intact bridges and easily fanned out into the Belgian plain.

The out-flanked Belgians now fell back to a defensive line between Leuven and Antwerp. The British and French, distracted by the thrust into Belgium, moved in to help stem the German tide. However, as the British reinforced the Belgians between Leuven and Wavre and the French advanced to the Huy-Tienen line, French defenses were breached at Sedan on May 14. Guderian and Reinhardt's panzer divisions of von Rundstedt's Army Group shoved through the 75 miles of the Ardennes in Luxembourg and Belgium brushing aside weak Belgian resistance and reached the French frontier on May 13. By passing through heavily wooded hilly country with few roads, most of which were quite narrow, the Germans confounded traditional military wisdom and surprised the French beyond the western end of the Maginot Line. The panzers continued their drive to the west and reached the mouth of the Somme on the English Channel by May 20.

In Belgium, after the Germans captured Antwerp, Leuven, and Brussels, the Allies desperately fell back toward the sea to avoid being cut off. Leopold, who had assumed direct command of the Belgian army, had agreed to cover the British and French retreat but when the Germans broke through Belgian defenses on either side of Kortrijk, the king capitulated on May 27. Leopold, like his father Albert, did not wish Belgium to become a mere appendage of the interests of the Allies. He regarded the defeat of his forces as the end of the conflict for Belgium, and he felt that he was obliged to remain in Belgium with his troops.

British and French reached the beaches between Dunkirk in France and De Panne in Belgium. From those beaches between May 27 and June 4 the bulk were withdrawn in a remarkable rescue effort. The Belgian cabinet, headed by Hubert Pierlot, which had disapproved of the personal surrender of the king, withdrew to France and announced that Leopold as a German captive was no longer able to act as king. A rump meeting of the Belgian parliament on May 31 at Limoges, France repeated the government's condemnation of Leopold. After France fell, Pierlot believed that the war was irrevocably lost. He attempted to achieve reconciliation with Leopold, but was rebuffed. Leopold had received strong public support for his decision to remain in Belgium. Pierlot and his ministers, on the other hand, were decried for leaving. At the end of August Pierlot and his foreign minister, Paul-Henri Spaak, made their way to London and established a Belgian government-in-exile. The Pierlot government along with Charles de Gaulle's Free French vowed to continue the war with the support of Great Britain and placed the resources of the Belgian Congo at the disposal of the Allied cause.[5]

## German Occupation

On May 18, before the fighting ended, the Eupen, Malmédy, and Moresnet districts were incorporated into the Third Reich. A military government nominally under General Alexander von Falkenhausen, the final governor general of occupied Belgium during World War I, ruled the remainder of conquered Belgium. In reality, von Falkenhausen's chief of military administration, Eggert Reeder, was "de facto ruler of Belgium for the subsequent four years."[6] Day to day administration, however, was carried out by Belgian civil servants. Most secretaries general, the professional civil servants who headed government departments, "became compliant accessories of German policy."[7] In fact a law enacted by the Belgian parliament on May 10 had directed the civil service, in the event of a German occupation of the country, to remain at their posts to protect, as much as possible, the interests of the Belgians.[8] In July 1944 the military government was replaced with a Reichs Commissioner, Josef Grohe, who combined in one person military, police, and SS authority. At that time it was the intention of the Nazi leadership to transform Belgium into two districts (*Reichsgaue*), the Reichsgau Vlaanderen, and the Reichsgau Wallonia, both of which would be directly annexed by Germany.[9]

Contrary to the situation during World War I, Belgian industry resumed production after the surrender. Belgian businessmen agreed to produce under German supervision. The Belgian economy, as a result, was integrated into needs of the German economy and thus "aided the German war effort."[10] Workers were compelled to join a single labor organization and relations between managers and workers were regulated by the authorities of the occupation regime.

The German military administration gave its support to "emphatically collaborationist groups." The appeal did not go unheeded. Léon Degrelle's Rexist movement among the francophones responded with enthusiasm. The Flemish National Front sought German support for the establishment of a Flemish state. The pro-Nazi Flemish DEVLAG movement supported the absorption of Flanders into a Greater German Reich. The "progressively more emphatic espousal of the Nazi cause [by these groups] created a gulf between them and a large majority of the Belgian population, both French and Dutch speaking."[11] The King, for his part, refused to have anything to do with the government-in-exile. He did meet with Hitler at Berchtesgarten in November 1940 to plea for a restoration of Belgian independence after the war, but he also declared that since he was technically a prisoner of war he could not engage in political activity as long as Belgium was occupied.

Life for the Belgians under German occupation became increasingly difficult after the fortunes of war turned against the Germans. One observer wrote in 1942: "The people of most occupied countries live in a mental state hardly understandable to the American reader. Their mind is dominated by an all-absorbing anxiety—food, the bare nourishment necessary to sustain physical existence."[12] The monthly consumption of bread and cereals by the average adult dropped from 16.7 kilograms in 1929 to 12.84 kilograms at the beginning of 1943. The consumption of butter was cut by 66 percent to .64 kilograms. Meat dropped from 3.15 kilograms to 1.29. Though the consumption of potatoes dropped from 18.7 kilograms in 1929 to 8.6 in May of 1941, it increased to 23.4 kilos at the beginning of 1943.[13] Perhaps the increase in the consumption of potatoes is related to the fact that vegetable gardening became the principal leisure-time activity of the Belgians.[14] Studies of the weight of Belgian miners and steel workers during the war found that 64 percent were at least 4 kilos under-weight and 89 percent of the younger workers were under weight.[15] Coal was rationed and during the winter of 1941–1942 many Belgian families suffered from the cold. The winter of 1942–1943 was better, not because there was more coal, but because the temperature was unusually mild. Cafés were less frequently visited. The price of beer had doubled while quality declined and the size of the glasses decreased. Nevertheless, some Belgians were still drawn to cafés in search of heat.[16] But cafés closed early; ordinarily there was a general curfew at 11 P.M. Following anti-German incidents the Germans would clear the streets at 7 or 8 P.M.[17] Tobacco was severely rationed and replaced by all sorts of substitute smokes. The reading matter of many Belgians before 1940 had been newspapers. Since most Belgians found the press controlled by the Germans of little interest, reading declined. There were hardly any sports. Life retreated to the home, and the kitchen became the gathering place for the family circle. Often it was the woman who, through her resourcefulness and frequently her self-abnegation, kept enough food on the table to keep the family going.[18]

## Liberation

The liberation of Belgium began in September 1944. The Allies reached Brussels on September 3, and shortly afterwards liberated Ghent, Bruges, Ostend, and Antwerp. The Americans also reached Charleroi, Mons, and Namur on September 3, and by September 10 had reached Luxembourg and Liège. Hitler attempted to exploit the weak center of the Allied line in the December offensive in the Ardennes, the Battle of the Bulge. In a last desperate effort 38 German divisions attacked along a 50-mile (80-kilometer) front on December 16. Mechanized units overran several U.S. Army positions and Field Marshall Walter Model's forces almost reached the Meuse. However, when the Germans sent an ultimatum to the Americans surrounded in Bastogne, Brigadier General Anthony C. McAuliffe of the 101st Airborne Division responded "Nuts!" His forces were relieved by the 3rd US Army, which drove through the Germans from the south. By early January 1945 the Germans had again been pushed beyond the Belgian frontier. Today an American cemetery and monuments at Bastogne and a museum at Arlon commemorate the battle. The response of the surrounded McAuliffe to the Germans is remembered in the annual "Nuts" festival in Bastogne.

### The Nazi Occupation and the Jews of Belgium

When the Germans overran Belgium there were 65,696 Jews in the country.[19] A majority of these were not Belgian citizens. They were Jews who had fled anti-Semitism in Poland and Germany and after the *Anschluss* of March 1938 from Austria and then from Czechoslovakia. The Belgian government had worked with religious and civic organizations to assist Jewish refugees. The government had allocated six million francs to assist German Jewish refugees in 1938. The support of the general population for this receptive policy was demonstrated by the rebuff by Belgian voters in 1938 of the Rexists and other fascistic groups. 80 percent of the Jews of Belgium lived in Brussels and Antwerp, where they dominated the diamond trade. According to the Nazi statistics 30,000 Jews lived in Brussels, and 22,000 lived in Antwerp.[20] Most of the others lived in Charleroi, Liège, and Ghent. In addition to two government supported Jewish schools in Antwerp, there were many afternoon Jewish schools. There were some wealthy Belgian Jewish families, but the majority of the Jews in Belgium were "either poor or very poor."[21] They worked in the leather, fur, textile, and diamond trades.

Germany overwhelmed Belgium in May 1940. On October 28, 1940, a decree applied the 1935 Nazi Nuremberg Law's definition of Jewishness to Belgium and ordered all Jews in Belgium to register. Their identity cards were marked "*Juif-Jood*" and they were barred from public entertainment: theaters, the cinema, bars, and restaurants. Jews were excluded from the civil service, teaching, the legal profession, and the press. The Jews were required to set up a version of the later eastern European "*Judenrat*," the Association of the Jews of Belgium (AJB), a body of Jews, which was to exercise self-enforcement of the anti-Jewish measures. At the same time the Nazi authorities directed the Belgian governmental departments to remove Jews from the economic life of the country. The Belgian bureaucrats initially refused to comply. The Belgian government-in-exile declared on January 10, 1941, that all decrees of the German occupiers were to be ignored. The Germans then issued decrees on their own and the Belgian administrators cooperated in their enforcement.[22]

On April 14, 1941, the Anti-Jewish League and other extreme-rightists in Antwerp staged their version of *Kristallnacht*, the German anti-Jewish pogrom of November 1938. During the "Antwerp pogrom" the hooligans broke the windows of 200 Jewish shops and burned two synagogues. On May 31, 1941, Jewish businesses were required to be registered, and the "Aryanization" of Jewish property began. In July the 7,600 Jewish businesses still operating were closed. By the middle of 1943 all Jewish property had been seized.

Jews in the fall of 1941 were ordered to adhere to a curfew and were forbidden to leave the city where they resided. They were excluded from parks and ordered not to walk around the streets. Jewish children were ousted from public schools on December 31, 1941. Antwerp Jews were subjected to forced labor in the spring of 1942, and all Jews in Belgium were ordered to wear the Star of David on May 27, 1942.[23] Underground newspapers denounced the measure and a number of non-Jews expressed their sympathy with the Jews by wearing yellow Stars of David.[24]

The underground left-wing Zionist Workers' Party refused to cooperate with the AJB. Its clandestine newspaper, *Unser Vort*, warned, "the time has come when we must, calmly, refuse to submit to Nazi orders."[25] On July 25, 1942, a Jewish section of the partisan movement in Brussels burned the work mobilization files of the AJB, but unfortunately there were duplicates. The following month the same group assassinated the Jewish head of the Jewish Department of Labor Mobilization as a collaborator, or at least, an enabler of the Nazis. Non-Jews resisted too. *La Libre Belgique* reappeared during this second German occupation. It admonished Belgians, "Citizens, out of hate for the Nazis and through loyalty to yourselves, do what you haven't been doing: Greet the Jews." In June 1941 the City Council of Brussels informed the local Nazi commander that it would not let its municipal offices be utilized for handing out the compulsory Stars of David.[26]

Gay Block and Malka Drucker ascribe the survival of so many of the Jews living in Belgium to the fact that Belgium had been occupied by the Germans in World War I. The Belgians "saw the German threat as collective, and they transformed their compassion into organized cooperation."[27] The Belgian resistance movement was committed to the rescue of Jews from the Nazis. Dan Michman believes that the close ties, which had developed between Belgian Jews and the parties of the Left in Belgium, contributed to the support of the left-wing resistance for the Jews.[28] The Jewish *Comité de Défense des Juifs* (CDJ, Committee for the Defense of Jews) was set up to warn Jews of impending deportations and to provide them with money, false identity papers, and hiding places. The CDJ had contacts with the Catholic Church and helped to find hiding places for Jews. Cooperating with the *Oeuvre nationale de l'enfance* (National Children's Committee), headed by Yvonne Nejean, it found hiding places for Jewish children.[29] According to Block and Drucker, "although Jews worked in resistance movements throughout Europe, Belgian Jews did more to help their own people than Jews in any other country."[30] The Belgian Catholic

Church was also deeply involved in the work of the Committee. Together the Committee and Catholics, both lay and religious, saved many lives, especially those of children. 25,000 Jews escaped to France trying to reach the unoccupied south. Most of those, however, were eventually apprehended and deported to concentration and death camps. But at least 20,000 people were hidden in Belgium.[31] Non-Jews worked with the CDJ. "Belgian government departments and banks provided material assistance and ration cards"[32] for the hidden Jews.

The deportation of Jews from Belgium began in 1942. On July 25, 1942, the ABJ received an order for 10,000 Jews to report for "labor mobilization." They were told to report to the Dossin barracks in Mechelen. The Queen and Cardinal Joseph-Ernest van Roey appealed on behalf of those Jews who were Belgian citizens. The cardinal denounced the treatment of Jews as "inhuman," "brutal," and "cruel."[33] Falkenhausen at first mollified them but the Germans eventually also deported Jews, who were Belgian citizens. Between the middle of 1942 and mid-1944 25,257 Jews were deported from Belgium to Auschwitz by way of the transit camp in Mechelen. Almost all of the children and most of the women were executed as soon as they arrived at Auschwitz. Only 1,207 of the 9,000 adults "spared" for slave labor survived the Holocaust.[34]

The first train left Dossin for Auschwitz on August 4, 1942. When most Jews refused to voluntarily present themselves for "labor mobilization," the Nazis resorted to force. On the night of August 15 the Antwerp police took 1,000 Jews into custody. These unfortunates, 28 percent of whom were children, were deported to the east two days later. There were additional night raids in Antwerp on August 28 and in Brussels on September 3, 11, and 12. 61.8 percent of the Jews who had lived in Belgium in 1940 were exterminated in Auschwitz-Birkenau. Several thousand others died in Belgium as a result of overwork, hunger, abuse, or formal or informal execution.[35] 17,000 Jewish adults and 3,000 children survived in Belgium; many were saved by the efforts of individual Belgians and religious communities.[36] The Communist Jewish Defense Committee helped Jews find hiding places, but their special concern was for the children whose parents had been deported. The organization arranged for the children to be housed and paid for their up-keep. Despite the threat of death many Christian Belgians took in these children and saved at least 3,000 from the death camp.[37]

## Breendonk

In addition to Jews, members of the resistance movement, suspects, and hostages were housed at Fort Breendonk, near Mechelen. On September 20, 1940, Breendonk was designated a concentration camp, or more precisely an *Auffangslager* or holding camp, for "Jews and certain dangerous internees."[38] Breendonk, constructed between 1906 and 1914, was one of the forts designed to protect Antwerp. It fell to the Germans in World War I and for 18 days in May 1940 it served as the General Headquarters of the Belgian Army and King Leopold. Its present appearance is the result of the labor of Jews and other political prisoners, who were forced to excavate the earth covering the reinforced concrete heart of the fortress. The camp was administered by the German army, the Wehrmacht, until the invasion of Russia by Nazi Germany on June 22, 1941. The camp was then taken over by the SS. The number of prisoners held at one time varied between 30 and 600. The camp, in comparison to other German concentration and death camps was quite small, but atrocities occurred there, which were similar to those in better-known camps. Dan Michman writes that "conditions [at Breendonk] were among the worst in the camps of western Europe: overcrowded and dilapidated housing, bad food, and harsh punishment; but worst of all was the violence."[39] The officer in charge of forced labor, Untersturmführer Arthur Preuss, had a particular reputation for cruelty. Occasionally prisoners would be buried to their necks and then be beaten or kicked to death. The precise number of Jewish and Gentile prisoners who died of hunger, disease, or mistreatment is not known.[40] It is estimated that 3,456 prisoners endured Breendonk. At the execution ground, which has been preserved, 21 resistance fighters were hung and approximately 164 hostages were shot in revenge for acts of the resistance. 108 other prisoners were killed elsewhere in the complex, and an additional 98 died as a result of beating, torture, or starvation.[41]

Jean Améry, who was born in 1912 in Vienna, the son of a Jewish father and a German Catholic mother, had fled to Belgium after the Germans annexed Austria in March 1938. He later participated in the Belgian resistance was captured and sent to Breendonk, where he was tortured before being sent on to Auschwitz. In his *At the Mind's Limits* he described the Breendonk he knew. He wrote

> watchtowers arise along the moat that rings the castle. Barbed-wire fences wrap around them . (. . .) The creators of the National Museum have left everything the way it was between 1940 and 1944. Yellowed wall cards: "Whoever goes beyond this point will be shot." (. . .) One steps through the main gate and soon finds oneself in a room that in those days was mysteriously called the "business room." A picture of Heinrich Himmler on the wall, a swastika flag spread as a cloth over a long table, a few bare chairs. The business room. Everyone went about his business, and theirs was murder. Then the damp cellarlike corridors, dimly lit by the same thin and reddishly glowing bulbs as the ones that used to hang there. Prison cells, sealed by inch thick wooden doors. Again and again one must pass through heavy barred gates before one finally stands in a windowless vault in which various iron implements lie about. From there no scream penetrated the outside. There I experienced it: torture.[42]

On May 6, 1944, all of the prisoners confined in Breendonk were transported to concentration and death camps in the east. It was filled again, but on August 30,

1944, all of its prisoners were transported to the Vught camp in the Netherlands. When Allied troops reached Breendonk on September 3, 1944, it was empty.[43]

## Resistance and Retribution

During the war most Belgians concentrated their efforts on survival for themselves and their families. However, extreme Flemish nationalists and followers of Léon Degrelle formed Flemish and Walloon SS regiments, which were sent to the eastern front.[44] The Germans also deported a half million Belgians for forced labor in the Third Reich. There, however, was a Belgian resistance movement. One of its more spectacular achievements occurred on April 20, 1943. 1,500 Jews were being transported from Mechelen to death camps in Poland in cattle cars when three partisans, one of whom was Jewish, stopped the train outside Mechelen near Boortmeerbeek. This was "the only recorded instance of an armed attack in Europe on a train taking Jews to their death."[45] The participation of Jews in partisan resistance was not unusual in Belgium. 1,000 Jews fought with the resistance and 140 of them were killed. The partisans in this incident overpowered some of the guards, opened the cars, and distributed money to the deportees. Germans, however, opened fire killing 20 of the people attempting to escape and wounding 40. 600 did get away and were able to find hiding places in the Brussels area.[46]

A small Belgian armed force accompanied the Allies as they entered Belgium in September 1944. Members of the Belgian resistance also cooperated with the Allied forces when they arrived. Belgians took a number of German stragglers captive and also rounded up suspected collaborators.

After the war, some of the perpetrators from Fort Breendonk were apprehended, tried, found guilty, and executed. Among them was SS Sturmbannführer Schmidt, the commandant, eight Belgian SS men, three Belgian workers, and three former inmates, a Belgian and two German Jews, who assisted their captors in the fort's hellish torture chamber.

In the immediate post-war years hundreds of Jewish orphans and many members of Zionist youth groups emigrated from Belgium to Palestine. However, the Jewish communities of Antwerp and Brussels were re-established, though they were much smaller than before. Elsewhere the Jewish communities, if they existed, were miniscule.[47]

# CHAPTER 16

# Belgium Since 1945

## Leopold and the Royal Question

L eopold, who succeeded his father on February 17, 1934, was a tragic figure. His wife, Astrid of Sweden, was killed when a car driven by Leopold crashed in 1935. The dead Astrid became a cult-like figure against whom Leopold and his future behavior were negatively compared. Leopold had served as a regular soldier in World War I, but his conduct in World War II suffered in comparison to that of his father, Albert, in World War I. In May 1940 most of Belgium was quickly over-run by the Germans. The Belgian army had its back to the sea. On May 26 the center of the Belgian line gave way. There were no reserves, the rear was packed with civilians, and the situation was really hopeless. Winston Churchill appealed for continued resistance, an appeal that he himself characterized as "asking them to sacrifice themselves for us."[1] The Belgians were surrounded and they were well aware that the British were desperately attempting to evacuate. Leopold refused to escape by plane, saying that his duty demanded that he "must stay with his Army and people."[2] When Leopold ordered the army to cease fighting on May 27, the Belgian government-in-exile in France declared him deposed. If what he did was, in hindsight, not wise, it was in his mind what honor required.[3]

Leopold was accused of treasonous coziness with the Germans during the occupation of Belgium. In November 1940 he had a personal meeting with Hitler at Berchtesgaden at which he appealed for the continued independence of Belgium. Leopold's personal life too was a matter of controversy. In September 1941 he married Mary Liliane Baels, the daughter of the pro-German Mayor of Ostend, and the couple spent their honeymoon in German Austria. In 1944 Leopold was taken from Belgium by the retreating Germans but was comfortably lodged in a castle in Austria. With the liberation, the anti-Leopold vituperation of the clandestine Walloon press was no longer muted by the Nazi occupation. The provisional Belgian government declared Leopold "incapable of ruling" and asked him to remain in Geneva, where he had sought refuge. His brother Charles was named regent. A Commission of Information was established on July 14, 1946, to examine the "royal question." Its March 25, 1947 report found that the king's actions from May 25, 1940, until the Germans deported him to Austria on June 6, 1944, were within his constitutional authority. However, the government rejected the commission's narrow formulation of its inquiry.

## Referendum

To end the stalemate between the king and the government a referendum was held on March 12, 1950. The total tally was in support of the king. He was supported by 57.7 percent of those who voted. A two-year stalemate between king and government followed. The vote bared a significant regional split. 72 percent of the Flemish voters, strengthened undoubtedly by women who were enfranchised in Belgium in 1948, supported the king, but 58 percent of the Walloons and 52 percent of the voters in Brussels voted against the king. The Catholic People's Party, which had won an absolute majority in the parliament, invited him to return and resume his functions as king. When Leopold announced his decision to return, his announcement was greeted with strikes, massive demonstrations, and violence organized by the Communists and Socialists in Wallonia. Leopold and the government reconsidered and he submitted his abdication to parliament on August 3. Leopold's son Baudouin (Boudewijn) became king and was formally crowned on July 16, 1951. Leopold died in Brussels on September 25, 1983.[4]

## Baudouin

Baudouin, the eldest son of Leopold and Astrid, was born on September 7, 1930. The constitutional powers of king were transferred to Baudouin on August 11, 1950. He formally became king on July 17, 1951, the day after his father's abdication. Baudouin restored the prestige of the monarchy after the controversy surrounding his father. He made the office a symbol of national unity for Belgium's fractured society.

Baudouin contributed to the peaceful transformation of Belgium into a federal state. His deep religious convictions, however, did lead to an impasse with the parliament over abortion. In April 1990 he was unwilling to sign legislation legalizing abortion. Baudouin then voluntarily stepped aside for 44 hours. After the law was promulgated, parliament voted to reinstate the king. Baudouin and his Spanish wife Fabiola de Mora y Aragon had no children. Following his unexpected death on July 30, 1993, his brother Albert became king.[5]

## Internationalization

Following World War II Belgium was transformed in a number of ways. It experienced dramatic economic change. It attained new levels of prosperity but its economic base shifted from heavy industry to the service and technical sector. There was also a shift in the center of economic gravity from Wallonia to Flanders. The economic resurgence was connected to new international bonds and a growing process of integration between the states of Western Europe. The new economic, social, and political ties with the states of Western Europe compensated for the process of decolonization which saw the end of Belgian rule in the Congo, Rwanda, and Burundi. Belgium's growing integration into Europe also provided the context for the transformation of Belgium from a unitary state to a federation of cultural-geographic regions.

Belgium, which had formed an economic union with Luxembourg in 1922, formed a customs union with Luxembourg and the Netherlands in 1948. On February 3, 1959, the three countries signed the Benelux Treaty. When it went into effect in 1960 it provided for the free movement of labor, capital, and services between the three. Belgium was also one of the driving forces behind the broader economic integration of Europe through the European Coal and Steel Community of 1952 and the European Economic Community of 1957. Paul-Henri Spaak, who served as Belgian foreign minister from 1939 to 1947 and prime minister from 1947 to 1950, was one of the leading promoters of European cooperation and integration. He played a central role in the development of Benelux. In 1948 he signed the Treaty of Brussels, which established a defensive alliance of Britain, France, and the Benelux countries, and this Western European Union paved the way for the North Atlantic Treaty Organization (NATO) formed the following year. From 1952 to 1953 Spaak presided over the newly formed European Coal and Steel Community, and from 1957 to 1961 was the secretary general of NATO. He was an architect of the European Community and helped to formulate the 1957 Treaty of Rome, which established the European Common Market. From 1961 to 1966 he served again as Belgian foreign minister and deputy premier. In 1966 he left the government for private business and died on July 31, 1972.

## Decolonization

After the Congo had been wrested from King Leopold II in 1908, it had been dominated by Belgian business interests and the Catholic Church. Primary education was dominated by the church and financed by the state. However, there were few secondary schools and, apart from seminaries, higher education did not exist until 1954. By 1960 40 percent of the Congo's population was Christian, and 80 percent of the Christians were Catholic. The economy was dominated by the Belgian holding company, Société Générale. Wealth, generated by the mining of copper, gold, diamonds, and uranium, flowed into Belgium.

Belgium had not prepared its colonies for independence, but by 1958 Belgian politicians realized that independence was inevitable. It came much sooner than they had calculated. Riots in Leopoldville (Kinshasa) in 1959 awakened the Belgians to the reality of the situation. Belgium did not attempt to hold on in a futile fashion. According to Emile Lamberts, "Belgian public opinion, not particularly attached to the colony, clearly rejected the use of violence against the African inhabitants."[6] The Belgian government granted the Congo independence on June 30, 1960. The aftermath of Congelese independence was tragic. Belgium had failed to train a cadre of African administrators. The new country was fractured by a military mutiny and the province of Katanga under the leadership of Moise Tshombe temporarily seceded. Unity was restored but at the expense of a corrupt military dictatorship under Joseph Mobutu. Mobutu's regime was toppled in 1999. But civil war and foreign intervention further fractured the country.

The fate of Rwanda and Burundi, which became independent on July 1, 1962, has not been better. Both have experienced ethnic violence between the Hutus and the Tutsis, who had received special privileges under the Belgians. The hostility of the Hutus culminated in the tragic genocide inflicted upon the Tutsi of Rwanda in 1994. The aftermath of colonialism in these former Belgian colonies certainly gives lie to the assertion of the civilizing mission of the Europeans.

### Cleavages

*Twentieth century Belgium often appears to be a "labyrinth" of compartmentalized communities that have contended for influence and have been forced to compromise with each other——Flemings and French-speakers, Catholics and anticlericals, big business, labor, farmers, and small commerce.*

—Carl Strikwerda[7]

The controversy over Leopold brought to the surface deep cleavages in Belgian society. The Flemish National Front (VNV), which had received growing support between the wars, collaborated with the Germans.[8] Coupled with the Walloon antagonism toward the king was a hostility inspired by the courting of the Flemish by the Nazis. While Walloon prisoners of war were held by the Nazis until the end of the war, Flemish prisoners of war were allowed by the Germans to return to Belgium.[9] The prosecution of collaborators,[10] and the denunciations of Leopold were issues which demonstrated and exacerbated divisions in Belgian society. These divisions followed the fault lines of the pre-World War II politics. Most Catholics, particularly

Flemish ones, approved of the return of Leopold, and Flemish Catholics often regarded the post-war prosecutions as acts of repression against Flemish patriots.[11] Many Flemish believed that Catholic Flemish militants were being persecuted to promote a left-wing agenda.[12] This feeling was exacerbated by the destruction in 1946 of the Ijzer Tower, which had been erected after World War I to commemorate the Flemish soldiers who had died along the Ijzer front and had become a symbol of the Flemish community.

The Christian Democrats[13] regarded the abdication as a humiliating defeat of the Catholics and the Flemish at the hands of the anti-clericals and the Walloons. In the 1950s the tension continued and culminated in the 1954–1958 School War between the Catholics and a Socialist-Liberal coalition. The Catholics whose Christian Peoples'/Social Christian party won a narrow but absolute majority in the 1950 elections, enacted the Harmel Laws. These laws provided subsidies to Catholic secondary schools and placed representatives of the Catholic schools on educational supervisory commissions. In 1954 Socialists and Liberals together won a majority. The Socialist-Liberal government of Achille Van Acker enacted the Collard Laws, which dismissed teachers who possessed degrees from Catholic normal schools, which the government regarded as substandard. In addition, state funds were paid directly to the teachers in Catholic schools rather than to the schools themselves. In the 1958 election the Catholics won a majority in the senate, but in the lower house the Catholics and the anti-clericals were tied. As a result of this deadlock a Catholic-Liberal coalition was formed and a compromise was worked out.[14] The outcome of the acrimonious struggle was the School Pact of 1958. Public and private, principally Catholic, schools would co-exist and both would be financed by the state. Free secondary education was provided to students in both public and private secondary schools and this was subsequently extended to higher education.

This school compromise led the Liberals to jettison their doctrinaire anti-clericalism and re-dub themselves the Party of Freedom and Progress. It also set the stage for agreements on social and cultural issues. The state assumed financial responsibility while the "pillarized" social institutions managed the insurance for unemployment, sickness, and disability. (The Flemish use the word *verzuiling*, which is often translated as "pillarization," to refer to the social organizations and subcultures of the various political "cultures," Catholic, Socialist, and Liberal.) The legislation concerning education and social security thus ended Belgium's "religious and ideological tensions without undermining the country's pillarized structures."[15]

## Labor and the Welfare State

Following the war, the labor movement, despite being divided into socialist, Catholic, and small liberal segments, made significant progress. Unions were an essential part of the social market approach to the economy, which was adopted as Belgium embarked on the post-war period.[16] A consultative collective bargaining system was hammered out between the trade unions and employers. Labor unions were recognized as the legal representatives of workers. By law they represented the workers' interests on the national, sectoral, and company levels. By the late 1950s a neo-corporativist system of social bargaining between trade unions and employers with tri-partite bodies representing labor, management, and the public was operating on the national and sectoral level, establishing standards for wages, benefits, and conditions of labor. Out of these developments emerged a comprehensive social security system, which was extended to all employees. In addition to unemployment benefits and pensions, the system provided health care, industrial accident and disability insurance, supplementary payments for families with children, and paid vacations. The system was financed by payments by workers, employers, and the self-employed, but it was administered by the existing "pillarized" social institutions. These Catholic, Socialist, and Liberal (secular) groupings or "pillars" characterized Belgium's politically segregated civil society. They enabled very divergent ideological communities to mitigate their conflicts and conduct a peaceful and stable social life—even if society was divided into three compartments. Tony Judt says that each was

> (. . .) a closed social, economic, and cultural community. (. . .) Much of daily life was arranged within hermetically separated and all-embracing nations-within-a-nation, including child care, schooling, youth groups, cafés, trade unions, holiday camps, women's groups, consumer cooperatives, insurance, saving societies, banking, and newspapers.[17]

Economic and social changes after 1960, however, have made inroads into the ideological bases of the compartments. In Flanders the influence of the Catholic Church significantly declined. This was visible in decreased church attendance and in falling birth rates. In 1973 a 1923 law forbidding the sale of contraceptives was repealed, and abortion was legalized in 1990. However, the pillarized institutions endured because "they were so closely intertwined with the state apparatus, and because of their services and social usefulness."[18]

Nevertheless, as the twentieth century drew to a close, new opposition parties challenged "the organized interest groups and large intermediate groups, which served as intermediates between the state and its citizens."[19] In 1981 the Flemish party, AGALEV (To Live Differently), was the first environmental party in the world to win parliamentary representation. In 1988, ECOLO, the francophone environmental party, won 10 percent of the vote in the European parliamentary election, the highest percent achieved by any Green party in Europe.

## Nationalities Politics

*The crisis of the Belgian state, that model of nineteenth century modernization may well be terminal.*

—William Wallace[20]

*[T]here can be no doubt that in Belgium, as elsewhere in Europe, the forces of nationalism are effecting social and political change so far-reaching as to threaten the cohesion of the nation-state.*

—Louis Vos[21]

After 1970 Belgium was transformed from a unitary state, with a single government and administration centered in Brussels, into a complex federal state. To the out-sider the new Belgian arrangement, which consists of bipartite and tripartite struc-tures, can have the appearance of a three dimensional maze. The evolution away from the unitary state was rooted in Flemish resentment of the francophone nature of the kingdom. Flemish assertiveness itself triggered a reaction among the franco-phone Walloons who tended to be much more secular and socialist than the ar-dently Catholic Flemish Dutch speakers.

Tension was high after World War II. The Germans courted the Flemish during both wars. Following the defeat of the Nazis, anger and desire for revenge against collaborators was particularly strong among the Walloons. Though the Walloons en-joyed temporary ascendancy, post-war demographic and economic change worked against them. Although Brussels was becoming more and more francophone, the total Walloon percentage of the Belgian population declined from 40.3 in 1900 to 32.9 in 1962. The Walloon leaders sought institutional guarantees for their predom-inantly socialist minority against a Flemish Christian Democratic majority.

Although the Walloons advanced a federalist transformation, the idea was quite congenial to the Flemish, who resented the continued role of French in business, higher education, and culture, and the preponderance of French in the national capital. Economically, Wallonia, which had been the site of the heavy industry that made Belgium a pioneer in the industrial revolution, declined in the post-war pe-riod. Foreign investment and new industry spread inland from the ports of Flanders into what had previously been a rather poor agricultural region. During the 1950s 200,000 miners lost their jobs when mines in the Walloon Sambre-Meuse region shut down. Along with coal, the steel and textile industries of Wallonia experi-enced precipitous decline. In 1998 Belgium produced only two million tons of coal from its Walloon coalmines, while in 1961 it had produced 21 million tons.[22] On the other hand Flanders experienced a dramatic economic upsurge. In 1947 20 per-cent of the Flemish workers were employed in agriculture. By the end of the twenti-eth century less than three percent of the Flemings were so employed. The service, commercial, and technological sectors in the meantime surged.[23] Thus the previous economic situation in Belgium was reversed. Instead of a developed and prosperous Wallonia confronting an undeveloped and poor Flanders, Flanders prospered while Wallonia languished. The fact that most young Flemish people became quite fluent in English can be viewed both as an effect of and as a factor contributing to the modernization and internationalization of the Flemish economy. It, however, can also be viewed as a reaction against the previous cultural hegemony of the French language.[24]

A general strike was called by the socialist trade unions in December 1960 to protest the government's Unity Law for economic recovery, an austerity program. When the strike failed due to the lack of support in Flanders, the Walloon unionists vented their anger against the de-industrilization of Wallonia. The Popular Walloon Movement (*Mouvement Populaire Wallon*, MPW), headed by its charismatic leader André Renard, bolted from the Belgian Socialist Party and gave rise to a number of Walloon nationalist parties. The MPW hoped to combat the economic decline of Wallonia by setting up a regional government. Although the MPW faded quickly after the death of Renard in 1962, the French-speaking socialist labor movement quickly absorbed its goals.

In response to developing national sentiments both among the Flemish and the Walloons, a coalition government of Flemish Christian Democrats and Walloon Socialists formed after the March 1961 elections introduced a new constitutional arrangement. The coalition wanted to provide guarantees to the Walloon minority and to address the language grievances of the Flemish. However, constitutional changes failed because it was impossible to gain the required two-thirds majority in parliament.

The coalition did pass legislation which reflected its compromising accommodations to both Walloon and Flemish concerns. A 1962 law determined the language boundary. This removed the uncertainty of a boundary which would fluctuate from census to census. Four provinces were designated as French speaking: Hainaut, Liège, Luxembourg, and Namur. Four were designated Flemish speaking: Antwerp, East Flanders, Limburg, and West Flanders. Brabant was divided into Flemish and French segments, and Brussels was designated as bi-lingual. 1963 language legislation affirmed and strengthened the dominance of Dutch and French in their respective regions and bilingualism for Brussels. The latter move, however, caused resentment among the francophone majority in Brussels. They formed the *Front démocratique des Francophones*. In coalition with the *Mouvement Populaire Wallon* it opposed the compromise and demanded the establishment of a tri-partite federal state. They called for the transformation of an expanded Brussels into a full third region. The Flemish naturally rejected this demand and responded with their own demand for full autonomy for Belgium's two language communities.

The aim of the government in establishing the linguistic borders was to put an end to the controversy over language. However, by creating linguistic areas, which were as homogeneous as possible, the new arrangement underlined the differences between the Flemish and French speakers and encouraged some Flemish to intensify their efforts to create a monolingual Flemish state.[25]

In addition to the problem area of Brussels the 1962 law granted special "facilities" to minorities in a few border communities. This created resentment among Flemish proponents of unilingualism. In 1968 the linguistic/nationality conflict reached a new level of intensity. The issue concerned the nature of the Catholic University at Louvain/Leuven. Flemish speaking students in the university town, the inhabitants of which were predominantly Flemish, first demanded that every course offered in French be simultaneously offered in Dutch. Francophone professors and staff members of the university responded by calling for Leuven to become a bi-lingual city like Brussels.[26] To the Flemish this raised the prospect of the "ink blot" of Brussels spreading further into Flemish Brabant. Eventually the university was split along language lines. A sensible compromise to separate the two faculties but to maintain the coherence and unity of the university, which would have been very feasible because the linguistic divide runs along the southern outskirts of Leuven, gave way to monetary and political deals. An entirely new French speaking institution, Louvain-la-Neuve, was established some 28 kilometers from Leuven at Ottinges. It is said that money and new facilities were promised to other institutions and cities to seal the deal. A Dutch language counterpart to the French language Free University of Brussels was set up and new Dutch speaking university campuses were established at Diepenbeek, Kotrijk, and Antwerp. Just as the old premier university was divided, so were the Christian Democratic Party in 1968 and the Liberal Party in 1972. The socialists followed suit in 1978, and after that there were no longer any national parties.[27]

According to Lamberts, "the Leuven question sealed the fate of the Belgian unitary state, setting in motion the process which would lead to the regionalization and federalization of the country."[28] The expulsion of the French-language section of the university fueled anti-Fremish sentiment in Wallonia and among the French speakers of Brussels.[29] It stimulated support for regionalist nationalist parties in Flanders as well as in francophone Belgium: the People's Union (Volksunie) among the Flemish, the Walloon Rally (Rassemblement Wallon), and the Brussels Front démocratique des Francophones. After the split of the Belgian Socialist Party in 1978, the Parti Socialiste, now sporting Walloon identity, absorbed the Walloon nationalist parties. The cultural separation was thus replicated on the terrain of parties. The Christian Democrats were the dominant political party among the Flemish. The Socialists predominated among the Walloons, and the Liberals were a principal factor in Brussels.

The six new linguistically separated parties all moved rapidly toward a federalist transformation of Belgium. Steps in this direction had occurred in 1970 and 1971. The autonomy of the Flemish, French, and German "communities" was legally recognized in December 1970 and three economic regions were established in Flanders, Wallonia, and Brussels. Linguistic proportional representation was legislated for the cabinet. With the exception of the prime minister cabinets had to have an equal number of French and Dutch speakers. Then two linguistic community councils were set up with exclusive control over cultural issues with the exception of education in their respective linguistic regions.

Although the inhabitants of Voeren (Fourons) in the Flemish province of Limburg speak a dialect of German among themselves, two-thirds consider themselves French speakers. They elected José Happart, a militant advocate of the French language, mayor in 1987. Because he refused to speak Flemish or to submit to a test of his capacity to speak Dutch language, Happart was declared unqualified for the office by the Belgian Supreme Court. The national government collapsed over the issue. Three Flemish ministers threatened to resign if he were not forced to resign. In response to his ouster three French-speaking ministers resigned. The prime minister, Wilfried Martens, exasperated and angry, was nevertheless forced to resign over the issue, which had split his cabinet. Happart, for his part, emerged as a very popular spokesman for Walloon rights and was elected to the European Parliament. In response to the Voeren (Fourons) dispute, power sharing was introduced for linguistically mixed communities in 1992.

Legislation in 1980 gave regional authorities in Flanders, Wallonia, and bilingual Brussels competence over social and economic matters such as planning, housing, the environment, and local government. Because the French speakers were unsatisfied with the territory allocated to the Brussels region, regional institutions were not set up for the city, but they were implemented in both Flanders and Wallonia. The new regional council and executive for Flanders was merged with the Flemish community institutions, which had been established in 1971, thus forming the Flemish Council and Executive. Among the francophones there was concern in Wallonia that the French speakers of Brussels might challenge the socialist domination of the Walloon Regional Council, so for the French speakers regional institutions and community institutions were not at first merged. To mediate between the government and the federal executives a Consultative Committee was established. A Court of Arbitration with an equal number of Dutch and French speakers was also set up in 1985.

Finally in 1988 a two-thirds majority in the Belgian parliament agreed on comprehensive constitutional reforms. The two communities assumed responsibility for education within their areas. They were given a limited right to tax, and they were even permitted to enter into international agreements. Control over economic policy, energy, public works, and transportation devolved to the regions. In addition, the Brussels region was established in 1989 with the guarantee that two of its five ministers would be Dutch speakers. It was divided into 19 boroughs, each with its own mayor and aldermen, and possessed a parliament.

Additional measures of devolution were implemented in 1993. Belgium was transformed into "a federal state with an asymmetrical construction of 'communities' and 'regions' that now became states within a state. Four states—the Flemish and the German 'communities,' and the 'regions' of Brussels and Wallonia—would now choose their own parliaments."[30] The former bi-lingual province of Brabant was divided into Flemish Brabant and Walloon Brabant. As the splintering continued the French Community divided some of its competencies between the Walloon Region and the French Linguistic Group of the Council of the Brussels Capital Region.

The constitution was re-drawn to reflect all of these devolutionary changes. It was signed by Albert II on February 17, 1994, and was promulgated on May 21, 1995. The function of the upper house of the parliament was decreased transforming it into a body for political "reflection." Proportional representation was maintained in both houses of the parliament, but in matters judged to be of significant impact to a linguistic community a majority of the representatives from each community and a two thirds composite vote was required. The Council of the French Community was established. It consisted of the 75 members of the Walloon Regional Council and the 19 representatives of the French Linguistic Group of the Brussels Council. The Flemish Council was composed of the 118 representatives of Flemish Region and 6 representatives of the Dutch Linguistic Group of the Brussels Council.

As a result of the constitutional changes since 1988 the competence of the national government was reduced to "national economic and monetary policy, justice, defense, foreign policy, social security, and the police."[31] The Communities and Regions had jurisdiction over everything else. Within the national government, most appointments, even within the military, were made according to proportionality. However, through agreements and deals, friends and clients from the various "pillars" were advanced by their patrons.[32] As the twentieth century ended Flemish politicians were demanding control over income tax and social security. If this happens, Judt writes, "the unitary state will effectively have ceased to exist."[33]

With the developing economic disparity between the regions and the promulgation of federalism, "a cultural curtain developed between Flanders and Wallonia."[34] The Flemish people stressed their cultural identity and distinctiveness in an assertive fashion. The memory of second-class status and the disparagement of their language are still alive among many Flemish. The Flemish have oriented themselves economically and culturally toward the English-speaking world. The French-speakers, especially those in Brussels, have increasingly identified with the French-speaking world. A separate Walloon identity, however, is emerging. This is characterized by different interests and different values on the part of the French-speakers in Wallonia proper and those in Brussels.[35] Few Walloons identify with French culture or France, and the question of Walloon identity is a recurrent one in their literature.[36]

## The German-speaking Community

In 1984 cultural autonomy was also granted to the German-speaking Community. The offices of this community are located in Eupen and administer the social and cultural affairs of the 70,000 German speakers in nine municipalities located near the German frontier in the Province of Liège of the Walloon Region.[37] This area had historically been part of the Prince-archbishopric of Liège. It was transferred to Prussia by the Congress of Vienna in 1815 but, against the will of its inhabitants and following a bogus referendum, became part of Belgium following World War I. In addition, there are another 50,000 German-speaking Old Belgians (*Deutschsprachige Altbelgier*), who live in three distinct areas which belonged to Belgium at the time of its inception in 1830. The area inhabited by the German-speaking Old Belgians, Montzener Land in the northeastern part of the province of Liège, the area around Bocholz (Beho) in the northeastern part of the province of Luxembourg, and Areler Land near the border of the Grand Duchy of Luxembourg, have been structurally integrated into the Walloon Region and the French Community. French in those three areas is the sole official language and there has been no demand for education in German or Letzebürgish, the third official language of the Grand Duchy of Luxembourg. In contrast to the areas inhabited by the German-speaking Old Belgians, the 70,000 Germans of the eastern-most part of the province of Liège (Eupen, Malmedy, and St. Vith) "have been given a wide range of autonomous competencies as the Third Community in the Federal State."[38]

Despite the desire of a majority of the inhabitants of the Eupen, Malmedy, St. Vith area for re-union with Germany before the rise of Adolf Hitler, and the welcome given by many to the Nazi invaders in 1940, the experiences of Nazi Germany and post-war purges were cathartic. Young men from the region, born between 1890 and 1927, were drafted into the German army. Of the 8,700 draftees, 2,200 died, largely on the Eastern Front; 1,800 were declared missing and were presumed dead or prisoners in Russia; and 1,900 returned wounded or amputees. In addition to wartime devastation (St. Vith was destroyed), the exit of the Nazis was followed by a harsh persecution of accused collaborators who were imprisoned and whose houses and possessions were confiscated. 16,400 people, 25 percent of the inhabitants of the region, were indicted. Though only 10 percent of the accused were tried, this amounted to 2.5 percent of the population in contrast to .68 percent of the population in the rest of Belgium.[39]

The Belgian government imposed a program of total assimilation centered in the schools, where all instruction was conducted in French. There was a pragmatic realization among the population that they now had no alternative but "to learn to live with the Belgian state."[40] A turning point, however, came with the assertion by the Flemish of their linguistic and cultural claims. The German-speaking Belgians realized that Belgium consisted of "different competing ethno-linguistic groups." Hubert

Jenniges has written "the knowledge that the Flemings, who constituted the major-ity of the population, were sympathetic toward the German Belgians was crucial."[41] The German-speaking Belgians did not question "the reality of living in a Belgian state," but they did question the notion of living in a homogeneous francophone state. Inspired by the Flemish and empowered by political-cultural developments, an autonomous German-speaking Community with its own government and insti-tutions was established in 1984. According to Jenniges, "as the European integra-tion movement gains momentum and the notions of state and citizenship become layered with new meanings, the German-Belgian identity crisis may be expected to fade away into the past."[42]

## The Nationalist Right and the Vlaams Blok (VB)

After the defeat of Germany, the extreme right in Belgium, which had found more support among the Flemish than the Walloons, assumed a low profile. Though sen-sitive to the charge of collaboration with the Germans, ultra-rightists sought to form a political organization to promote an amnesty for collaborators and to agitate for autonomy for the Flemish areas. The Popular Union (*Volksunie*, VU) was founded in 1954. Although the VU was a democratically oriented Flemish-national party, it did provide a home for arch right-wingers.

The Order of Flemish Militants (*Vlaamse Militanten Orde*, VMO), a para-military organization founded in 1949 to protect gatherings of Flemish nationalists, originally supported the VU. The VU, however, soon became too tame for the ex-treme right. The monthly magazine *Dietsland-Europa* (Netherlands-Europe) of the radical right-wing group *Were Di* (Arm Yourself) advocated a corporate path as a compromise between capitalism and communism and called for the amalgamation of Flanders with the Netherlands. In 1981, having become more radical and vio-lent, the VMO was outlawed under a law banning private militias.[43]

The objective of VU was a reorganization of the Belgian state rather than its de-struction and in 1977 a representative of VU was asked to join the cabinet of a coali-tion Belgian government. The VU desired the transformation of Belgium from a uni-tary state into a federal state, which would give local control to the Flemish in the areas where they constituted the majority. This enraged the intransigent extreme-right, which wished ultimately to destroy the Belgian state. Disgruntled Flemish na-tionalists, who wanted an independent mono-racial and mono-cultural Republic of Flanders, founded the Flemish Bloc (*Vlaams Blok*, VB) on October 2, 1977. It gained support in Antwerp and Mechelen, both of which have visible immigrant commu-nities, on the basis of its anti–immigrant and law-and-order positions.

In the December 1978 election the VB only attracted 76,000 votes or 2.2 percent of the vote and won only one seat in parliament. However, aided by "a wide-spread feeling of political and social malaise,"[44] and intensified Flemish assertiveness, the VB advanced steadily. In 1995 it won 475,000 votes or 12 percent of the national vote and became the fourth largest party in Flanders. It won 28 percent of the vote in Antwerp, the most important city in Flanders, and was only prevented from controlling the city by a coalition of all other parties. If the VB's success in Antwerp was significant, it was not an aberration. In the 1995 election the VB elected 32 members to the national parliament, two to the European parliament, and 204 councilors in 86 municipalities.[45]

## The New Belgians

Immigrants are a principle target of VB invective. A tenth of Belgium's population has foreign passports, but, as a matter of fact, if naturalized citizens and citizens with foreign-born parents or grand-parents are included approximately a quarter of Belgium's population has recent immigrant roots.[46] Nevertheless, as a result of Belgium's nationalities politics and the formation of the linguistic communities, the children of immigrants are being pressed to "choose a camp." According to Anne Morelli and Jean-Philippe Schreiber, the VB is not alone in advancing such a position. They write

> one cannot even have a good relationship with both linguistic communities without being suspected of being a renegade or, as some would have it, a traitor or enemy agent. This is because the communities are busy forging backward-looking regional identities (. . .) in which aliens have hardly any place.[47]

Brussels is an example of changing urban demographics in Belgium, but perhaps also something of an exception to the contention of Morelli and Schreiber concerning the uncomfortable insertion of immigrants into the national cleavages of Belgium. At the same time that Brussels experienced a demographic decline, it also experienced a growth of its immigrant population. Between 1971 and 1994, as the population of Brussels declined from 1,075,136 to 949,070, an 11.72 percent decrease, its foreign population grew from 173,507 to 274,590, a 58.25 percent increase. In 1995 there were 281,245 foreigners in Brussels. The remaining 667,825 inhabitants of Brussels included both nationalized Belgians and the children of immigrants. New Belgians (naturalized citizens) have been elected to borough councils and the Brussels Parliament. According to Serge Govaert, "a strong community feeling (in the social, not institutional sense of the word) has developed since the seventies through a dense web of associations," especially on the borough level. This, plus the political success of New Belgians, he asserts, has had "an effect on the way these people experience their identity and on the forms of political representation they develop."[48]

## Conclusion

Belgium is not without problems. It suffers from the ills of a post-industrial society. Its elaborate welfare state is proving increasingly difficult to fund. It has its rust belt and urban blight. Its two principal national communities seem, at times, determined to split the country in half. They, perhaps, have not done so yet because of the francophone island of Brussels in the midst of a Flemish area. However, the Belgians, even if they differ, seldom resort to extremes. They are a familial and humane people. American students are struck by the safety of the streets of Leuven. The almost complete absence of violent crime in Belgium is a refreshing contrast to America. It was moving to watch 100,000 Belgians from around the country pour into the streets of Brussels to demonstrate against violence and administrative inefficiency following the shocking discovery of a ring of sex perverts and murderers in 1996. It is hard to imagine two murders, no matter how brutal, bringing an equivalent percentage of the American people, 3.5 million, into the streets for a peaceful manifestation of concern. It is a credit to the people of Belgium that they are still capable of being shocked, and have not yet been completely anesthetized by mass society.

# APPENDIX I

# Kings, Prime Ministers, and Governments

## Kings of Belgium

| | |
|---|---|
| Leopold I | 1831–1865 |
| Leopold II | 1865–1909 |
| Albert I | 1909–1934 |
| Leopold III (1st time) | 1934–1944 |
| Charles (regent) | 1944–1950 |
| Leopold III (2nd time) | 1950 |
| Baudouin I (regent 1950–1951) | 1950–1993 |
| Albert II | 1993- |

## Prime Ministers

| | |
|---|---|
| Charles Latour Rogier (acting) (1st time) | 1830–1831 |
| Erasme Louis, baron Surlet de Chokier | 1831 |
| Charles de Brouckère (acting) | 1831–1832 |
| Charles Latour Rogier (2nd time) | 1832–1834 |
| Barthélemy Théodore, comte de Theux de Meylandt (1st time) | 1834–1840 |
| Joseph Lebeau | 1840–1841 |
| Jean Baptiste, baron Nothomb | 1841–1845 |
| Jean Sylvain van de Weyer | 1845–1846 |
| Barthélemy Théodore, comte de Theux de Meylandt (2nd time) | 1846–1847 |
| Charles Latour Rogier (3rd time) | 1847–1852 |
| Henri de Brouckère | 1852–1855 |
| Pierre Jacques François de Decker | 1855–1857 |
| Charles Latour Rogier (4th time) | 1857–1868 |

| | |
|---|---|
| Hubert Joseph Walther Frère-Orban | 1868–1870 |
| Jules Joseph, baron d'Anethan | 1870–1871 |
| Barthélemy Théodore, comte de Theux | |
| de Meylandt (3rd time) | 1871–1874 |
| Jules Malou (1st time) | 1874–1878 |
| Hubert Joseph Walther Frère-Orban | 1878–1884 |
| Jules Malou (2nd time) | 1884 |
| Auguste Marie François Beernaert | 1884–1894 |
| Jules Philippe Marie de Burlet | 1894–1896 |
| Paul de Smet de Nayer (1st time) | 1896–1899 |
| Julius Vandenpeereboom | 1899 |
| Paul de Smet de Nayer (from 1900, Paul, | |
| comte de Smet de Nayer) (2nd time) | 1899–1907 |
| Jules de Trooz | 1907–1908 |
| Frans Schollaert | 1908–1911 |
| Charles, baron de Broqueville (1st time) | |
| (1914–18 in exile) | 1911–1918 |
| Gerhard Cooreman | 1918 |
| Léon Delacroix | 1918–1920 |
| Henri, comte Carton de Wiart | 1920–1921 |
| Georges Theunis (1st time) | 1921–1925 |
| Aloys, Burgrave van de Vyvere | 1925 |
| Prosper, vicomte Poullet | 1925–1926 |
| Henri Jaspar | 1926–1931 |
| Jules Renkin | 1931–1932 |
| Charles, comte de Broqueville (2nd time) | 1932–1934 |
| Georges Theunis (2nd time) | 1934–1935 |
| Paul van Zeeland | 1935–1937 |
| Paul Emile Janson | 1937–1938 |
| Paul Henri Spaak (1st time) | 1938–1939 |
| Hubert Pierlot (1940–45 in exile) | 1939–1945 |
| Achille van Acker (1st time) | 1945–1946 |
| Paul Henri Spaak (2nd time) | 1946 |
| Achille van Acker (2nd time) | 1946 |
| Camille Huysmans | 1946–1947 |
| Paul Henri Spaak (3rd time) | 1947–1949 |
| Gaston Eyskens (1st time) | 1949–1950 |
| Jean Pierre Duvieusart | 1950 |
| Clovis Louis Marie Emmanuel Joseph Pholien | 1950–1952 |
| Jean Marie van Houtte | 1952–1954 |
| Achille van Acker (3rd time) | 1954–1958 |

| | |
|---|---|
| Gaston Eyskens (2nd time) | 1958-1961 |
| Thiodore Lefhvre | 1961-1965 |
| Pierre Charles Josi Marie Harmel | 1965-1966 |
| Paul Vanden Boeynants (1st time) | 1966-1968 |
| Gaston Eyskens (3rd time) | 1968-1972 |
| Edmond Leburton | 1973-1974 |
| Gaston Eyskens (3rd time) | 1968-1972 |
| Edmond Leburton | 1973-1974 |
| Léo Tindemans | 1974-1978 |
| Paul Vanden Boeynants (2nd time) | 1978-1979 |
| Wilfried Martens (1st time) | 1979-1981 |
| Mark Eyskens | 1981 |
| Wilfried Martens (2nd time) | 1981-1992 |
| Jean-Luc Dehaene | 1992-1999 |
| Guy Verhofstadt | 1999- |

## Governments (Cabinets) of Belgium since 1945

The Catholic Party was no longer called the Conservative or Catholic Party but in Flanders the Christian People' s Party and in Wallonia the Social Christian Party, or generically the Christian Democrats (CD).

| | |
|---|---|
| Achille van Acker<br>Feb. 1945–Feb. 1946 | Socialist- Liberal -CD |
| Paul Henri Spaak<br>Mar. 1946 | Socialist |
| Achille van Acker<br>Mar. –Jul. 1946 | Socialist—Liberal |
| Camille Huysmans<br>Aug. 1946–Mar. 1947 | Socialist—Liberal |
| Paul Henri Spaak<br>Mar. 1947–Nov. 1948 | CD—Socialist |
| Paul Henri Spaak<br>Nov. 1948–June 1949 | CD—Socialist |
| Gaston Eyskens<br>Aug. 1949–June 1950 | CD—Liberal |
| Jean Pierre Duvieusart<br>June–Aug. 1950 | CD |
| Joseph Pholien<br>Aug. 1950- Jan. 1952 | CD |

| | |
|---|---|
| Jean van Houtte | CD |
| Jan. 1952–Apr. 1954 | |
| Achille van Acker | Socialist—Liberal |
| Apr. 1954–Jun. 1958 | |
| Gaston Eyskens | CD |
| June–Nov. 1958 | |
| Gaston Eyskens | CD—Liberal |
| Nov. 1958–Mar. 1961 | |
| Théodore Lefèvre | CD—Socialist |
| Apr. 1961–July 1965 | |
| Pierre Harmel | CD—Socialist |
| July 1965- Feb. 1966 | |
| Paul Vanden Boeynants | CD -Liberal |
| Mar. 1966–Feb. 1968 | |
| Gaston Eyskens | CD—Socialist |
| June 1968–Nov. 1971 | |

From this point the parties fracture into Walloon and Fremish units and new parties are formed:

CVP-Christian People's Party (Flemish)
PLP-Liberal Party
PRL-Liberal Reformation Party
PSB-Socialist Party (French)
PSC-Social Christian Party (French)
PVV-Party for Freedom and Progress
BSP-Socialist Party (Flemish)
VB-Flemish Bloc
VLD-Flemish Liberals and Democrats—the Citizen's Party

| | |
|---|---|
| Gaston Eyskens | CVP-PSB-PSC-BSP |
| Jan.–Nov. 1972 | |
| Edmond Leburton | PSB-CVP-PVV-PSC-BSP-PLP |
| Jan. 1973–Jan. 1974 | |
| Léo C. Tindemans | CVP-PSC-PVV-PLP |
| Apr.1974–Oct. 1978 | |
| Paul vanden Boeynants | seats virtually unchanged |
| Oct. 1978–Apr. 1979 | |
| Dr. Wilfried Martens | CVP-PSC-SP-PS -FDF |
| Apr. 1979–Jan. 1980 | |

| Dr. Wilfried Martens | CVP-PSC-SP-PS |
| Jan. 1980–Apr. 1980 | |
| Dr. Wilfried Martens | PRL-PVV-CVP-PSC-SP-PS |
| May 1980–Oct. 1980 | |
| Dr. Wilfried Martens | CVP-PSC-SP-PS |
| Oct. 1980–Mar. 1981 | |
| Mark Eyskens | CVP-PSC-SP-PS |
| Apr. 1981–Sept. 1981 | |
| Dr. Wilfried Martens | PRL-PVV-CVP-PSC |
| Dec. 1981–Nov. 1985 | |
| Dr. Wilfried Martens | PRL-PVV-CVP-PSC |
| Nov. 1985–Oct. 1987 | |
| Dr. Wilfried Martens | CVP-PSC-SP-PS-VB |
| May 1988–Mar. 1992 | |
| Jean-Luc Dehaene | |
| March 1992–June 1999 | CVP-PSC-SP-PS |
| Guy Verhofstadt | |
| June 1999– | VLD-PRL-Greens |

# APPENDIX II

## *Leuven*

According to local legend Leuven (Louvain), which now has 85,000 inhabitants, grew up around a camp established by Caesar. A local guide once assured me that the remains in Sint Donatus Park were from the Roman wall. Actually the remains are of city ramparts constructed between the twelfth and fifteenth centuries. The first written references to the location date from the ninth century. The Vikings or Normans, who pushed their way up the coastal rivers including the Dijle, had an encampment in the area. Arnold of Carinthia defeated them. Around his castle on the Keizerberg the town began to grow. Around 1000 Lambert, the first count of Leuven, built a church, which was located on the site of the present Sint Pieter. At the end of the twelfth century Leuven became the capital of Henry II the Duke of Brabant. In the thirteenth century the town prospered with the cloth trade. With 50,000 inhabitants it was a very large city. During the fourteenth century there was a prolonged conflict between the city's citizens and the local nobles. The Old Guild Hall, the center for the town's powerful cloth guilds, was constructed between 1317 and 1345. Its baroque upper story was added in 1619 after the building had been donated to the university. When Wenceslas of Luxembourg acquired Brabant through marriage in 1356, he was forced by the guilds to sign a declaration of town rights, the *Blijde Inkomst*. In 1379 the guildsmen threw seventeen nobles from the Guild Hall onto the pikes of the crowd waiting below. Wenceslas responded quickly and brutally. Many guildsmen fled to England and the capital of Brabant was transferred to Brussels.

Nevertheless, the town was prosperous enough to erect the striking Stadhuis on the Grote Markt between 1448 and 1463. Because of financial difficulties the 230 large and 52 small niches were only furnished with statues between 1828 and 1850. The Stadhuis was built opposite Sint Pieterkerk, which was constructed between 1425 and 1497 on the site of two earlier Romanesque churches, both of which had been destroyed by fire. The towers of the earlier Romanesque church were removed in 1507. Grandiose Gothic towers were begun, the central tower was planned to rise

170 meters, which would have surpassed the spire of the Ulm cathedral, at that time the world's highest structure, by nine meters.[1] However, due to the marshy ground the foundations eventually failed, and the project was abandoned in 1541. In the early 17th century the unfinished towers were reduced to roof level. The church was burned by the Germans in 1914 and the choir suffered bomb damage in 1944. Of interest are chapels eight and nine dedicated to St. Margaret of Leuven. Margaret was a servant at an inn. She was abducted by robbers who had killed her master and mistress. According to legend, after refusing to marry one of her abductors, she was murdered and thrown into the River Dijle. A series of paintings in the ninth chapel by Pieter Verhagen depict the events including her body which, according to legend, miraculously returned to the city by floating up-river. The fourteenth chapel contains the *Triptych of the Last Supper* painted by Dirk Bouts. From the fifteenth century Burgundian interior in the painting two windows look out on none other than Leuven's Grote Markt.

The university, founded in 1425, became central to the history and life of the city. This was the first university established in the Low Lands. Despite the importance of the cathedral school at Liège in the eleventh and twelfth century it did not develop into a university. A number of possible explanations have been offered for this deficiency. The political fragmentation of the Low Lands, their small size in comparison to France or Germany, and the high importance of commercial capitalism have all been cited as reasons.[2] However, once established the university at Leuven initially flourished. Among the scholars at Leuven were Erasmus, Mercator, and the future Pope Adrian VI. Jansenius was head of the Dutch College from 1618 to 1636. His tower was built in 1616 on the remains of the 12th century town wall. The counter-reformation, however, had a stultifying impact upon the university and the anti-clerical French agents of the revolutionary Directory closed it in 1797. After the defeat of Napoleon and the unification of the old Austrian Netherlands with the Netherlands proper, the Dutch set up a secular college in 1817. Its character, however, was offensive to the Catholic clergy. After the independence of Belgium, a Catholic university was reestablished in Mechelen in 1833 and returned to Louvain in 1835. In 1970 the nationalities struggle between the Flemish and the Walloons led to the division of the university. A French speaking university, Louvain-la-Neuve, was set up at Ottinges, 28 kilometers south of Leuven; the university in the city of Leuven became the Catholic University of Leuven, a Flemish speaking institution.

In the eighteenth century the building of a canal from Leuven to Rupel gave Leuven access to the canal and river systems of Belgium. In addition the Austrians also built paved roads to connect Leuven with Brussels and other cities. The canal spurred the growth of Leuven's Artois brewery and the city experienced a rapid growth in population. The most important economic development of the nineteenth century was the linking of Leuven to Belgium's developing rail system. A station was built on the ring road, where the last city wall had been, and a new avenue, today called the Bondgenotenlaan, was constructed to connect the station with the Grote Markt.

Leuven possesses one of the most impressive béguinages, the Groot Begijnhof, founded before 1232 along two branches of the Dijle outside the first city wall, which was erected in the 1100s. Béguinages were self-contained lay sisterhoods. The name has been ascribed to St. Begga, the daughter of Pepin of Landen, but stems more probably from Lambert le Bègue. Lambert, a Liège priest, who died in 1187, devoted himself to the bereaved families of crusaders. He encouraged the establishment of communities for widows and other women, who could have the support of a religiously oriented community life without taking vows.

The béguinage in Leuven was on the village model in contrast to the Bruges béguinage constructed around a court or yard. It was located in an area called "Ten Hove" near the Wolvenpoort, or Wolves' Gate. After the second city wall was constructed in the 1300s the area became part of Leuven proper. The architectural style of the béguinage today is predominantly seventeenth century, when the community reached its peak of approximately 300 members. The French Revolution destroyed the béguinage as a living community. The Belgian Social Welfare Council, which had inherited the complex, sold it to the university in 1962. The university renovated the property, which had fallen into disuse, and now uses it for student and faculty housing.

The agents of revolutionary France also closed Park Abbey, an abbey of the Premonstraten order, established in 1129 by Godfrey of Brabant. Monks returned to the abbey in 1836, after Belgium gained its independence from the Netherlands. The abbey church was built in Romanesque style in the thirteenth century, but was redone in Baroque style in 1729. The abbey buildings date from the seventeenth and eighteenth centuries, the restored gate dates to 1722, and the farm buildings from the late seventeenth century.

The Chateau of Arenberg (Heverlee) built in 1511 is located in a park on the outskirts of the city. Faced with its expropriation as part of German war reparations, its owner, a German duke, presented it to the University in 1921. Today the chateau houses university offices and university buildings have been constructed on the grounds of the old estate.

In addition to architectural treasures and the university, Leuven is also famous for its beer. Some call it "the beer capital of Belgium."[3] It is the site of the largest brewery in Belgium, the maker of "Stella Artois." The brewery first appeared in ducal levy records as *Den Horen* (The Horn) in 1366. By 1537 the brewery had become the most important industry in Leuven. In 1717 the master brewer, Sebastien Artois, ran the operation. It passed from father to son in the Artois family for more than a century. Around the beginning of the twentieth century the brewery began producing a low fermentation golden pils. In 1926 the brewery began producing a barley beer and called it *Stella* or star. Leuven is also home to a mini-brewery, Domus, which is unique in Belgium because of the pipeline connecting its vats with the taps in its next-door bar. Leuven is not only a beer capital, in January 1995 when the province of Brabant was divided into Flemish and French-speaking sections, Leuven became the capital of Flemish Brabant (Vlaams Brabant).

# Notes

## Chapter 1

1. Derek Blyth, *Flemish Cities Explored* (London: Pallas Athene, 1998), 14.
2. L.J.R. Milis, "A Long Beginning: The Low Countries through the Tenth Century," in *History of the Low Countries*, edited by J.C.H. Blom and E. Lamberts (New York: Berghahn Books, 1999), 7–8.
3. Lamberts, 10.
4. Patricia Carson, *Flanders in Creative Contrasts* (Leuven: Davidfonds, 1989), 37.
5. Pieter Geyl, *The Revolt of the Netherlands (1555–1609)* (London: Ernest Benn Limited, 1958), 26.
6. Geyl, 25. Another exception is the present-day north western corner of France which was long a predominantly Flemish speaking region.
7. Blyth, 15. Charles H. Haskins is correct in asserting that "the linguistic frontier has never coincided with a political frontier, and has never stood in the way of the formation of political groupings. The same holds true of the racial and geograpic divisions." Haskins, "Belgian Problems," Inquiry Document 207, 30 November 1918, M 1107, roll 43, National Archives. This was one of the reports prepared for Woodrow Wilson, the American president, in preparation of a post-World War I peace conference.
8. Milis, 6–7, and 10.
9. The third grandson, Louis the German, received the eastern section of Charlemagne's empire.
10. Milis, 20–21, and 25. Kas Deprez and Louis Vos, "Introduction," in *Nationalism in Belgium: Shifting Identities, 1780–1995*, edited by Kas Deprez and Louis Vos (New York: Macmillan, 1998), 1–2.
11. Victor J. Dossogne, "From Caesar to 1814," in *Belgium*, ed. by Jan-Albert Goris (Berkeley/Los Angeles: University of California Press, 1946), 16–17.
12. Geyl , 27.
13. Carson, 49.
14. Milis, 33. The villages created in cleared forest land can still be identified by the Flemish suffix -rode, and the French suffix -sart, or the more evident French suffix -bos(ch) and Flemish suffixes -hout and -woud. The bringing of new land into production produced a need for labor which led to an improvement of the conditions of peasants. They had traditionally been assigned thirty-five acres for their own needs.

By the end of the twelfth century peasants were granted written contracts stipulating their obligations which were greatly reduced. By the thirteenth century the arrangements often amounted to three-year contracts with set annual rent payments.

15. Milis, 28. For legal evolution see 40.
16. Milis, 30–31.
17. Milis, 28.
18. Arthur Frommer, A *Masterpiece Called Belgium* (New York: Prentice Hall, 1989), 220.
19. Kas Deprez and Louis Vos, "Introduction," 1.
20. Milis, 20.
21. Milis.
22. Milis, 25.
23. Milis, 50–51.
24. Derek Blyth, *Flemish Cities Explored* (London: Pallas Athene, 1998), 98.
25. Blyth, 16, quoting Matthew of Westminster.
26. W.P. Blockmans, "The Formation of a Political Union, 1300–1600," in *History of the Low Countries*, 80.
27. Blockmans, 60.
28. Frommer, 202–203.
29. Blockmans, 59.

## Chapter 2

1. Pieter Geyl, *The Revolt of the Netherlands (1555–1609)* (London:Ernest Benn Limited, 1958), 31.
2. W.P. Blockmans, "The Formation of a Political Union, 1300–1600," in *History of the Low Countries*, edited by J.C.H. Blom and E. Lamberts (New York: Berghahn Books, 1999), 61.
3. Hendrik Conscience, a Flemish romantic and outstanding proponent of Flemish cultural nationalism in the first half of the nineteenth century, published his *Lion of Flanders* in 1839. This book inspired the Flemish flag and anthem and popularized Breydel and De Coninck as Flemish national heroes. In 1867 a committee was set up in Bruges to erect a statue in their honor. When the municipal authorities intervened and set the date for the 1887 dedication on August 15, thousands of people assembled for a gigantic outpouring of Flemish national sentiment on the anniversary of the Battle of the Golden Spurs, July 11. They marched past the new statue and sang *The Flemish Lion* over and over. Shepard B. Clough, A *History of the Flemish Movement in Belgium: A Study in Nationalism* (New York: Richard R. Smith, 1930), 71 and 123.
4. Demand for Flemish woolen cloth had eventually outstripped local supplies of wool. The cloth producers of Flanders then turned to England for raw wool. The earliest reference to imports of English wool date from 1113. L.J.R. Milis, "A Long Beginning," in *History of the Low Countries*, 38.
5. W.P. Blockmans, 61.
6. Arthur Frommer, A *Masterpiece Called Belgium* (New York: Prentice Hall, 1989), 13–14.
7. Blockmans, 62.
8. Blockmans, 60.
9. Blockmans, 70.

10. Patricia Carson, *Flanders in Creative Contrasts* (Leuven: Davidfonds, 1989), 148. A statue of Jakob van Artevelde by Peter de Vigne-Quyo was unveiled in Ghent's Friday Market Square in 1863. Contrary to a popular image of van Artevelde as a democrat, David Nicholas writes that he "was actually a wealthy broker whose career fell within the framework of the political traditions and economic interests of the narrow elite that had governed Ghent during the thirteenth century." David Nicholas, *The van Arteveldes of Ghent: The Variety of Vendetta and Hero in* History (Ithaca, NY: Cornell University Press, 1988), x. Nicholas quotes Mollat and Wolff to the effect that van Artevelde was "the opposite of a people's man (. . .) although raised to power by an insurrection." Nicholas, xi, quoting Michel Mollat and Philippe Wolff, *The Popular Revolutions of the Late Middle Ages,* translated by A. L. Lytton-Sells (London: Allen & Unwin, 1973), 61.
11. Blockmans, 71
12. Blockmans, 70.
13. Carson, 148.
14. Nicholas, 30–32.
15. Nicholas, 117.
16. Nicholas, 189. Nicholas writes that "the refusal to recognize the Prince of Wales as count of Flanders was simply a pretext to cloak the enmities that his personal conduct, some of which must be difficult for the most persistent of van Artevelde partisans to excuse, had aroused in his city."
17. Nicholas, 190.
18. Blockmans, 70–1.

Chapter 3

1. W.P. Blockmans, "The Formation of a Political Union, 1300–1600," in *History of the Low Countries,* ed. by J.C.H. Blom and E. Lamberts (New York: Berghahn Books, 1999), 65–66. Estates-General will be used in this book to designate the representative bodies in individual duchies which brought together representatives of the nobles, the clergy, and the merchants and guildsmen. States-General will be used to indicate assemblies representing a number of duchies or other political units.
2. Victor J. Dossogne, "From Caesar to 1814," in *Belgium,* ed. by Jan-Albert Goris (Berkeley/Los Angeles: University of California Press, 1946), 117–118.
3. Pieter Geyl, *The Revolt of the Netherlands (1555–1609)* (London: Ernest Benn Limited, 1958), 29.
4. Geyl, 31.
5. Blockmans, 73. Another impact of the plague was the decimation of the scholars in the hard-hit religious communities and, as a result, the replacement in Flanders of a creative philosophy and theology, such as that of John of Ghent, by an imitative and stagnant scholasticism.
6. Patricia Carson, *Flanders in Creative Contrasts* (Leuven: Davidfonds, 1989), 57–61.
7. Derek Blyth, *Flemish Cities Expolred* (London: Pallas Athene, 1998), 100.
8. Blyth, 17.
9. Geyl, 29.
10. Geyl, 30.

11. Geyl, 32.
12. Blyth, 17.
13. Blockmans, 114.
14. Geyl, 32.
15. Geyl.
16. Geyl, 33.
17. Geyl, 30.
18. During his youth, Charles' aunt, Margaret of Austria, had served as governor-general in his name from Mechelen. Charles moved the administrative capital to Brussels in 1531.
19. Kas Deprez and Louis Vos, "Introduction," in Kas Deprez and Louis Vos, eds., *Nationalism in Belgium: Shifting Identities, 1780–1995* (New York: Macmillan, 1998), 2. L. Wils, *Histoire des nations belges. Belgique, Flandre, Wallonie: quinze siècles de passé commun* (Ottignies: Quorum, 1996), 65.
20. The Coudenberg Palace, which dated from the end of the eleventh century, burned in 1713. The present royal palace built by the Austrian Hapsburgs in the 1730s covers part of the site of the former Coudenberg.

Chapter 4

1. L.J.R. Milis, "A Long Beginning: The Low Countries through the Tenth Century,"in *History of the Low Countries*, edited by J.C.H. Blom and E. Lamberts (New York: Berghahn Books, 1999), 40. The "hanse"was at first a fee which merchants had to pay to trade in another city. Hanse eventually became trade organizations. The Flemish Hanse of London, controlled by Bruges, regulated trade between Flanders and England and Scotland. The Hanseatic League of the later Middle Ages controlled trade in the Baltic. It had warehouses in London and member cities from Bergen in Norway, Lübeck in Germany, to Riga in the eastern Baltic.
2. W.P. Blockmans, "The Formation of a Political Union,"in *History of the Low Countries*, 100.
3. L.J.R. Milis, "A Long Beginning," 48. Milis writes that "even in late medieval times, traders from Lübeck or anywhere in northern Germany had few problems understanding their counterparts in Deventer or Bruges. The case was probably similar in the southwest. As long as Calais or Saint-Omer remained Dutch speaking—which they did until the late Middle Ages—their inhabitants had relatively little difficulty communicating with the English across the Channel."
4. Blockmans, 108–109.
5. Arthur Frommer, *A Masterpiece Called Belgium* (New York: Prentice Hall, 1989),158–159.
6. Patricia Carson, *Flanders in Creative Contrasts* (Leuven: Davidfonds, 1989), 12–14.
7. The church completed in 1320 also contains the mausoleums of Charles the Bold, whose remains were ordered returned from his burial place near Nancy by Charles V, and Mary of Burgundy, who died five years after her father in 1482 after falling from her horse on a hunt.
8. See Frommer, 157–159.

9. Carson, 23.

10. Carson, 168.

11. Carson, 170.

12. H.W. Janson, *History of Art* (Englewood Clifffs, N.J.: Prentice-Hall, 1970), 290.

13. Janson.

14. Janson, He dismisses those who have questioned the very existence of Hubert.

15. Blockmans, 102.

16. Blockmans, 121–123.

17. Hieronymus Bosch (1474–1516), known particularly for his fantastic and indecipherable *The Garden of Delight* (c.1500), was born in 's Hertogenbosch and spent most of his life there. 's Hertogenbosch is now known as den Bosch and is located in the Netherlands.

18. Blockmans, 124.

19. Blockmans, 125–126. The building, which housed Erasmus' college, is located on an cul-de-sac off the Vismarkt in Leuven. At the beginning of the twenty–first century a restaurant, appropriately called *Drei Tongen*, occupied the building.

20. Frommer, 221.

21. Frommer, 220–222, and 235.

22. Milis, 44 and 47.

23. W. A. Olyslager, *The Groot Begijnhof of Leuven* (Leuven: Leuven University Press, 1983), 9.

24. Olyslager, 132–135.

## Chapter 5

1. W.P. Blockmans, "The Formation of a Political Union," in *History of the Low Countries*, ed. by J.C.H. Blom and E. Lamberts (New York: Berghahn Books, 1999), 131.

2. "Ce n'est qu'un tas de gueux" or "They are only a bunch of beggars."

3. Blockmans, 133.

4. Bruneel, "The Spanish and Austrian Netherlands, 1585–1780," in *History of the Low Countries*, 233.

5. Bruneel.

6. Blockmans, 129.

7. Vezio Melegari, "Antwerp," *The Great Military Sieges* (New York: Thomas Y. Crowell, 1972), 142–143.

8. Blockmans, 139–40.

9. A number of conditions were imposed upon Isabella and Albrecht, her husband. If they did not produce an heir the territory would return to Spain. If they had an heir, the king of Spain had to approve of his or her marriage. The archdukes had to be Catholic under pain of losing their territory. Their lands could not trade with Spanish America. Protestants were to be banned and, in particular, were forbidden the right to public services. Spain would continue to garrison specified fortresses and the king of Spain would appoint the governors of the Southern Netherlands. Finally, the archdukes were forced to promise to submit to the will of Philip II. Bruneel, 224.

10. Bruneel, 224–227.

11. Derek Blyth, *Flemish Cities Explored* (London: Pallas Athene, 1998), 15.

12. Blyth, 19.

13. Bruneel, 232.

14. Bruneel, 230–232. There were also some experiments with workhouses, but the funding was insufficient and as in England in the nineteenth century these did not prove to be a real solution to the problem of pauperism.

15. Patricia Carson, *Flanders in Creative Contrasts* (Leuven: Davidfonds, 1989), 162 and 171.

16. Bruneel, 234–6. Jansenism made its way to Ireland during the time of the Penal Laws of the 1600 and 1700s, when Irish students studied Theology in the Spanish or Austrian Netherlands.

17. Carson, 162.

18. St. Michael's in Leuven provides a magnificent example of a Baroque facade. Less successful, at least to my taste, is the cluttering of the interior of St. Baaf's in Ghent and the beautiful cathedral of Our Lady in Antwerp.

19. Vezio Melegari, "Maastricht," *The Great Military Sieges*, 154–156.

20. Vezio Melegari, "Namur," *The Great Military Sieges*, 162–165.

21. Arthur Frommer, *A Masterpiece Called Belgium* (New York: Prentice Hall, 1989), 41.

22. Victor J. Dossogne, "From Caesar to 1814," in *Belgium*, ed. by Jan-Albert Goris (Berkeley/Los Angeles: University of California Press, 1946), 117–118.

## Chapter 6

1. Jan Roegiers, "Belgian Liberties and Loyalty to the House of Austria," in Kas Deprez and Louis Vos, eds., *Nationalism in Belgium: Shifting Identities, 1780–1995* (New York: Macmillan, 1998), 24–5.

2. C. Bruneel, "The Spanish and Austrian Netherlands," in *History of the Low Countries*, edited by J.C.H. Blom and E. Lamberts (New York: Berghahn Books, 1999), 249.

3. Adrien de Meeüs, *History of the Belgians*. Tr. by G. Gordon (New York: Praeger, 1962), 224. Jan Craeybeckx points out that pauperism was not unique to the Austrian Netherlands. He writes, "before the Industrial Revolution the great bulk of the population of Europe lived on the brink of or even below the minimum subsistence level." Craeybeckx, "The Brabant Revolution: A Conservative Revolution in a Backward Country?" *Acta Historiae Neerlandica*, IV (1970): 64–5.

4. Craeybeckx, 50, quoting A. D. Gomicourt, who wrote as Dervial, *Le voyageur dans les Pays-Bas autrichiens* (Amsterdam, 1782), I:9.

5. Craeybeckx, 63.

6. Bruneel, 255–256. Maria Theresa's governor-general, Charles of Lorraine, was a dedicated francophile and French was the language of the court in Brussels. With the spread of French ideas, tastes, and fashions after mid-century the ability to speak French became increasingly a symbol of social status.

7. Quoted by Adrien de Meeüs, 224.

8. De Meeüs, 225.

9. De Meeüs, 229–230.

10. Roegiers, 23–24.

11. Due to Amiot's influence, Maria Elizabeth threw her support behind Pope Clement XI's 1713 condemnation of Jansenism. Students at the University of Leuven were

forced to take an oath against Jansenism, and the Catholic Church in the Austrian Netherlands became Ultramontanist, that is obedient to the directives of the pope. See Bruneel, 251.

12. Bruneel, 248.
13. Bruneel, 255. See 252–255.
14. Janet Polansky, *Revolutions in Brussels 1783–1793* (Hanover, NH: University Press of New England, 1987), 35, quoting Maria Theresa to Joseph II, July 22, 1780 in A. von Arneth, *Briefe der Kaiserin Maria Theresa an Ihre Kinder und Freunde* (Vienna: 1881), I:3.
15. Ellen L. Evans, *The Cross and the Ballot: Catholic Political Parties in Germany, Switzerland, Austria, Belgium and the Netherlands, 1785–1985* (Boston: Humanities Press, 1999), 18.
16. De Meeüs, 237. According to Janet Polansky, 37, "the Belgians' unquestioning respect for privilege and their celebration of tradition clashed with his ideal. (. . .) [I]nstead of good laws, he found a myriad of legal customs varying from province to province, elaborate internal customs regulations. (. . .) Furthermore, the complex of local authorities and the Church inhibited the power of the central Austrian state."
17. Craeybeckx writes that "open and more or less general opposition to the government" occurred only when Joseph attempted to rationalize the administration and the judiciary. Craeybeckx, 50.
18. De Meeüs, 237.
19. Polasky, 34.
20. J. Roegiers and N.C.F. van Sas, "Revolution in the North and South," in *History of the Low Countries*, 289.
21. Despite general discontent with Joseph, the revolt was centered in the Third Estate, the middle class and the artisans. The risk of popular rebellion frightened the other Estates. Polasky, 81.
22. Craeybeckx, 50. However, Craeybeckx indicates that the peasants did not always oppose Joseph II. In 1788 a riot erupted at Schorisse and the area around Oudenaarde against the collection of taxes and feudal dues. The rioters in this case appealed to the Emperor against the provincial Estates and the local administrators. The same was true of wider disturbances in 1789 and 1790. Craeybeckx, 72–3.
23. "Billet mortuaire, " January 26, 1789, *Écrits politiques du XVIIIe siècle*, vol. 60, 367, Archives générales du Royaume, Brussels, quoted by Polasky, 84.
24. According to Van der Noot, these constitutional provisions "(. . .) contained only that which a good prince owed to his people: they have equity for their principal and justice for their foundation, which alone are the most solid and firm base of kingdoms, provide for the peace and tranquility of families, the happiness of the people, support for the throne and the glory of the prince." Polasky, 48, quoting Henri Van der Noot, "Mémoire sur les Droits du peuple brabançon," April 24, 1787, in *Révolution belge*, vol. 35, pam. 4, Bibliothèque Royale, Brussels.
25. According to Evans, 20, Vonck, the son of peasants, was a wholesale wine dealer. Craeybeckx, in his "The Brabant Revolution: A Conservative Revolution in a Backward Country?", 55, states that Vonck and his followers "(. . .) wanted to see a centuries-old self government adapted to the new economic and social structures; hence they were not opposed to any strengthening of the central government provided that it was not done at the expense of the sovereignty of the people."
26. Polasky, 121–123.

27. E.H. Kossmann, *The Low Countries, 1780–1940* (Oxford: At the Clarendon Press, 1978), 60. Its source was the 1776 Articles of Confederation of the United States of America, which were in turn influenced by the 1579 Union of Utrecht.

28. Evans, 20. See Craebeckx, 60–61.

29. According to Evans, 19, Vonck was a practicing Catholic opposed to Joseph's religious ordinances. A small group of Jacobin-style democrats within the Vonckist movement was anti-clerical, and Vonck in exile in France broke with them over this issue.

30. Craeybeckx, 81. Craeybeckx, 74–79, argues that it is not accurate to speak of a mobilization of the people by the Statists and Vonckists. He contends that in Ghent supporters of Third Estate championed the sovereignty of the people against the "Statists," and threw their support to the Austrians rather than be dominated by the noble and clerical leaders of the Estates of Flanders. He also asserts that support for the revolution was not general through the Southern Netherlands. The Land of Herve and Hainault supported the Emperor. While the Estates of Limburg were very anti-Austrian, the farmers and middle class of Limburg supported Joseph and the Austrians, who had protected the industry of that province and tolerated its numerous Protestants. In addition, many "enlightened" burgers in Flanders, Hainault, and Tournai were not at all displeased with the return of Austrian authority.

31. Roegiers and van Sas, 285–289. Roegiers and van Sas assert that the opposition between the clericals and anticlericals during the Brabantine Revolt "would have a lasting effect on the nation's political composition" and that the opposition between the two would become "the deepest divide in [Belgian] national politics." Following the collapse of the republic the democrats blamed the clericals for its failure. Roegiers and van Sas, 289.

32. W.P. Blockmans, "The Formation of a Political Union, 1300–1600," in *History of the Low Countries*, 64–65.

33. Blockmans, 65.

34. Patricia Penn Hilden, *Women, Work, and Politics: Belgium, 1830–1914* (Oxford: Clarendon Press, 1993), 88.

35. Craeybeckx, 53.

36. De Meeüs, 246.

## Chapter 7

1. Adrien de Meeüs, *History of the Belgians*, Tr. by G. Gordon (New York: Praeger, 1962), 253.

2. Sidney Pollard, *Peaceful Conquest: The Industrialization of Europe, 1760–1970* (Oxford: Oxford University Press, 1981), 87.

3. E.H. Kossmann, *The Low Countries 1780–1940* (Oxford: At the Clarendon Press, 1978), 68–71.

4. J. Roegiers and N.C.F. van Sas, "Revolution in the North and South," in *History of the Low Countries*, edited by J.C.H. Blom and E. Lamberts (New York: Berghahn Books, 1999), 291.

5. Lode Wils, "The Two Belgian Revolutions," in Kas Deprez and Louis Vos, eds., *Nationalism in Belgium: Shifting Identities, 1780–1995* (New York: Macmillan, 1998), 34–5.

6. Roegiers and van Sas, 292.

7. Philippe Raxhon, "Henri Conscience and the French Revolution," in *Nationalism in Belgium: Shifting Identities*, 72–3. Even the francophone writers of nineteenth century Belgium, in order to develop a Belgian literature distinct from French utilized Belgian themes which were in essence Flemish. Among them was a winner of the Nobel Prize for literature, Maurice Maeterlinck. Christian Berg, "The Symbolic Deficit. French Literature in Belgium and 19th Century National Sentiment," in *Nationalism in Belgium: Shifting Identities, 1780–1995*, 61 and 70.

8. Wils, 34–5.

9. Ellen Evans writes that Flemish in the eighteenth century "(. . .) was already in jeopardy. French was used more and more for official business in the Estates, and the Austrian government favored French over Flemish as the more prestigious and international tongue." Van der Noot and his followers, the nobility, and the upper clergy spoke French. She adds that during the French occupation "(. . .) Flemish almost ceased to be a written language altogether, being used mainly by the illiterate rural population and the lower clergy." Ellen L. Evans, *The Cross and the Ballot: Catholic Political Parties in Germany, Switzerland, Austria, Belgium and the Netherlands, 1785–1985* (Boston: Humanities Press, 1999), 20.

10. Roegiers and van Sas, 295.

11. Kas Deprez, "The Language of the Flemings," in *Nationalism in Belgium: Shifting Identities, 1780–1995*, 97.

12. Roegiers and van Sas, 295.

13. De Meeüs, 258.

14. Patricia Penn Hilden, *Women, Work, and Politics: Belgium, 1830–1914* (Oxford: Clarendon Press, 1993), 19.

15. J. Craeybeckx, "The Brabant Revolution: A Conservative Revolution in a Backward Country?" *Acta Historiae Neerlandica*, IV (1970), 65.

16. Arthur Frommer, *A Masterpiece Called Belgium* (New York: Prentice Hall, 1989), 221.

17. Penn Hilden, 7.

18. Penn Hilden, 8.

19. Penn Hilden, 19. See J. Dhondt, "Notes sur les ouvriers gantois à l'époque française," *Revue du Nord* 34 (1954): 313, 310.

20. Karl Marx and Friedrich Engles, *La Belgique des insurrections* (Paris: n.d.), 190.

21. Penn Hilden, 20.

22. De Meeüs, 260.

## Chapter 8

1. I would like to express my appreciation to Salem Press for its permission to reprint from *Chronology of European History* (Pasadena: Salem Press, 1997), ed. by John Powell, *pp.* 819–821 of my "Belgian Revolution of 1830." By permission of the publisher, Salem Press, Inc. Copyright, c. by Salem Press, Inc.

2. Charles H. Haskins, "Belgian Problems," Inquiry Document 207, November 30, 1918, M 1107, roll 43, National Archives.

3. John W. Rooney, *Revolt in the Netherlands: Brussels 1830* (Lawrence, KS: Coronado Press, 1982), 2.

4. Simon Schama, "The Rights of Ignorance: Dutch Educational Policy in Belgium 1815-30," History of Education, 1 (1972): 86.
5. Schama, 84.
6. In 1998 the university had 27,126 students, 2,330 of whom were non-Belgians, who came from 100 countries.
7. Patricia Carson, Flanders in Creative Contrasts (Leuven: Davidfonds,1989), 12; Shepard B. Clough, A History of the Flemish Movement in Belgium: A Study in Nationalism (New York: Richard R. Smith, 1930), 33-35.
8. Lode Wils, "The Two Belgian Revolutions," in Kas Deprez and Louis Vos, eds., Nationalism in Belgium: Shifting Identities, 1780-1995 (New York: Macmillan, 1998), 38-9.
9. Rooney, 15.
10. Ellen L. Evans, The Cross and the Ballot: Catholic Political Parties in Germany, Switzerland, Austria, Belgium and the Netherlands, 1785-1985 (Boston: Humanities Press, 1999), 24. Evans (22-23) quoting de Lamennais, Correspondance Générale (Paris: Armand Colin, 1973), 4. See Bernard Cook, "Lammennais, Félicité de," The Encyclopedia of 1848, ed. by James Chastain, <http://www.cats.ohiou.edu/~Chastain/>.

## Chapter 9

1. I would like to express my appreciation to Salem Press for its permission to reprint my "Belgian Revolution of 1830" from Chronology of European History (Pasadena: Salem Press, 1997), ed. by John Powell, pp. 819-821. By permission of the publisher, Salem Press, Inc. Copyright by Salem Press, Inc.
2. John W. Rooney, Revolt in the Netherlands: Brussels 1830 (Lawrence, KS: Coronado Press, 1982), 20.
3. Rooney, 22-23. Armand Julien, "La condition des classes laborieuses en Belgique, 1830-1930," Annales de la Société Scientifique de Bruxelles, ser. D, 55 (1935): 248 and 256.
4. Rooney asserts that the Belgian Revolution was a specifically Belgian affair. According to him "the effect that the July Revolution [in France] had on that in Brussels was minimal." Yet he admits that "news of the July Revolution in France brought great excitement in Brussels," and that placards had appeared on August 24 predicting that revolution would occur on the the the twenty-fifth. He also states that during the working class rioting shouts were raised for France and Napoleon II. Rooney, 24, 27, and 30.
5. "Sacred love of the Fatherland."
6. Rooney, 49-50 and 70-99.
7. Rooney, 85.
8. Rooney. However, Rooney (107) states that "help from the outside which was received by the Brussels streetfighter was minimal at best, while the participation of foreigners was virtually nonexistent."
9. Rooney, 86-87 and 110-117. Day laborers constituted the largest number of rebels, followed by workers in the building trades. Over half were single and 60 percent were Flemish speakers. Most resided in Brussels but over half had been born elsewhere. However, they were predominantly from towns of over 5,000 inhabitants. They were not from the peasantry. They came from levels of the working class which, especially if they were married, would have experienced a rather constant struggle to subsist.

Rooney drawing on Alan Kittell, "The Revolutionary Period of the Industrial Revolution: Industrial Innovation and Population Displacement in Belgium, 1830–1880," *Journal of Social History*, I (Winter 1967): 136–7, assumes that the bulk of those who had moved to Brussels were displaced linen weavers from Flanders, who had come to an expanding Brussels in hopes of eking out a living. Rooney, 113–4. If the street fighters numbered 1,700, that would have amounted to 1.65 percent of Brussels' population, which was 103,000.

10. Rooney, 87 and 100. Rooney wrote that "great significance must be attached to the role played by the Brussels street fighter in 1830, for it was he, at the moment of crisis, who won for Belgium its right to independence. During the critical September Days, he fought leaderless against an imposing army. What is surprising is that it was he and not the army who prevailed."

11. Rooney, 98. See 91–97. According to Rooney, Henri Pirenne is wrong in attributing the withdrawal of the royal forces to a ferocious rebel attack upon royal troops in the Parc. See Henri Pirenne, *Historie de Belgique* (Brussels, 1928–30), VI:403.

12. Rooney, 118–119.

13. Rooney, 107.

14. Rooney, 172. See 145–174.

15. Though this might well have been a problematic assertion for many other Catholics at this time, it was not for Belgian Catholic leaders influenced by de Lamennais, who had argued that "(. . .) popular sovereignty derives ultimately from God." Ellen Evans, *The Cross and the Ballot: Catholic Political Parties in Germany, Switzerland, Austria, Belgium and the Netherlands, 1785–1985* (Boston: Humanities Press, 1999), 25.

16. E. Lamberts, "Belgium since 1830," in *History of the Low Countries*, ed. by J.C.H. Blom and E. Lamberts (New York: Berghahn Books, 1999), 314.

17. Evans, 25.

18. In 1814 Leopold of Saxe-Coburg had married Princess Charlotte, the presumed heiress to the British crown. His sister was the mother of Victoria, and in the 1830s he played a key role in the marriage of his niece, Victoria, to his nephew, Albert of Saxe-Coburg.

19. Baron de Gruben, "Consolidation and Expansion of the Kingdom (1814–1914)," in *Belgium*, ed. by Jan-Albert Goris (Berkeley/Los Angeles: University of California Press, 1946), 38.

20. Lamberts, 316.

21. Evans, 25.

22. Cook, "Belgian Revolution of 1830."

Chapter 10

1. "*Haast en spoed is zelden goed.*"

2. Pope Gregory XVI in 1832 issued the encyclical *Mirari Vos*, in which he condemned the ideas of de Lamennais, and specifically denounced "(. . .) liberty of conscience, freedom of the press, revolution, separation of church and state, and alliance between Catholics and liberals." However, no specific mention of Belgium was made and the Belgian constitution was never specifically condemned. Archbishop Englbert Sterkx of Malines/Mechelen was able to convince Rome of the practical advantages of the constitution for the Church. Ellen L. Evans, *The Cross and the Ballot: Catholic Political*

*Parties in Germany, Switzerland, Austria, Belgium and the Netherlands, 1785-1985* (Boston: Humanities Press, 1999), 26. See Henri Haag, *Les origines du Catholicisme libéral en Belgique (1789-1839)* (Louvain: Bibliothéque de l'université, 1950), 216.

3. Patricia Carson, *Flanders in Creative Contrasts* (Leuven: Davidfonds, 1989), 165.

4. Carl Strikwerda, *A House Divided: Catholics, Socialists, and Flemish Nationalists in Nineteenth Century Belgium* (Lanham/Boulder/New York/London: Rowman & Littlefield, 1997), 27-28.

5. E. Lamberts, "Belgium since 1830," in *History of the Low Countries*, ed. by J.C.H. Blom and E. Lamberts (New York: Berghahn Books, 1999), 315. By 1840 seven colleges of the Jesuit order had been established. The number of male and female members of religious orders grew from less than 4,800 in 1829 to 12,000 in 1847 and 18,000 in 1866. Evans, 28 and 136.

6. Patricia Penn Hilden, *Women, Work, and Politics: Belgium, 1830-1914* (Oxford: Clarendon Press, 1993), 28.

7. Leopold, who resented the resistance of Belgian Catholic leaders to his effort to play a more significant role in the governing of the country, persuaded Pope Gregory XVI to send a Papal Nuncio, a personal representative, to the country to apply pressure on the local church and to appoint conservative bishops. As a result the leaders of the Belgian church became tied to the government and identified with social conservatism. Lamberts, 316.

8. Under the July Monarchy in France (1830-1848) approximately three percent of the adult males could vote. In Britain as a result of the Great Reform Bill of 1832 the right to vote was extended to six percent of the male population.

9. Baron de Gruben, "Consolidation and Expansion of the Kingdom (1814-1914)," in *Belgium*, ed. by Jan-Albert Goris (Berkeley/Los Angeles: University of California Press, 1946), 41.

10. David Shub, *Lenin: A Biography* (Baltimore: Penguin, 1966), 79.

11. Penn Hilden, 30.

12. Evans, 28 and 136. The law gave local authorities practically complete control over elementary education. In most locales this meant that clericals possessed control over both personnel and curriculum.

13. Brison D. Gooch and John W. Rooney, Jr., "Belgium in 1848," The Encyclopedia of 1848, edited by James Chastain, <http://www.cats.ohio.edu/ ~chastain/ac/ belgium. htm>.

## Chapter 11

1. Patricia Penn Hilden, *Women, Work, and Politics: Belgium, 1830-1914* (Oxford: Clarendon Press, 1993), 22.

2. Penn Hilden.

3. Demetrius C. Boulger, *Belgian Life in Town and Country* (New York: G.P. Putnam's Sons, 1904), 114.

4. Hubert Watelet, *Une Industrialisation sans dévéloppement: Le Bassin de Mons et le charbonnage du Grand-Hornu du milieu du XVIIIe siècle* (Ottawa: Editions de l' Université d' Ottawa, 1980), 454 and 256.

5. Georges Jacquemyns, *Histoire de la crise écomnomique des Flandres (1845-1850)* (Brussels: Maurice Lamertin, 1929), 13.

6. W.O. Henserson, *The Industrialization of Europe 1780-1914* (New York: Harcourt, Brace & World, 1969), 20. According to E.J. Hobsbawm, *The Age of Revolution: 1789-1848* (New York: The New American Library, 1962), 211, "the earliest and best-planned of these [railway] networks was the Belgian, projected in the early thirties, in order to detach the newly independent country from the (primarily waterborne) communications system based on Holland."

7. E. Lamberts, " Belgium since 1830," in *History of the Low Countries*, ed. by J.C.H. Blom and E. Lamberts (New York: Berghahn Books, 1999), 321.

8. Édouard Ducpétiaux, *De la condition physique et moral des jeunes ouvriers et des moyens de l' améliorer* (Brussels: Meline, Cans et compagnie, 1843), I:25–26 and 128–129.

9. Jacquemyns, 295 and 13–66. According to Jacquemyns " before the great distress of 1845, the misery of Flanders had become proverbial" (296). According to Édouard Ducpétiaux, due to the decline of the linen industry, misery had become "(. . .) permanent, hereditary and in certain locales it seemed to have become a chronic state; from that arises the label pauperism." Édouard Ducpétiaux, *Mémoire sur le paupérisme dans les Flandres* (Brussels: M. Hayez, 1850), x.

10. Hobsbawm, 244.

11. Penn Hilden, 50, 63, 42, and 61.

12. Boulger, 93 and 95.

13. Lamberts, 321.

14. Jürgen Kuczynski, *The Rise of the Working Class* (New York: McGraw-Hill, 1971), 57. Boulger, 96–97.

15. Penn Hilden, 24–25.

16. Hobsbawm, 359.

17. Hobsbawm, 361; Jacquemyns, 13–66 and 264–266. Due to the failure of its own crops, Belgium was forced to import 92,817,000 kilos of wheat in 1847 compared to 31,634,000 in 1845, and 46,897,000 kilos of rye in 1847 compared to 9,121,000 in 1845. Prices rose accordingly. A hectoliter of wheat, which cost 17.36 francs in 1844, brought 31.15 in 1847.

18. Jacquemyns, 210–215.

19. Ducpétiaux, *Mémoire sur le paipérisme*, 91.

20. Boulger, *Belgian Life in Town and Country*, 100.

21. Ducpétiaux, *Mémoire sur le paupérisme*, 81-2. Ducpétiaux offered a comprehensive program for the economic, social, and moral improvement of the working class in his *De la condition physique et moral des jeunes ouvriers et des moyens de l' améliorer*, II:313–320.

22. Denise De Weerdt, *En de vrouwen? vrouw vrouwenbeweging en feminisme en Belgie, 1830-1960* (Ghent: Masereelfonds, 1980), 22 in Penn Hilden, 58–59.

23. Jacquemyns, 298.

24. Jacquemyns, 283–288 and 302–303.

25. Jacquemyns, 321, 314–315.

26. Jacquemyns, 329. See 324–331.

27. Jacquemyns, 333.

28. Ducpétiaux, *Mémoire sur le paupérisme dans les Flandres*, 44. The numbers elsewhere were less dramatic, but in Ypres, they grew from 70 in 1845 to 250 in 1847, and in Kotrick from 116 to 331.

29. Ducpétiaux, *De la condition physique et moral des jeunes ouvriers et des moyens de l' améliorer*, I:433.

30. Eduard Ducpetiaux, *De l' état de l' instruction primare et populaire en Belgique* (Brussels: Maline, Cans and Co., 1838), II:357, 552–553, 8, 110, and 120.

31. Ducpétiaux, *De la condition physique et moral des jeunes ouvriersr*, I:305.

32. Boulger, 102.

33. Ducpétiaux, *De la condition physique et moral des jeunes ouvriers*, I:386–388 and 390.

34. Penn Hilden, 94, 71 and 76.

35. A model of one of the "modern and scientific" prisons can be viewed in the museum of the Gravensteen in Ghent. One of the actual "model" prisons is easily viewed from the ring road to the south of the station in Leuven.

36. Penn Hilden, 29.

37. Lamberts, 320.

38. Boulger, 128–131.

39. Boulger, 132.

40. Boulger, 133.

41. Boulger, 135.

42. Evans, 168.

43. Boulger, 96.

44. Lamberts, 321 and 335. Boulger wrote in 1904 "it is quite true that in regard to housing, the Belgian operatives were, until recently, very badly off. In the towns they occupied on the tenement system the older streets which fashion and respectability had long abandoned. Crowded together, under conditions which precluded all considerations of sanitation and even of decency, up side-streets or alleys, which the rest of the world carefully avoided, the quarters occupied by them presented all the repellant features of England's old rookeries. These may still be found in all of the great cities, but a movement of reform has been set on foot, and the communal authorities have commenced a campaign for purging them of these plague spots. The execution of these reforms must take a certain time, but already the displacement of the working classes from their restricted quarters to the suburbs, where workmen's cottages have been specially constructed for them, has to a certain extent taken place. In some towns more progress has been made than in others. For instance Brussels has carried the campaign of expulsion much further than Liége or Antwerp. This has been rendered possible by the excellent systems of tramways and light railways, which bring the workman to his place of labour rapidly and cheaply." 121–122.

45. Boulger, 124–125.

Chapter 12

1. Carl Strikwerda, *A House Divided: Catholics, Socialists, and Flemish Nationalists in Nineteenth Century Belgium* (Lanham/Boulder/New York/London: Rowman & Littlefield, 1997), 29.

2. Strikwerda.

3. Ellen L. Evans, *The Cross and the Ballot: Catholic Political Parties in Germany, Switzerland, Austria, Belgium and the Netherlands, 1785–1985)* (Boston: Humanities Press, 1999), 168.

4. Strikwerda, 2–3 and 13.
5. Strikwerda, 5–6.
6. Strikwerda, 11.
7. Strikwerda, 12–13.
8. Evans, 139.
9. Evans, 140 and 167.
10. Strikwerda, 31.
11. Evans, 140–141. See Julius Vuylsteke, "Introduction," to "A Brief Statistical Description of Belgium [1865–9]," Document 21, in Theo Hermans, Louis Vos, and Lode Wils, eds., *The Flemish Movement: A Documentary History, 1780–1990* (Atlantic Highlands, NJ: Athlone Press, 1992), 142.
12. Strikwerda, 32.
13. At the time of independence there were pronounced and proudly acknowledged variations in the dialects of French spoken in Charleroi, Liège, and Verviers, and even between the French of Charleroi and the Borinage. Likewise the Flemish of Ghent was noticeably distinct from that of Antwerp and of Leuven. Alexander B. Murphy, *The Regional Dynamics of Language Differentiation in Belgium: A Study in Cultural-Political Geography* (Chicago: University of Chicago, 1988). Kas Deprez writes that "only a small elite in Brussels and in the towns, in both Flanders and Wallonia, spoke standard French. The remainder spoke dialect (Flemish, Brabant, Limburg, Walloon and Picardy dialects)." Deprez, "The Dutch Language in Flanders," in *The Flemish Movement: A Documentary History*, 63–4.

  Charles H. Haskins says that "It was inevitable that at the outset French should have a decided advantage. The Flemish dialects had no literary common denominator, and Dutch was extremely unpopular as the language of the foreign government which had just been overthrown and of the officers whom it had appointed throughout the country. The leaders of the movement for independence spoke French, and the impulse for the movement had largely come from France, while French had behind it a long tradition of use by the upper classes and the bourgeoisie, and had been re-enforced by the legislation of the Napoleonic occupation. Some of the leaders openly favored French as the future language of the whole kingdom. Under these conditions for more than a generation French was the language of the middle and higher schools, the central administration, the army, the courts, and public life." Haskins, "Belgian Problems," Inquiry Document 207, 30 November 1918, M 1107, roll 43, National Archives.
14. Louis Vos, "Nationalism, Democracy, and the Belgian State," in Richard Caplan and John Feffer, eds. *Europe's New Nationalism: States and Minorities in Conflict* (New York/Oxford: Oxford University Press, 1966), 89–90.
15. Tony Judt, "Is there a Belgium?," *The New York Review*, December 2, 1999, 50.
16. Evans, 137.
17. Louis Vos, "The Flemish National Question," in Kas Deprez and Louis Vos, eds., *Nationalism in Belgium: Shifting Identities, 1780–1995* (New York: Macmillan, 1998), 84.
18. Patricia Carson, *Flanders in Creative Contrasts* (Leuven: Davidfonds, 1989), 260. According to Willem Verkade, "the language barrier became almost comparble to the colour bar in colonial societies." *Democratic Parties in the Low Countries and Germany* (Leiden: Universitaire Pers, 1965), 34.

19. Evans, 138.

20. F.A. Snellaert, "Report of the Commission established by the Royal Decree of 27 June 1856 to investigate and Recommend to the Government Appropriate Measures to Ensure the Development of Dutch Literature and Regulate the Use of the Dutch Language in Relation to Various Government Departments," Document 18 in *The Flemish Movement: A Documentary History*, 125–134.

21. Kas Deprez, "The Language of the Flemings," in *Nationalism in Belgium: Shifting Identities*, 98.

22. Kas Deprez, "The Language of the Flemings."

23. The Flemish Cultural Council adopted Dutch as the official language of the Flemish Community in 1973. In 1980 the Flemish Community signed a treaty with the Netherlands establishing the Dutch Language Union. However, Flemish and Netherlandic speakers of Dutch can quite easily be identified on the basis of their speech. Kas Deprez, "The Language of the Flemings," in *Nationalism in Belgium: Shifting Identities, 1780–1995*, 104–5. Deprez adds on p. 107 that "the Dutch do not identify with the Flemings and neither do the vast majority of the Flemings identify with the Dutch. As a result most Flemings refuse to speak like the Dutch." Yet, he admits that "Flemish is actually Dutch." And according to the *Flanders Fact Sheet* of the Ministry of the Flemish Community, "Dutch is spoken in Flanders. The very same language that is used in the Netherlands." (nr. 9, 1994, 14).

24. W.P. Blockmans, "The Formation of a Political Union," in *History of the Low Countries*, edited by J.C.H. Blom and E. Lamberts (New York: Berghahn Books, 1999), 124.

25. Shepard B. Clough, *A History of the Flemish Movement in Belgium: A Study in Nationalism* (New York: Richard R. Smith, 1930), 71 and 123.

26. Piet Couttenier, "National Imagery in 19th Century Flemish Literature," in *Nationalism in Belgium: Shifting Identities*, 57–9.

27. Clough, 105.

28. Clough, 105.

29. Piet Couttenier, "National Imagery in 19th Century Flemish Literature," in *Nationalism in Belgium: Shifting Identities*, 57–9. See the sketch of Gezelle's life and work in Clough, 102–106.

   Gezelle's most famous follower was another poet–priest, Hugo Verriest, who was a founder of the *Flemish Flag*, a Flemish student journal. Verriest's student, Albrecht Rodenbach, brought his contagious Flemish enthusiasm to the University of Leuven before dying in his mid–twenties in 1880. He drew his watchword from Conscience, "*Vliegt die blauwvoet, storm op zee*" (The gull flies, a storm is on the sea), and launched a Flemish student movement, *Blauwvoeterie*. Clough, 106–109.

30. Mercier, an important Belgian intellectual, who founded the Higher Institute of Philosophy at the University of Leuven, was a dedicated supporter of the French language.

31. Carson, 258–261. The bishops of Belgium at the end of the nineteenth century were overwhelmingly francophone and were "not inclined to modify the system of private francophone schools in Flanders, even to the extent of offering Flemish courses in them." Evans, 171. See Val R. Lorwin, "Linguistic Pluralism and Political Tensions in Modern Belgium," *Canadian Journal of History*, 5 (1970), 10.

32. Roland Renson, "Sport and the Flemish Movement. Resistance and Accommodation 1868–1914," in *Nationalism in Belgium: Shifting Identities, 1780–1995*, 123–4. A Cath-

olic Flemish Student Movement, inspired by but eventually repudiated by Gizelle because of their protest actions, was formed in the 1880s. Piet Couttenier, "National Imagery in 19th Century Flemish Literature," 59. In 1906 a Flemish sociologist, Lodewijk De Raet published *Over Vlaamsche Volkskracht* (On the Vitality of the Flemish People), in which he asserted that there was a direct connection between economic development and technical and the availability of higher education in a people's national language. Vos, "The Flemish National Question," 85.

33. Kas Deprez and Louis Vos, "Introduction," in Kas Deprez and Louis Vos, eds., *Nationalism in Belgium: Shifting Identities*, 8.
34. Vos, "The Flemish National Question," 84.
35. Vos, "Nationalism, Democracy, and the Belgian State," 90.
36. Vos, "Nationalism, Democracy, and the Belgian State," 90.
37. Tony Judt, "Is there a Belgium?," 50.
38. Baron de Gruben, "Consolidation and Expansion of the Kingdom (1814–1914)," in *Belgium*, ed. by Jan-Albert Goris (Berkeley/Los Angeles: University of California Press, 1946), 50.
39. Evans, 167.
40. Louis Vos, "The Flemish National Question," 85.
41. Clough, 176.
42. Clough
43. Clough, 178.
44. Clough.
45. E.H. Kossmann, *The Low Countries, 1780–1940* (Oxford: At the Clarendon Press, 1978), 378–380. My thanks to two of my students, Anne Finney and Coleen Schmidt, for bringing to my attention some of the information in this section on the Congo.
46. Adam Hochschild, *King Leopold's Ghost: A Story of Greed, Terror, and Heroism in Colonial Africa* (New York: Houghton Mifflin, 1998), 45 and 58.
47. Hochschild, 87.
48. Kossmann, 382, "(. . .) the Americans had not the slightest idea what Leopold was actually doing."
49. Kossmann, 383.
50. Kossmann, 382.
51. Kossmann, 384.
52. Samuel Nelson, *Colonialism in the Congo Basin* (Athens, OH: Center for International Studies, 1994), 84 and 165. Adam Hochschild, 116.
53. Morel, who worked for a Liverpool shipping company, was initially struck by the fact that ships arriving at Ostend from the Congo were full of ivory and rubber, but that they did not bring commodities back to the Congo. Instead, they were filled with weapons and soldiers. Hochschild, 2.
54. Kossmann, 394.
55. Jules Marchal quoted by John Miller, "Art of Darkness," *The Bulletin* (*The Newsweekly of the Capital of Europe*), 1 July 1999, 11. See Jules Marchal, *L'Etat libre du Congo: paradis perdu: l'histoire du Congo 1876–1900* (Borgloon: Bellings, 1996), and *E.D. Morel contre Léopold II: l'histoire du Congo, 1900–1910* (Paris: Harmattan, 1996).
56. Miller, "Art of Darkness," 11. Also E. Lamberts, "Belgium since 1830," in *History of the Low Countries*, 347.

57. Patricia Penn Hilden, *Women, Work, and Politics: Belgium, 1830-1914* (Oxford: Clarendon Press, 1993), 33.

58. Barbara Tuchman, *The Proud Tower: A Portrait of the World Before the War: 1890-1914* (New York: Macmillan, 1966), 490; Evans adds that it "(. . .) was probably the most relentlessly anticlerical of any socialist party of Europe." Evans, 167.

59. Strikwerda, 15.

60. Strikwerda, 34. In 1877, 80 percent of students left school before the age of 12. Carson, 204.

61. Strikwerda, 33.

62. Demetrius C. Bolger, *Belgian Life in Town and Country* (New York: Putnam, 1904), 262.

63. Penn Hilden, 7. See 4-7.

64. De Gruben, 49.

65. Bonnie S. Anderson, and Judith P. Zinsser, *A History of Their Own: Women in Europe from Prehistory to the Present* (New York: Oxford University Press, 2000), II:200. All adult women did not receive the right to vote in Belgium until 1948.

66. Lieve Gevers, "The Catholic Church and the Flemish Movement," in *Nationalism in Belgium: Shifting Identities*, 114.

67. Helleputte, a member of the Peoples League/League of Democratic Christians (a faction within the Catholic Party), became Minister of Agriculture in 1907. Evans, 170.

68. Evans, 169. Evans indicates that there are conflicting estimates of the strength of the Catholic and Socialist unions. Felix Morlion, "The History of Christianity in Belgium," in *Belgium*, ed. by Jan–Albert Goris, 223, wrote that the Catholic unions had 800,000 members in 1938, 100,000 more than the Socialist unions. Max Gottschalk, "Social Legislation" in Goris's *Belgium*, 189, stated that the strength of the Socialist unions in 1939 was 581,951 or 237,333 more than the Catholic unions. Evans suggested that Morlion included the membership of Catholic organizations, which Gottschalk did not regard as bona fide unions.

   At the end of World War II membership in the Catholic unions numbered around 340,000, about half the size of the socialist unions. By 1980, with a sizeable component of Flemish white as well as blue collar workers, they were slightly larger than the socialist unions. Evans, 253.

69. In fact, the Christian democratic National League of Christian Workers was the political arm of the Confederation of Christian Syndicates.

## Chapter 13

1. I would like to thank Garland Publishers for the permission to include in this section much of my "Belgium: Neutrality of," published in *The European Powers in the First World War: An Encyclopedia*, ed. by Spencer Tucker (New York: Garland Publishers, 1996), 118-119.

2. "The Von Schlieffen Plan," World War I Documentary Archive, <http://www.lib.byu.edu/~rdh/wwi/1914m/schlieffen.html>.

3. Niall Ferguson, *The Pity of War: Explaining World War I* (New York: Basic Books, 1999), 67.

4. "4 August, 1914 Origin of the Term 'A Scrap of Paper,'" *The World War Document Archive*, <http://www.lib.byu.edu/~rdh/wwi/1914/ paperscrap. html>.

5. John E. Rodes, *Germany: A History* (New York: Holt, Rinehart and Winston, 1964), 461–462; "The German Demand for Free-Passage through Belgium," *The Belgian Grey Book: Diplomatic Correspondence Respecting the War, July 24–August 29, 1914*, No 21, <http:// www.lib.byu.edu/~rdh/wwi/papers/belgrey.html> "The Response of the Belgian Government," *The Belgian Grey Book*, No. 22, <http://www.lib.byu.edu/~rdh/wwi/papers/belgrey.html>4 August, 1914, The Imperial Chancellor Defends the Invasion of Belgium," *The World War Document Archive*, <http://www.lib.byu.edu/~rdh/wwi/ 1914/theobelg.html>.

6. Ferguson, 170–171, and 287–288.

7. Bethmann-Hollweg's speech of August 4 to the Reichstag. See Ernst Müller-Meiningen, *Who are the Huns? The Law of Nations and its Breakers* (New York: Stechert, 1915), 4–5; John F.V. Keiger, *France and the Origins of the First World War* (New York: St. Martin's Press, 1983), 339.

8. Quoted by David A. Boileau, *Cardinal Mercier: A Memoir* (Leuven: Peeters,1996), 194. See Mercier's courageous denunciation of the German occupiers of Belgium, his December 1914 pastoral *Patriotism and Endurance*, in David A. Boileau, *Cardinal Mercier*, 383–393.

9. Georges Theunis, "In the First World War" in *Belgium*, ed. by Jan-Albert Goris (Berkeley/Los Angeles: University of California Press, 1946), 55.

10. Charles H. Haskins, "Belgian Problems," Inquiry Document 207, 30 November 1918, M 1107, roll 43, National Archives.

11. "King Albert's Speech to the Belgian Nation," *World War One Document Archive*, 1914, <http://www.lib.byu.edu/~rdh/wwi/ 1914/alberto. html>.

12. Spencer Tucker, *The Great War 1914–18* (Bloomington: University of Indiana Press, 1998), 95.

13. "General Leman's Account of the Fall of Liège," *The World War I Document Archive*, <http://www.lib.byu.edu/~rdh/wwi/ 1914/liege. html>.

14. Henri Pirenne, *La Belgique et la Guerre Mondiale.* (Paris: Les Presses universitaires de France, 1928), 44.

15. Pirenne, 45.

16. Pirenne.

17. E.H. Kossmann, *The Low Countries 1780–1940* (Oxford: At the Clarendon Press, 1978), 519.

18. G.L. McEntee, *Military History of The World War* (New York: Charles Scribner's Sons, 1943), 16–17.

19. Arnold J. Toynbee, *The German Terror in Belgium: An Historical Record* (New York: George H. Doran Co, 1917), 88.

20. For a contemporary account from the *New York Times* see *The World War I Document Archive 1914*, <http://www.lib.byu.edu/~rdh/ wwi/1914/louvburn.html>.

21. In this battle the French and the British thwarted the von Schlieffen Plan and thus prevented a German victory in World War I.

22. John Keagan, *The First World War* (New York: Alfred A. Knopf, 1999) 128.

23. Charles H. Haskins, "Belgian Problems," Inquiry Document 207.

24. Tucker, 95.

25. Georges Theunis, "In the First World War," 60.

26. In Flanders Fields Museum. Ypres.

27. B.H. Liddell Hart, *The Real War 1914-1918*. (Boston: Little, Brown, and Co., 1930), 68.

28. Adapting John McCrae's "In Flanders Fields."

29. Due to the circuitous route of the trench lines they stretched approximately 450 miles from the North Sea to Switzerland.

30. James L. Stokesbury. *A Short History of World War I*. (New York: William Morrow and Co., 1981), 95.

31. As early as October 1914 the Germans had sprayed French trenches with petroleum and then ignited it with incendiary bombs. In a dress rehearsal on February 26, 1915, they tried out bona fide flamethrowers against the French on the Verdun front. The Hooge attack on the night of July 29-30, 1915, was the first tactical use of flame-throwers and it was very successful. According to Michael Dewar, "the Germans had achieved complete surprise, and the employment of flamethrowers was not only to-tally effective within the limited area in which they were used, but also terrorized the troops in the peripheral area of the attack." Michael Dewar, "The First Flame At-tacks," in *Tanks and Weapons of World War I*, ed. By Bernard Fitzsimons (New York: Beekman House, 1973), 50.

32. Stokesbury, 95.

33. Tucker, 139

34. Tucker.

35. "Eyewitness accounts of the Great War," *Guide to Quotations in Flanders Fields Museum* (Ieper: Flanders' Fields Museum, 1999), 13.

36. "Eyewitness accounts of the Great War," 13-14.

37. "Eyewitness accounts of the Great War," 14.

38. Adolf Hitler, *Mein Kampf* (Boaston: Houghton Mifflin, 1971), 201.

39. Keegan, 31, lists Hitler's regiment as the 6th Bavarian Reserve Regiment.

40. Hitler, *Mein Kampf*, 163.

41. Hitler, 201.

42. Hitler, 202. Joachim C. Fest, *Hitler* (New York: Harcourt Brace Jovanovich,1974), 67 and 77.

43. Martin Gilbert, *Atlas of the First World War*. (London: Dorset, 1984), 58.

44. His work can be seen at the Imperial War Museum in London.

45. Eye witness accounts of the Great War, *Guide to Quotations In Flanders Fields Museum*, 28.

46. The web site of the Imperial War Museum, *http://www.iwm.org.uk/online/fww_rem/fww-art5.htm*, accessed March 22, 2001. My thanks to Williamson's son, Paul Wil-liamson, for permission to quote this passage from his father's archives.

47. Keagan, 131 and 359. See Jünger's *Storm of Steel*. Introduction by R. H. Mottram. (New York: H. Fertig, 1975).

48. Tucker, *The Great War 1914-18*, 198.

49. I would like to thank Garland Publishers for the permission to include in this section much of my "Belgium: Occupation of, 1914-18," published in *The European Powers in the First World War: An Encyclopedia*, ed. by Spencer Tucker (New York: Garland Pub-lishers, 1996), 119-120.

50. John Horne and Alan Kramer, "German 'Atrocities' and Franco-German Opinion, 1914: The Evidence of German Soldiers' Diaries," *Journal of Modern History*, 66 (March 1994): 16. They wrote "the official German case that the Belgians in particu-

lar had fought a savage but coordinated irregular war may have been a genuine belief or a cynical cover for preemptive action against the civilian population. It was certainly invoked by the commanders of the three main armies that swept through central and southern Belgium to justify what they admitted were harsh measures."

51. Nicoletta F. Gullace, "Sexual Violence and Family Honor: British Propaganda and International Law during the First World War," *American Historical Review*, 102 (June 1997), 3:731–732. Gerhard Von Glahn, *Law among Nations: An Introduction to Public International Law*, 4th ed. (New York: Macmillan, 1981), 219

52. J. Bédier, *Les crimes allemandes d'après témoinages allemands* (Paris: A. Colin, 1915), 10–11, 12, and 26. John Horne and Alan Kramer, "German 'Atrocities,'" 7 and 11.

53. John Horne and Alan Kramer, "German 'Atrocities,'" 22. Henri Pirenne, *La Belgique et la guerre mondiale*, 64.

54. Kossmann, 525.

55. Charles H. Haskins, "Belgian Problems."

56. Ellen L. Evans, *The Cross and the Ballot: Catholic Political Parties in Germany, Switzerland, Austria, Belgium and the Netherlands, 1785–1985* (Boston: Humanities Press, 1999), 171.

57. Charles H. Haskins, "Belgian Problems." Ellen L. Evans, *The Cross and the Ballot*, 173; Shepard B. Clough, *A History of the Flemish Movement in Belgium: A Study in Nationalism* (New York: Richard R. Smith, 1930), 189, names a physician, R. Speleers, as the rector of the university.

58. "Memorandum: The Content of the Inquiry," Inquiry, Document 885, M 11.07, roll 43, National Archives.

59. Clough, 200–205.

60. Charles H. Haskins, "Belgian Problems."

61. Louis Vos, "Nationalism, Democracy, and the Belgian State," in Richard Caplan and John Feffer, eds. *Europe's New Nationalism: States and Minorities in Conflict* (New York/ Oxford: Oxford University Press, 1966), 91.

62. "Council of Flanders: Declaration of Independence," Doc. 34 in Theo Hermans, Louis Vos, and Lode Wils, eds., *The Flemish Movement: A Documentary History, 1780–1990*. (Atlantic Highlands, NJ: Athlone Press, 1992), 238–239. See Shepard B. Clough, *A History of the Flemish Movement in Belgium*, 198.

63. Charles H. Haskins, "Belgian Problems."

64. The members of the Council of Flanders fled to Germany at the end of the war. Ellen L. Evans, *The Cross and the Ballot*, 173.

65. Evans, 172. When the Belgian government introduced conscription in 1913, it had exempted workers in strategic industries. Since Belgian industry, at the time, was concentrated in the francophone parts of the country, it has been estimated that up to 80 percent of the Belgian soldiers were Flemish speakers, commanded by a francophone officer corps.

66. In Flanders Fields Museum display "Life at the Front." See also Henri Pirenne, 209–228.

67. "Eye witness accounts of the Great War,"*Guide to Quotations In Flanders Fields Museum*, 3–4.

68. "Eye witness accounts of the Great War," 4. See Adiel Debeuckelaere, "Open Letter to the Belgian King Albert I," Document 35 in Theo Hermans, Louis Vos, and Lode Wils, eds., *The Flemish Movement: A Documentary History*, 227–237.

69. In Flanders Fields Museum display "Life at the Front."
70. Charles H. Haskins, "Belgian Problems."
71. A German proclamation of November 15, 1916 had stated "The German Authority informs the population that it will force civilians to work, if there are not enough voluntary workers." Those refusing work would be sent to prison or be placed in labor battalions. Poster "Avis Relatif au travail volontaire exigé des Civils," in the Photographic Archive of the Imperial War Museum, London, Q33040.
72. Kossmann, 533.
73. Bernard Cook, "Belgium: Occupation of," in *The European Powers in the First World War: An Encyclopedia*, 119–120.
74. S. William Halperin, *Germany Tried Democracy, A Political History of the Reich from 1918 to 1933* (New York: W.W. Norton & Co., 1974), 91–92.
75. Elizabeth D. Schafer, "Albert I, King of Belgium," *The European Powers in the First World War*, 33–34; Evans, 172–173.

## Chapter 14

1. Jan-Albert Goris, "Belgium between the Two World Wars," in *Belgium*, ed. by Jan-Albert Goris (Berkeley/Los Angeles: University of California Press, 1946), 66.
2. Goris, 66–67.
3. E. Lamberts, "Belgium since 1830,"in *History of the Low Countries*, edited by J.C.H. Blom and E. Lamberts (New York: Berghahn Books, 1999), 351.
4. Louis Vos, "The Flemish National Question,"in Kas Deprez and Louis Vos, eds., *Nationalism in Belgium: Shifting Identities, 1780–1995* (New York: Macmillan, 1998), 87.
5. According to Vos, the VNV was influenced by nineteenth century West Flanders Catholic traditionalism. The VNV wished to replace Liberalism and democracy with a Catholic New Order. Louis Vos, "The Flemish National Question," 89. In 1931 the *Frontpartij* also spawned a fascist off-shoot *Verdinaso* (*Verbond van Dietsche Nationaal-solidaristen*, The League of Dutch National Solidarity), led by Joris Van Severen. Van Severen was arrested on May 10, 1940, on the order of the minister of justice, Paul-Emile Janson, along with 2,000 to 3,000 Belgians suspected of being potential collaborators with the invading Germans. As the Germans over-ran Belgium he was transferred to a French prison where he and 20 others were executed on May 20. Martin Conway, *Collaboration in Belgium: Léon Degrelle and the Rexist Movement* (New Haven, CN: Yale University Press, 1993), 28.
6. Louis Vos, "The Flemish National Question,"88.
7. Vos.
8. Lamberts, "Belgium since 1830," 362.
9. Conway, *Collaboration in Belgium*, 8.
10. Bonnie S. Anderson, and Judith P. Zinsser, *A History of Their Own: Women in Europe from Prehistory to the Present* (New York:Oxford University Press, 2000), II:200. All adult women did not receive the right to vote in Belgium until 1948.
11. In 1921 the Catholic party recognized that it contained quite distinct socio-economic and linguistic factions. It reorganized itself as the Catholic Union, consisting of the conservative and francophone Federation of Catholic Circles and of Workers' Associations, the Christian democratic and Flemish National League of Christian Work-

ers, the political arm of the Confederation of Christian Syndicates, the Federation of Farmers' Associations, itself divided between the small Walloon *Alliance agricoles* and the Fremish *Boerenbond*, and the Christian Federation of Middle Classes. In 1936 the fractured Catholic Union confronting the success of Belgian fascists reorganized into the Belgian Catholic Bloc, which consisted of the Catholic Flemish Federation and the Catholic Social Party. Ellen L. Evans, *The Cross and the Ballot: Catholic Political Parties in Germany, Switzerland, Austria, Belgium and the Netherlands, 1785-1985* (Boston: Humanities Press, 1999), 174-175.

12. Lamberts, "Belgium since 1830,"358 and 360.

13. Lamberts, 352.

14. Conservative Catholics were not placated by greater state support for Catholic primary education. Women were granted the right to vote in local elections but both Socialists and Liberals feared that granting women the right to vote for the parliament would have resulted in a stronger Catholic vote.

15. Mark Mazower, *Dark Continent: Europe's Twentieth Century* (New York: Penguin, 1998), 22-24.

16. Lamberts, "Belgium since 1830,"315.

17. Lamberts, 354.

18. Conway, *Collaboration in Belgium*, 12.

19. Conway. Support for the Catholic party dropped from 38.5 percent in the 1932 election to only 27.6 in the 1936 election.

20. Conway, 16.

21. Conway, 18.

22. Conway, 17-18. Degrelle envisioned himself involved in a struggle for a "New European Order" against a corrupt democratic order, Marxism, and "the occult forces of freemasonry and Jewish finance." Conway, 17. Degrelle, though arrested and deported to France in May 1940, survived, was discovered by colleagues in a Vichy detention camp in the south of France, was released, and returned to Brussels on July 30, 1940. Conway, 28. Ellen L. Evans, *The Cross and the Ballot*, 176; David Zabecki, "Degrelle, Léon," in *World War II in Europe: An Encyclopedia*, ed. by David Zabecki, (New York: Garland, 1999), 274. See Martin Conway, "'Building the Christian Community': Catholics and Politics in Interwar Francophone Belgium," *Past and Present*, 128 (1990), 117-151; J.-M. Etienne, "Les origines du rexisme," *Res Publica*, IX (1967), 87-110; and Martin Conway, *Collaboration in Belgium*, 8-20.

The Rexists in 1936 won 16 of their 21 seats in direct contests with the Catholic party. The Rexists were particularly strong in Wallonia with 15.6 percent of the vote. They won 18.5 percent in Brussels but only 7.01 in Flanders. The weakness of the Rexists in Flanders was off set by the strength in Flanders of the Flemish National Alliance with which it agreed upon the need for the division of Belgium into two administrative units under an authoritarian government. Ellen L. Evans, *The Cross and the Ballot*, 176.

23. Conway, *Collaboration in Belgium*, 5.

24. Janson died in the Nazi concentration camp Buchenwald in 1944.

25. Evans connects the decline of the Rexists to the international situation: the distaste of francophone Belgians for Hitler and Franco and concern over the *Anschluss* of March 1938 in which Hitler took over Austria, led by the Catholic authoritarian

traditionalist Kurt von Schuschnigg. Ellen L. Evans, *The Cross and the Ballot*, 177. After the repudiation by Cardinal van Roey the Rex movement had increasingly mimicked foreign fascists. It won only 4.43 of the national vote in 1939, but won 7.58 in Liège and 12.74 in the province of Luxmbourg. Conway, *Collaboration in Belgium*, 14.

26. Conway, *Collaboration in Belgium*, 13–4.
27. Conway, 16.

## Chapter 15

1. *Trial of the Major War Criminals before the International Military Tribunal: The Judgment* (Nuremberg: The International Military Tribunal, 1947), 30. See "The Invasion Of Belgium, The Netherlands and Luxemburg," The Nizkor Project, <http://www.nizkor.org/hweb/imt/ tgmwc/judgment/j-invasion-belgium.html>.

2. *Trial of the Major War Criminals before the International Military Tribunal: The Judgment*, 30. See "The Invasion Of Belgium, The Netherlands and Luxemburg," The Nizkor Project. The full text of Hitler's briefing can be found in German in *Trial of the Major War Criminals before the International Military Tribunal*, Vol. XXVI, 334–5.

3. *Trial of the Major War Criminals before the International Military Tribunal*, vol. II, 202. See " Session 15, December 7, 1945 (Part 1 of 9)," The Nizkor Project, < http://www.nizkor.org/hweb/imt/tgmwc/ tgmwc-02/tgmwc-02-15-05.shtml>.

4. J.E. and H.W. Kaufmann, *Maginot Imitations: Major Fortifications of Germany and Neighboring Countries* (New York: Praeger, 1997).

5. Martin Conway, *Collaboration in Belgium* (New Haven, CN: Yale University Press, 1993), 22–23. Conway regards the support for Leopold as indicative of loyalty to the king as a symbol of national unity. He, however, adds "there were few Belgians at this time who felt any great affection for their former democracy." Conway, 24.

6. Conway.

7. Lucy S. Dawidowicz, *The War against the Jews 1933–1945* (New York: Bantam, 1986), 363.

8. Conway, 25.

9. Dan Michman, "Belgium," in *Encyclopedia of the Holocaust*, Israel Gutman, editor-in-chief (New York: Macmillan, 1990), 161.

10. E. Lamberts, "Belgium since 1830," in *History of the Low Countries*, edited by J.C.H. Blom and E. Lamberts (New York: Berghahn Books, 1999), 364.

11. Martin Conway, "Justice in Postwar Belgium: Popular Passions and Political Realities," in *The Politics of Retribution in Europe: World War II and its Aftermath*, ed. by István Deák, Jan T. Gross, and Tony Judt (Princeton, NJ: Princeton University Press, 2000), 135.

12. R. Ardenne, *German Exploitation of Belgium* (Washington: The Brookings Institution, 1942), 36.

13. G. Jacquemyns, *La Société Belge sous l'Occupation Allemand 1940–1944: Alimentation et état de santé* (Brussels: Nicholson & Watson, 1950), 286.

14. G. Jacquemyns, *La Société Belge sous l'Occupation Allemand 1940–1944 Mode de vie, Comportement moral et social* (Brussels: Nicholson & Watson, 1950), 211 and 217.

15. Jacquemyns, *La Société Belge sous l'Occupation Allemand 1940–1944: Alimentation et état de santé*, 133.

16. Jacquemyns, *La Société Belge sous l'Occupation Allemand 1940–1944: Mode de vie, Comportement moral et social*, 209, 211, and 217.

17. R. Motz, *Belgium Unvanquished* (London: Linsay Drummond, 1942), 69–70. See Herman Bodson, *Agent for the Resistance: A Belgian Saboteur in World War II* (College Station: Texas A&M University Press, 1994).

18. Jacquemyns, *La Société Belge sous l'Occupation Allemand 1940–1944: Mode de vie, Comportement moral et social*, 212 and 143–144.

19. Michman, 160. The figure given by the Jewish Museum of Deportation and Resistance in Mechelen is 60,000. The estimate of the Nazi occupiers was 56,000. But, perhaps, many of the recently arrived refugees were not officially counted. According to Michman, estimates prior to 1980 that the Jewish population in Belgium was as large as 90,000 are erroneous. Michman, 161.

20. According to some estimates the Nazi figure for Antwerp is much too small.

21. "Guide to the Museum," of the the Museum van Deportatie en Verzet—Pro Museo Judaico V.Z.W., Mechelen (Mechelen Museum of Deportation and Resistance).

22. Dan Michman, 164.

23. Dawidowicz, 364–5. The date for the compulsory wearing of the star given by Dawidowicz is June 6. The May date is given by the Museum van Deportatie en Verzet, see "Belgium under the German Occupation of 1940–1942: Setting the Trap for the Jewish Community," <http:www. cicb.be/belgiumgermanoccu. html>.

24. Michman, 164–165.

25. Museum van Deportatie en Verzet, <http://www.cicb.be/ reactiontothetrap. html>.

26. Museum van Deportatie en Verzet.

27. Gay Block and Malka Drucker, *Rescuers: Portraits of Moral Courage in the Holocaust* (New York: Holmes & Meier Publishers, 1992), 91.

28. Michman, 160.

29. Michman, 168.

30. Block and Drucker, 91.

31. Eva Fogelman, *Conscience & Courage: Rescuers of Jews during the Holocaust* (New York: Anchor, 1994), 36 and 326–327. Michman says 25,000 were hidden. Michman, 165

32. Block and Drucker, 92.

33. Block and Drucker , 91. Although he has been accused of facilitating the deportation by only protesting against the deportation of certain groups of Jews. Van Roey protested against the arrest and imprisonment in Breendonk of Rabbi Salomon Ullmann and leaders of the ABJ. Michman, 165.

34. Museum van Deportatie en Verzet, <http://www.cicb.be/hell.html>.

35. Dawidowicz, 364–5; Museum van Deportatie en Verzet, http://www. cicb.be/ 100days1942.html.

36. The number given by the Museum van Deportatie en Verzet, <http://www.cicb.be/ memo.html>, is 20,000 Jews including 3,000 children. The numbers given by Fogelman are 20,000 adults and 8,000 children. Fogelman, 36 and 326–327.

37. Museum van Deportatie en Verzet, <http://www.cicb.be/100days1942.html>.

38. Museum van Deportatie en Verzet. See "Belgium under the German Occupation of 1940–1942: Setting the Trap for the Jewish Community," <http:www.cicb.be/facingthe deportation.html>.

39. Dan Michman, "Breendonck," in *Encyclopedia of the Holocaust*, 243.

40. "Breendonk (Belgium)," <http://www.jewishgen.org/Forgotten Camps/Camps/ForgottenEng.html> accessed 24 June 1999.

41. "Breendonk (Belgium)." According to Dan Michman 300 inmates died at Breendonk as a result of torture, over-work, and deprivation. He writes that 450 were executed by shooting and that 14 were hung. According to Michman 65 Jews died at the camp and 54 were transported to Auschwitz. Michman, "Breendonck,"243.

42. Jean Améry, At the Mind's Limit: Contemplations by a Survivor on Auschwitz and its Realities, Tr. by Sidney Rosenfeld and Stella P. Rosenfeld (New York: Schocken Books, 1986), 21–22.

43. "Breendonk (Belgium)," <http://web.forgottencamps.by.net/-june/Vincent/Camps/Breend/Eng.html>, accessed June 24, 1999.

44. During World War II Degrelle formed the Wallon Legion, which became the 28th SS Division of the Waffen-SS. Degrelle comanded this unit, which was never larger than a regiment, on the Eastern Front. After the war he reached Spain where he died in exile in 1993. David Zabecki, "Degrelle, Léon," in World War II in Europe: An Encyclopedia, ed. by David Zabecki, (New York: Garland, 1999), 274.

45. Michman, "Belgium," 168.

46. Overseas News Agency, August 2, 1943. Museum van Deportatie en Verzet, <http://www.cicb.be/facingthe deportation.html>. "The Holocaust in Belgium," <http://web.forgottencamps.by .net/-june/Vincent/Camps/BelgEngl.html>, accessed June 24, 1999.

47. Michman, "Belgium," 168.

Chapter 16

1. B.H. Liddell Hart, History of the Second World War. Volume I. (New York: Capricorn, 1972), 77.

2. Liddell Hart, 78.

3. See Roger Keyes, Outrageous Fortune: The Tragedy of Leopold III of the Belgians, 1901–1941 (London: Secker and Warburg, 1984).

4. Martin Manning, " Leopold III," in Europe since 1945: An Encyclopedia, edited by Bernard Cook (New York/London: Garland Publishers, 2001), 780–1. See Raymond E. Arango, Leopold III and the Belgian Royal Question (Baltimore: Johns Hopkins University Press, 1961).

5. Martin Manning, " Baudouin," in Europe since 1945: An Encyclopedia, 85.

6. E. Lamberts, " Belgium since 1830," in History of the Low Countries, edited by J.C.H. Blom and E. Lamberts (New York: Berghahn Books, 1999), 365.

7. Carl Strikwerda, A House Divided: Catholics, Socialists, and Flemish Nationalists in Nineteenth Century Belgium (Lanham/Boulder/New York/London: Rowman & Littlefield, 1997), 15.

8. See Hugo Claus' novel, The Sorrow of Belgium, for an account of Flemish sympathies during the war. The Sorrow of Belgium, tr. by Arnold J. Pomerans (London: Penguin, 1991).

9. Kas Deprez and Louis Vos, " Introduction," in Kas Deprez and Louis Vos, eds., Nationalism in Belgium: Shifting Identities, 1780–1995 (New York: Macmillan, 1998), 11. Arrests of collaborators were much more numerous after World War II than after World

War I. After the First World War 39 collaborators were sentenced to death in absentia, but not one of them was executed. After the Second World War 242 collaborators were executed. Ellen L. Evans, *The Cross and the Ballot: Catholic Political Parties in Germany, Switzerland, Austria, Belgium and the Netherlands, 1785–1985* (Boston: Humanities Press, 1999), 173.

According to Martin Conway, *Collaboration in Belgium: Léon Degrelle and the Rexist Movement* (New Haven, CN: Yale University Press, 1993), 277, a total of 57,052 individuals were tried for collaboration between 1944 and 1949. 53,005 were declared guilty. 21,709 were tried in Wallonia. 12,597 francophone Belgians were found guilty of military collaboration, and 7,258 of political collaboration.

According to Luc Huyse, 80,000 Belgians, accused of collaboration, were punished in one form or another by the government, and 48,000 received prison sentences. Luc Huyse, " The Criminal Justice System as a Political Actor in Regime Transitions: The Case of Belgium, 1944–50," in *The Politics of Retribution in Europe: World War II and its Aftermath*, ed. by István Deák, Jan T. Gross, and Tony Judt (Princeton, NJ: Princeton University Press, 2000), 161.

10. According to Conway, "In social terms, few of those prosecuted were powerful figures while (. . .) many of the modest servants of the German cause came from the least favored sections of society. (. . .) [N]one of the prewar political elite and very few major industrialists, local notables, or civil servants (other than German nominees) were held to account for their wartime actions." Martin Conway, "Justice in Postwar Belgium: Popular Passions and Political Realities," in *The Politics of Retribution in Europe*, 152. In fact the government in May 1945 decriminalized most instances of economic collaboration. Luc Huyse, "The Criminal Justice System as a Political Actor in Regime Transitions,"166.

11. Patrick Pasture, " Belgium," in *Europe since 1945: An Encyclopedia*, 92; Louis Vos, "Nationalism, Democracy, and the Belgian State," in Richard Caplan and John Feffer eds., *Europe' s New Nationalism: States and Minorities in Conflict* (New York/Oxford: Oxford University Press, 1966), 92.

12. Lamberts, " Belgium since 1830," 370. Ellen Evans writes " (. . .) there was no general stigma placed upon the Flemish as there had been before." Evans, *The Cross and the Ballot*, 246. Evans quotes the review in *The American Historical Review*, 94 (October 1994) 1347–8 by Werner Warmbrunn of Luc Huyse and Steven Dhondt, *La repression des collaboratios 1942–1952: un passé toujours présent* (Brussels: Centre de recherche et d' information socio-politiques, 1991) to the effect that recent Flemish historians contend that "contrary to generally received opinion, Flemish collaborators were not punished more frequently or more severely than francophone defendants."

13. The Catholic Party was no longer called the Conservative or Catholic Party but in Flanders the Christian People' s Party and in Wallonia the Social Christian Party, or generically the Christian Democrats.

14. Evans, *The Cross and the Ballot*, 248–9. According to the compromise law the construction of Catholic schools was not to be subsidized. This was altered by a 1973 law, which provided state subvention for the construction of Catholic schools and, in addition, equal state-provided pay for teachers who were members of religious orders or clerics.

15. Lamberts, " Belgium since 1830," 374.

16. According to Lamberts, " constructing a welfare state was the first order of business in post-war Belgium." Lamberts, "Belgium since 1830," 369.

17. Tony Judt, " Is there a Belgium?," *The New York Review*, December 2, 1999, 49.

18. Lamberts, " Belgium since 1830," 382.

19. Lamberts., 384.

20. William Wallace, "Rescue or Retreat? The Nation State in Western Europe, 1945–1993," *Political Studies*, 42 (Special issue 1994), 76.

21. Vos, "Nationalism, Democracy, and the Belgian State," 85.

22. Judt, " Is there a Belgium?," 45.

23. Judt, 50. Nevertheless, agriculture still produced 20 percent of the national income.

24. It is also true that the Flemish are more likely to know French than the francophones Flemish. John Edwards and Clare Shearn, "Language and Identity in Belgium: Perceptions of French and Flemish Students," *Ethnic and Racial Studies*, 10 (April 2, 1987), 138.

25. Judt, "Is there a Belgium?," 92.

26. Louis Vos, "The Flemish National Question," in Kas Deprez and Louis Vos, eds., *Nationalism in Belgium*, 93.

27. Lamberts, "Belgium since 1830," 378.

28. Lamberts.

29. Vos, "Nationalism, Democracy, and the Belgian State," 93.

30. Lamberts, "Belgium since 1830," 380.

31. Vos, "Nationalism, Democracy, and the Belgian State," 93.

32. Judt, "Is there a Belgium?," 49.

33. Judt, 50.

34. Pasture, "Belgium," 94.

35. Pasture.

36. Judt, "Is there a Belgium?," 49. In their 1984 study of student opinions, John Edwards and Clare Shearn found that while 81.8 percent of the francophone Belgian students they interviewed described themselves first as Belgian, 70.4 percent of the Flemish students identified themselves first as Flemish. John Edwards and Clare Shearn, "Language and Identity in Belgium," 140. Also see 144 and 147. In a 1979 study J. Lefèvre to the contrary, found that Walloon francophones identified themselves as Walloon rather than Belgian, and that Brussels francophones identified themselves as *Bruxellois* rather than Belgians. J. Lefèvre, "Nationalisme linguistique et identification linguistique: Le Cas de Belgique," *International Journal of the Sociology of Language*, 20 (1979), 37–58. V. Lorwin has written that "the [Belgian] nation has become an amalgam of one oppressed majority and two oppressed minorities. There are the old grievances of the Flemish, and the newer grievances of the Walloons, and those of the Bruxellois under Flemish pressure." V. Lorwin, "Linguistic Pluralism and Political Tension in Modern Belgium," in *Advances in the Sociology of Language*, ed. by J. Fishman (The Hague: Mouton, 1972), 401.

37. Lode Wils, " Belgium: Nationalities Politics," in *Europe since 1945: An Encyclopedia*, 97–99; and Pasture, "Belgium," 92–95. According to the 1910 census there were also 36,000 German speakers in the Arlon section of the province of Luxembourg. In 1895 a German cultural group was formed there, the *Deutscher Verien zur Hebung und Pflgung der Muttersprache in deutschredenden Belgien*. However, most of these people, as

are the rest of the Luxembourgeoisie, were thoroughly bi-lingual, and the two World Wars led them to emphasize their French character at the expense of the German. See Charles H. Haskins, "Belgian Problems," Inquiry Document 207, 30 November 1918, M 1107, roll 43, National Archives.

38. Hubert Jenniges, "Germans, German Belgians, German-Speaking Belgians," in *Nationalism in Belgium: Shifting Identities*, 241.
39. Jenniges, 243–45.
40. Jenniges, 246.
41. Jenniges, 247.
42. Jenniges, 247 and 248.
43. Marc Spruyt, "Belgium: The Flemish Extreme Right," in *Europe since 1945: An Encyclopedia*, 99.
44. Judt, "Is there a Belgium?," 49.
45. Spruyt, "Belgium: The Flemish Extreme Right," 99–100.
46. Anne Morelli and Jean-Philippe Schreiber, "Are the Immigrants the Last Belgians?," in *Nationalism in Belgium: Shifting Identities*, 249.
47. Morelli and Schreiber, 251.
48. Serge Govaert, " A Brussels Identity? A Speculative Interpretation," in *Nationalism in Belgium: Shifting Identities*, 237 and 234.

Appendix II

1. Derek Blyth, *Flemish Cities Explored*, 236.
2. L.J.R. Milis, "A Long Beginning: The Low Countries through the Tenth Century," in *History of the Low Countries*, edited by J.C.H. Blom and E. Lamberts (New York: Berghahn Books, 1999), 53.
3. "Interbrew, Stella Artois, and brewery Domus" Leuven homepage, <http://www.leuven.be/dtplv/inf.nsf/>, accessed April 24, 1999

# Bibliography

## Books

Améry, Jean. *At the Mind's Limit: Contemplations by a Survivor: On Auschwitz and its Realities*, Tr. by Sidney Rosenfeld and Stella P. Rosenfeld. New York: Schocken Books, 1986.

Anderson, Bonnie S. and Zinsser, Judith P. *A History of Their Own: Women in Europe from Prehistory to the Present*. New York:Oxford University Press, 2000.

Arango, Raymond E. *Leopold III and the Belgian Royal Question*. Baltimore: Johns Hopkins University Press, 1961.

Ardenne, R. *German Exploitation of Belgium*. Washington: The Brookings Institution, 1942.

Bédier, J. *Les crimes allemandes d'après témoinages allemands*. Paris: A. Colin, 1915.

Block, Gay and , Malka Drucker. *Rescuers: Portraits of Moral Courage in the Holocaust*. New York: Holmes & Meier Publishers, 1992.

Blom, J.C.H. and E. Lamberts, eds. *History of the Low Countries*. New York: Berghahn Books, 1999.

Blyth, Derek. *Flemish Cities Explored*. London: Pallas Athene, 1998.

Bodson, Herman. *Agent for the Resistance: A Belgian Saboteur in World War II*. College Station, Texas: Texas A&M University Press, 1994.

Boileau, David A. *Cardinal Mercier: A Memoir*. Leuven: Peeters, 1996.

Boulger, Demetrius C. *Belgian Life in Town and Country*. New York: G.P. Putnam's Sons,1904.

*Breendonk. Les débuts. . . .* Brussels: SOMA/CEGES, 1997.

Caplan, Richard and John Feffer, eds. *Europe's New Nationalism: States and Minorities in Conflict*. New York/Oxford: Oxford University Press, 1996.

Carson, Patricia. *Flanders in Creative Contrasts*. Leuven: Davidfonds, 1989.

Clough, Shepard B. *A History of the Flemish Movement in Belgium: A Study in Nationalism*. New York: Richard R. Smith, 1930.

Conway, Martin. *Collaboration in Belgium: Léon Degrelle and the Rexist Movement*. New Haven, CN: Yale University Press, 1993.

Cook, Bernard, *Europe since 1945: An Encyclopedia*. New York: Garland. 2001.

Dawidowicz, Lucy S. *The War against the Jews 1933–1945*. New York: Bantam, 1986.

Deák, István, Jan T. Gross, and Tony Judt, eds.*The Politics of Retribution in Europe: World War II and its Aftermath*. Princeton, NJ: Princeton University Press, 2000.

de Meeüs, Adrien. *History of the Belgians*. Tr. by G. Gordon. New York: Praeger, 1962.

Deprez, Kas and Louis Vos, editors, *Nationalism in Belgium: Shifting Identities, 1780–1995*. New York: Macmillan, 1998.

De Weerdt, Denise. *En de vrouwen? vrouw vrouwenbeweging en feminisme en Belgie, 1830–1960*. Ghent: Masereelfonds, 1980.

Ducpétiaux, Edouard. *De la condition physique et moral des jeunes ouvriers et des moyens de l'améliorer*. Brussels: Meline, Cans et compagnie, 1843.

_____. *De l'état de l'instruction primare et populaire en Belgique*. Brussels: Maline, Cans and Co., 1838.

_____. *Mémoire sur le paipérisme dans les Flandres*. Brussels: M. Hayez, 1850.

Evans, Ellen L.*The Cross and the Ballot: Catholic Political Parties in Germany, Switzerland, Austria, Belgium and the Netherlands, 1785–1985*. Boston: Humanities Press, 1999.

Fishman, J., ed. *Advances in the Sociology of Language*. The Hague: Mouton, 1972.

Fogelman, Eva. *Conscience & Courage: Rescuers of Jews during the Holocaust*. New York: Anchor, 1994.

Frommer, Arthur. *A Masterpiece Called Belgium*. New York: Prentice Hall, 1989.

Fest, Joachim C. *Hitler*. New York: Harcourt Brace Jovanovich,1974.

Ferguson, Niall. *The Pity of War: Explaining World War I*. New York: Basic Books, 1999.

Geyl, Pieter. *The Revolt of the Netherlands (1555–1609)*. London: Ernest Benn Limited, 1958.

Gilbert, Martin. *Atlas of the First World War*. London: Dorset, 1984.

Goris, Jan-Albert, editor. *Belgium*. Berkeley/Los Angeles: University of California Press, 1946.

*Guide to the Quotations in the Flanders' Fields Museum*. Ieper: Flanders' Fields Museum, 1999.

Gutman, Israel, editor-in-chief. *Encyclopedia of the Holocaust*. New York: Macmillan, 1990.

Haag, Henri. *Les origines du Catholicisme libéral en Belgique (1789–1839)*. Louvain: Bibliothéque de l'université, 1950.

Halperin, S. William. *Germany Tried Democracy, A Political History of the Reich from 1918 to 1933*. New York: W.W. Norton & Co., 1974.

Henderson, W.O., *The Industrialization of Europe 1780–1914*. New York: Harcourt Brace & World, 1969.

Hermans, Theo, Louis Vos, and Lode Wils, eds., *The Flemish Movement: A Documentary History, 1780–1990*. Atlantic Highlands, NJ: Athlone Press, 1992.

Hilden, Patricia Penn. *Women, Work, and Politics: Belgium, 1830–1914*. Oxford: Clarendon Press, 1993.

Hitler, Adolf. *Mein Kampf*. Boston: Houghton Mifflin, 1971.

Hobsbawm, E.J. *The Age of Revolution, 1789–1848*. New York: The New American Library, 1962.

Hochschild, Adam. *King Leopold's Ghost*, New York: Houghton Mifflin, 1998.

Jacquemyns, Georges. *Histoire de la crise écomnomique des Flandres (1845–1850)*. Brussels: Maurice Lamertin, 1929.

_____. *La Société Belge sous l'Occupation Allemand 1940–1944: Alimentation et état de santé*. Brussels: Nicholson & Watson, 1950.

_____. *La Société Belge sous l'Occupation Allemand 1940–1944: Mode de vie, Comportement moral et social*. Brussels: Nicholson & Watson, 1950.

Janson, H.W. *History of Art*. Englewood Clifffs, N.J.: Prentice-Hall, 1970.

Kaufmann, J.E. and H.W. Kaufmann. *Maginot Imitations: Major Fortifications of Germany and Neighboring Countries*. New York: Praeger, 1997.

Keagan, John. *The First World War*. New York: Alfred A. Knopf, 1999.

Keiger, John F.V., *France and the Origins of the First World War*. New York: St. Martin's Press, 1983.

Keyes, Roger. *Outrageous Fortune: The Tragedy of Leopold III of the Belgians, 1901–1941*. London: Secker and Warburg, 1984.

Kossmann, E.H. *The Low Countries, 1780–1940*. Oxford: At the Clarendon Press, 1978.

Kuczynski, Juergen. *The Rise of the Working Class*. New York: McGraw-Hill, 1971.

Liddell Hart, B.H. *History of the Second World War*. Volume I. New York: Capricorn, 1972.

_____. *The Real War 1914–1918*. Boston: Little, Brown, and Co., 1930.

Marchal, Jules . *E.D. Morel contre Léopold II: l'histoire du Congo, 1900–1910*. Paris: Harmattan, 1996.

_____. *L'Etat libre du Congo: paradis perdu: l'histoire du Congo 1876–1900*. Borgloon: Bellings, 1996.

Marx, Karl and Engles, Friedrich. *La Belgique des insurrections*. Paris: n.d.

Mazower, Mark. *Dark Continent: Europe's Twentieth Century*. New York: Penguin, 1998.

McEntee, G.L. *Military History of The World War*. New York: Charles Scribner's Sons, 1943.

Melegari, Vezio. *The Great Military Sieges*. New York: Thomas Y. Crowell, 1972.

Motz, R. *Belgium Unvanquished*. London: Linsay Drummond, 1942.

Müller-Meiningen, Ernst, *Who are the Huns? The Law of Nations and its Breakers*, Tr. by R. L. Orchelle. New York: Stechert (A. Hafner), 1915

Murphy, Alexander B. *The Regional Dynamics of Language Differentiation in Belgium: A Study in Cultural-Political Geography*. Chicago: University of Chicago, 1988.

Nelson, Samuel. *Colonialism in the Congo Basin*. Athens, OH: Center for International Studies, 1994.

Olyslager, W.A. *The Groot Begijnhof of Leuven*. Leuven: Leuven University Press, 1983.

Pirenne, Henri. *La Belgique et la guerre mondiale*. Paris:Les Presses universitaires de France, 1928.

_____. *Historie de Belgique*. Brussels: Renaissance du livre, 1948– 52.

Polansky, Janet. *Revolutions in Brussels 1783–1793*. Hanover, NH: University Press of New England, 1987.

Pollard, Sidney. *Peaceful Conquest: The Industrialization of Europe, 1760–1970*. Oxford: Oxford University Press, 1981.

Rodes, John E. *Germany: A History*. New York: Holt, Rinehart and Winston, 1964.

Rooney, John W. *Revolt in the Netherlands: Brussels 1830*. Lawrence, KS: Coronado Press, 1982.

Shub, David. *Lenin: A Biography*. Baltimore: Penguin, 1966.

Stokesbury, James L. *A Short History of World War I*. New York: William Morrow and Co., 1981.

Strikwerda, Carl. *A House Divided: Catholics, Socialists, and Flemish Nationalists in Nineteenth Century Belgium*. Lanham/Boulder/New York/London: Rowman & Littlefield, 1997.

Tuchman, Barbara. *The Proud Tower: A Portrait of the World Before the War: 1890–1914*. New York: Macmillan, 1966.

Tucker, Spencer, ed. *The European Powers in the First World War: An Encyclopedia*. New York: Garland Publishers, 1996.

_____. *The Great War 1914–18*. Bloomington: University of Indiana Press, 1998.

Toynbee, Arnold J. *The German Terror in Belgium: An Historical Record*. New York: George H. Doran Co, 1917.

Verkade, Willem, *Democratic Parties in the Low Countries and Germany*. Lieden: Universaitaire Pers, 1965.

Van Doorslaer, R., editor, *Les Juifs de Belgique de l'immigration au génocide, 1925–1945*, Brussels: SOMA/CEGES, 1994.

Von Glahn, Gerhard. *Law among Nations: An Introduction to Public International Law*, 4th ed. New York: Macmillan, 1981.

Watelet, Hubert. *Une Industrialisation sans dévéloppement:Le Bassin de Mons et le charbonnage du Grand-Hornu du milieu du XVIIIe siècle*. Ottawa: Editions de l'Université d'Ottawa,1980.

Wils, Lode. *Histoire des nations belges. Belgique, Flandre, Wallonie: quinze siècles de passé commun*. Ottignies: Quorum, 1996.

## Articles

Buyst, Erik. "Belgium: Economy."*Europe since 1945: An Encyclopedia*, Ed. by Bernard Cook. New York/London: Garland Publishers, 2001, 100–101.

Bernard Cook, "Belgian Revolution of 1830," in *Chronology of European History*, Ed. by John Powell. Pasadena: Salem Press, Inc.: 1997, 819–821.

_____. "Belgium: Neutrality of," and "Belgium: Occupation of," in *The European Powers in the First World War: An Encyclopedia*. Ed. by Spencer Tucker. New York: Garland Publishers, 1996, 118–120.

_____. "Dehaene, Jean-Luc." *Europe since 1945: An Encyclopedia*, 285.

_____. "Eyskens, Gaston." *Europe since 1945: An Encyclopedia*, 358. .

_____. "Martens, Wilfried." *Europe since 1945: An Encyclopedia*, 835–836.

_____. "Tindemans, Leo." *Europe since 1945: An Encyclopedia*, 1251.

Craeybeckx, Jan, "The Brabant Revolution: A Conservative Revolution in a Backward Country?" *Acta Historiae Neerlandica*, IV (1970), 49–83.

Deleek, Herman. "Belgium: Social Policy." *Europe since 1945: An Encyclopedia*, 101–104.

Duignan, Peter. "Spaak, Paul-Henri, and Western European Unity." *Europe since 1945: An Encyclopedia*, 1165–1166.

Edwards, John, and Clare Shearn. "Language and Identity in Belgium: Perceptions of French and Flemish Students." *Ethnic and Racial Studies*, 10 (April 2, 1987), 135–48.

Etienne, J.-M., "Les origines du rexism," *Res Publica*, IX (1967), 87–110.

Geller, Jay Howard. "Belgium: Decolonization,"*Europe since 1945: An Encyclopedia*, 95–96.

Gullace, Nicoletta F. "Sexual Violence and Family Honor: British Propaganda and International Law during the First World War." *American Historical Review*, 102 (June 1997), 3:731–732.

Horne, John, and Alan Kramer, "German 'Atrocities' and Franco- German Opinion, 1914: The Evidence of German Soldiers' Diaries," *Journal of Modern History*, Vol. 66, 1 (Mar. 1994), 1–33.

Judt, Tony. "Is there a Belgium?"*The New York Review*. December 2, 1999, 49–53.

Julien, Armand. "La condition des classes laborieuses en Belgique, 1830–1930." *Annales de la Société Scientifique de Bruxelles*, ser. D, 55 (1935).

Kittell, Alan. "The Revolutionary Period of the Industrial Revolution: Industrial Innovation and Population Displacement in Belgium, 1830–1880," *Journal of Social History*, I (Winter 1976), 136–7.

Lefèvre, J. "Nationalisme linguistique et identification linguistique: Le Cas de Belgique." *International Journal of the Sociology of Language*, 20 (1979), 37–58.

Lorwin, Val R. "Linguistic Pluralism and Political Tensions in Modern Belgium," *Canadian Journal of History*, 5 (1970), 1–24.

Manning, Martin. "Baudouin." *Europe since 1945: An Encyclopedia*, 85 .

————. "Leopold III." *Europe since 1945: An Encyclopedia*, 780–781.

Michman, Dan. "Belgium," in *Encyclopedia of the Holocaust*. Israel Gutman, editor-in-chief. New York: Macmillan, 1990, 160–169.

————. "Breendonck," in *Encyclopedia of the Holocaust*, 241–243.

Miller, John. "Art of Darkness," *The Bulletin (The Newsweekly of the Capital of Europe)*, July 1, 1999, 11.

Pasture, Patrick. "Belgium." *Europe since 1945: An Encyclopedia*, 92–95.

————. "Belgium: Civil Society and Pressure Groups."*Europe since 1945: An Encyclopedia*, 105–106.

Polasky, Janet. "Traditionalists, Democrats, and Jacobins in Revolutionary Brussels," *Journal of Modern History*, 56, 1 (June 1984), 227–262.

Schama, Simon."The Rights of Ignorance: Dutch Educational Policy in Belgium 1815–30." *History of Education*, 1 (1972), 81–89.

Schafer, Elizabeth D. "Albert I, King of Belgium." *The European Powers in the First World War: An Encyclopedia*. Ed. by Spencer Tucker. New York: Garland Publishers, 1996, 33–34.

Spruyt, Marc, "Belgium: The Flemish Extreme Right." *Europe since 1945: An Encyclopedia*, 99–100.

Tihon, André. "Belgium: Catholicism." *Europe since 1945: An Encyclopedia*, 104–105.

Vanke, Jeffrey William. "Belgium: Political Parties."*Europe since 1945: An Encyclopedia*, 96–97.

Wallace, William. "Rescue or Retreat? The Nation State in Western Europe, 1945–1993." *Political Studies*, 42 (Special issue 1994), 76.

Wielemans, Willy. "Belgium: Education." *Europe since 1945: An Encyclopedia*, 106–107.
Wils, Lode, "Nationalities Politics."*Europe since 1945: An Encyclopedia*, 97–99.
Zolberg, A.R., "The Making of Flemings and Walloons: Belgium 1830–1914," *Journal of Interdisciplinary History*, 5 (1974), 179–234.


Archival Material

Haskins, Charles H. "Belgian Problems," Inquiry Document 207, November 30, 1918, M 1107, roll 43, National Archives, Washingron, D.C.
"Memorandum: The Content of the Inquiry," Inquiry Document 885, M 1107, roll 43, National Archives, Washington, D.C.


Web Sites

"Belgium under the German Occupation of 1940–1942: Setting the Trap for the Jewish Community," Museum van Deportatie en Verzet—Pro Museo Judaico V.Z.W., Mechelen, http://www.cicb.be/facingthe deportation.html.
"Breendonk (Belgium)," http://www.jewishgen.org/Forgotten Camps/Camps/ForgottenEng.html
Cook, Bernard, "Lammennais, Félicité de." *The Encyclopedia of 1848*. Ed. by James Chastain, http://www.cats.ohiou.edu/ ~Chastain/ip/lamann.htm.
Davis, Harding, "The Burning of Leuven: A Contemporary Account," *New York Tribune*, August 31, 1914, *The World War I Document Archive 1914*, <http://www.lib.byu.edu/~rdh/ wwi/1914/louvburn.html>.
Gooch Brison D. and John W. Rooney, Jr. "Belgium in 1848." The Encyclopedia of 1848. Ed. by James Chastain, http://www.cats.ohio.edu/~chastain/ac/belgium.htm.

# Index

# Studies in Modern European History

The monographs in this series focus upon aspects of the political, social, economic, cultural, and religious history of Europe from the Renaissance to the present. Emphasis is placed on the states of Western Europe, especially Great Britain, France, Italy, and Germany. While some of the volumes treat internal developments, others deal with movements such as liberalism, socialism, and industrialization, which transcend a particular country.

The series editor is:

Frank J. Coppa
Director, Doctor of Arts Program
in Modern World History
Department of History
St. John's University
Jamaica, New York 11439

To order other books in this series, please contact our Customer Service Department:

(800) 770-LANG (within the U.S.)
(212) 647-7706 (outside the U.S.)
(212) 647-7707 FAX

or browse online by series at:

WWW.PETERLANGUSA.COM